D0900206

# The Victorian Gentleman

## ABOUT THE BOOK

The making, manners and morals of gentlemen in our great age of affluence and elegance. The age of our fathers and grandfathers was an age of easy money and of self-conscious manners, an age of immense social change when thousands made fortunes and became gentlemen and as many lost them and struggled to remain gentlemen. Military gentlemen, religious gentlemen, scandalous gentlemen, gentlemen involved in royal intrigue, in educational reform, in rebellion against the rigid morality of the Early Victorians — here is a complete panorama of gentlemen at work and at play in the Victorian age.

## ABOUT THE AUTHOR

Michael Brander lives in Scotland. Wounded in the War, he opted for life in the country with plenty of exercise and fresh air and writing on hunting and shooting, on dog-rearing and horse-training, as well as on Scottish touring and Scottish history. His work on *The Georgian Gentleman* is a witty and stimulating companion volume to *The Victorian Gentleman*

# Michael Brander

# The Victorian Gentleman

GORDON CREMONESI

Designed by Heather Gordon-Cremonesi
Produced by Chris Pye
Set by Preface Ltd, Salisbury
Printed in Great Britain by The Anchor Press Ltd

The publishers wish to thank
The Witch Ball Print Shop, Brighton
for their help in finding illustrations

ISBN 0-86033-004-4

Gordon Cremonesi Publishers
New River House
34 Seymour Road
London N8 0BE

# Contents

# Preface

My thanks are due to the many librarians throughout the country, from the Isle of Wight to Caithness, who have supplied me with material for this book, but particularly the staff of the National Library of Scotland and the Central Library in Edinburgh, also Mr Brian M. Gall and the staff of the East Lothian County Library. For his help with the research on the Victorians in India I must thank Mr M. M. Stuart, C.I.E., O.B.E. For the loan of their ancestor's diaries I must thank Mrs W. K. Simpson and the Rt. Hon. Earl of Mar and Kelly. I am grateful also to the readers in typescript and proof for their invaluable help – particularly Kenneth H. Grose, M.A., also my daughter Kathleen and my wife Evelyn. Without the help of the above it would have been impossible to write this book, but I must acknowledge at once that all the errors of omission and commission are mine also.

# Chronology

1815    Battle of Waterloo. Napoleon defeated and banished to Elba. Corn Law passed with a view to protecting agriculture.

1816    Income Tax repealed. Jane Austen, "Emma." Coleridge, "Kubla Khan." Scott, "The Antiquary."

1817    Disarming of the U.S.A. and Canadian boundary. Death of Jane Austen.

1818    Definition of the U.S.A. and Canadian boundary. Scott, "Heart of Midlothian"; Keats, "Endymion." Bowdler's Shakespeare.

1819    Queen Victoria born. Peterloo Massacre. Six Acts restricting free speech, print and assembly.

1820    George III died. Succeeded by George Augustus Frederick, Prince of Wales, as George IV. Attempt to divorce Queen Caroline ineffectual. Greek revolution against Turkish rule began. Keats, "Lamia," "Eve of St. Agnes," "Isabella." Shelley, "Prometheus Unbound." Scott, "Ivanhoe."

1821    Shelley, "Adonais." Scott, "Kenilworth." John Keats died, aged 26.

1822    George IV paid State Visit to Scotland. Lord Castlereigh died, Canning became Foreign Secretary. Matthew Arnold born. Percy Bysshe Shelley died, aged 30.

1823    The Monroe Doctrine. London Mechanics Institute founded. In Ireland O'Connell formed the Catholic Association.

1834    The Combination Acts were repealed. The Westminster Review was founded. Deaths of George Gordon, Lord Byron (aged 36).

1825    Opening of the Stockton to Darlington Railway. The Catholic Association declared illegal. Thomas Henry Huxley born.

1826    Peel acting as Home Secretary reformed the Penal Laws. Society For the Diffusion of Useful Knowledge formed.

1827    Combined English, French and Russian Fleets defeated the Turks at Navarino. University College, London, founded. Thomas Arnold became headmaster of Rugby. Tennyson, "Poems by two brothers." William Blake died.

1828    Test and Corporation Acts repealed. University College opened. The year of birth of Dante Gabriel Rossetti, George Meredith, Hyppolite Taine and A. J. Munby.

1829    Peel formed the police force in London, known as Peelers, or Bobbies. The Independence of Greece was acknowledged by the

Convention of London. Catholic Emancipation Act passed. Edinburgh Review founded. Carlyle, "Signs of the Times."

1830    George IV died, succeeded by William IV. Fall of Wellington government. Liverpool and Manchester Railway opened. July Revolution in Paris. Lyell, "Principles of Geology." Cobbett, "Rural Rides." Tennyson, "Poems." Death of William Hazlitt.

1831    First Reform Bill introduced. Rejected by the House of Lords. Captain Swing Riots. Cholera epidemic.

1832    Reform Bill passed. Anatomy Act regulated the supply of bodies to Anatomy Schools. Durham University was founded. The Penny Magazine and Chamber's Edinburgh Journal were established. First cheap weekly papers. Tennyson, "Poems." Sir Walter Scott died.

1833    Slavery abolished throughout British Empire. State Inspection of Factories introduced. Oxford Movement initiated by Pusey, Keble and Newman. End of cholera epidemic, 60,000 dead in a population of 14 million. East India Company's monopoly in China was ended. Carlyle, "Sartor Resartus."

1834    Poor Law Reform. Grey resigned as Prime Minister and succeeded by Melbourne. Robert Owen introduced the Grand National Consolidated Trades Union, an abortive attempt at Trade Union. First photograph taken by Fox Talbot. William Morris was born. Coleridge and Lamb died.

1835    Municipal Corporations Act. The appointment of the Ecclesiastical Commission. Bull-baiting made illegal. Augustus Hare born. Mrs Hemans and Cobbett died.

1836    Formation of London Working Men's Association. Start of the Chartist Movement. The Boer Farmers began their Great Trek. Dickens, "Pickwick Papers." Francis Burnand born.

1837    Death of William IV, succession of Victoria. Reform of Penal Code. Carlyle, "History of the French Revolution." Dickens, "Oliver Twist." Thackeray, "Yellow Plush Papers." Swinburne born. Constable died.

1838    The People's Charter promulgated. Formation of the Anti-Corn Law League. Start of Atlantic Steam service. Birmingham to London railway opened. Dickens, "Nicholas Nickleby." Lockhart, "Life of Scott."

1839    Rejection of Chartists Petition to Parliament resulted in riots. The annexation of Aden. First Afghan War. Penny Postage Act. Factory Inspector's Report. Darwin, "The Voyage of the Beagle." Carlyle, "Chartism."

1840    The Opium War with China started. The Bombardment of Acre. Canada Act united the two provinces. Annexation of New Zealand. Victoria married Albert, Prince of Saxe-Coburg-Gotha.

Dickens, "The Old Curiosity Shop," "Barnaby Rudge." Thomas Hardy born.

1841    Peel became Prime Minister. End of First Afghan War. Punch was founded. Carlyle, "Heroes and Hero Worship." Browning, "Bells and Pomegranates."

1842    Income Tax re-established. Chartist riots. Act regarding women and children's employment in mines. Chinese War ended with annexation of Hong Kong. Mudies Circulating Library began. Tennyson, "Poems," 2 vols. Dickens, "American Notes."

1843    Natal annexed to Cape Colony. Southey, Poet Laureate died and was succeeded by Wordsworth. Disruption of the Church of Scotland. Dickens, "Martin Chuzzlewit." Ruskin, "Modern Painters."

1844    Railway Act. Factory Act regulated employment of women and children. Royal Commission on health in towns. The Rochdale Pioneers began the Co-operative Movement. Disraeli, "Coningsby." Gerard Manley Hopkins was born.

1845    Irish potato crop failed. Newman joined the Roman Catholic Church. Carlyle, "Cromwell." Disraeli, "Sybil." Engles, "Condition of the Working Class in England." Sydney Smith and Mrs Fry died.

1846    Famine in Ireland. Corn Laws repealed. Start of commercial telegraph service. U.S.A. and Canadian border defined to the Pacific. Dickens, "Dombey and Son." Thackeray, "Book of Snobs." Lear, "Book of Nonsense."

1847    Fielden's Factory Act limited hours of work. Chloroform first used in Britain in an operation. Karl Marx's "Communist Manifesto" was published in London. Bennyson, "The Princess." Thackeray, "Vanity Fair." Charlotte Bronte, "Jane Eyre."

1848    Revolutions in France, Germany, Austria and Italy. Rebellion in Ireland set down after evictions and coercion. Orange River Colony annexed. Public Health Act. General Board of Health and Medical Officer of Health. Further outbreak of cholera. Chloroform and ether used in childbirth. Mills, "Political Economy." Macaulay, "History of England." Emily Bronte died, aged 30.

1849    The Punjab annexed. The Navigation Acts repealed. The cholera epidemic finally ended due to Dr. Snow's discovery that communicated by water. The Bedford College for Women founded. Dickens, "David Copperfield." Ruskin, "The Seven Lamps of Architecture."

1850    Restoration of the Roman Catholic hierarchy in England caused anti-R.C. feeling. Gold found in California. Oxford instituted degrees in Science. Public Libraries Act passed. On death of Wordsworth Tennyson made Poet Laureate. R. L. Stevenson born.

1851   Great Exhibition in Hyde Park. Gold found in Australia. Livingstone close to Zambezi in Africa.

1852   The Duke of Wellington died. Lord Derby Prime Minister. Disraeli Chancellor of the Exchequer. Independence of Transvaal, or the South African Republic acknowledged.

1853   Competitive examinations introduced for the Indian Civil Service. Cheltenham Women's College founded. Further epidemic of cholera. Thackeray, "The Newcomes."

1854   Workingmen's College founded in London. Crystal Palace moved to Sydenham. Outbreak of Crimean War. Orange River Free State granted independence until 1899. Dickens, "Hard Times." Oscar Wilde born.

1855   Palmerston Prime Minister. Fall of Sevastopol. Florence Nightingale reformed nursing and medical services in the Crimea. The "Daily Telegraph" founded. Charlotte Bronte died, aged 39.

1856   Treaty of Paris ended Crimean War. Canton bombarded. Bessemer steel making process introduced. George Bernard Shaw born.

1857   Outbreak of Indian Mutiny. Sepoy regiments at Meerut massacred white officers. Divorce Act passed. Hughes, "Tom Brown's Schooldays." Trollope, "Barchester Towers." Joseph Conrad born.

1858   Secretary of State for India superseded the East India Company. Derby P.M. Jews admitted to Parliament. Property qualifications for M.Ps removed. Gray's "Anatomy" published.

1859   Palmerston returned as P.M. in place of Derby. Gladstone Chancellor of the Exchequer. Franco-Austrian War. Livingstone on Lake Nyasa. Snow's theory on cholera proved correct. Charles Darwin, "The Origin of the Species." Macaulay, de Quincey died. A. E. Housman born.

1860   Franco-Austrian war ended with the unification of Italy. Nightingale Training School for Nurses established. Cholera outbreak in Britain ended. Dickens, "Great Expectations." "Cornhill Magazine" established.

1861   A legislative Council established in India. Outbreak of American Civil War. Victor Emmanuel crowned King of Italy. Elementary Education Act. Henry Gray died of smallpox. Elizabeth Barret Browning died aged 55. The Prince Consort died of typhus at Windsor. Victoria retired into mourning.

1862   The Companies Act established Limited Liability. Controversy followed the publication of Bishop Colenso's Pentateuch. Meredith, "Modern Love."

1863 Taiping rebellion. Huxley published "Man's Place in Nature." William Makepeace Thackeray died.

1864 Schleswig Holstein. Geneva Convention. Tennyson, "Enoch Arden." Browning, "Dramatis Personae." Dickens, "Our Mutual Friend."

1865 Fenian Conspiracy. Cattle plague rampant. Commons Preservation Society formed. Antiseptic surgery introduced. Insurrection in Jamaica. Russell Prime Minister. "Fortnightly Review" founded. Transatlantic cable began operating. Lewis Carroll, "Alice in Wonderland." Rudyard Kipling and William Butler Yeats born. Palmerston and Cobden died.

1866 Report of Jamaica Commission. Hyde Park Riots. Suspension of Habeus Corpus (Ireland). Derby Prime Minister. Disraeli Chancellor of Exchequer. H. G. Wells born. Keble died.

1867 Reform Bill extended franchise to working class in towns. Factory Acts extended. Disraeli Prime Minister for first time. Trial of Fenians at Manchester. British North America Act established the Dominion of Canada. Karl Marx, "Das Kapital." Ouida, "Under Two Flags." Arnold Bennett born.

1868 Abolition of Compulsory Church Rates. Gladstone Prime Minister for the first time. Abyssinian Campaign.

1869 Irish Protestant Church disestablished. First Women's college at Cambridge, Girton. Mills, "Subjection of Women." Tennyson, "The Holy Grail." Lord Derby died.

1870 Franco-Prussian War. Forster's Education Act resulted in compulsory Primary Education. Irish Land Act started Irish relief legislation. The Civil Service was opened to competitive examination. The Ballot Act was passed. Cardwell introduced drastic reforms in the Army. Commission by purchase abolished. Charles Dickens died aged 58.

1871 Religious Tests at Universities abolished. Local Government Boards introduced. Trade Unions legalised. Darwin, "The Descent of Man." Lewis Carroll, "Through the Looking Glass." De Morgan died.

1872 Secret Ballot introduced in General Elections. Agricultural Labourers Union founded. Darwin, "Expression of the Emotions." Butler, "Erewhon."

1873 Start of the agricultural depression with the introduction of cheap grain from the American Middle West. The Remington Typewriter invented. Mill, "Autobiography." Mill died, aged 62. Landseer and Livingstone also died.

1874 Ashantee War started. Famine in India. Public Worship Regulation Act. Disraeli Prime Minister. Parnell, Irish leader, elected to Parliament. Trollope, "The Way We Live Now." Hardy, "Far from the Madding Crowd."

1875 Artisan's Dwelling Improvement Act, first regarding housing. Employers and Workmen Act. Public Health Act. Prince of Wales visited India. Shares in Suez Canal purchased from Khedive of Egypt. Gilbert and Sullivan in first partnership in "Trial by Jury." Tennyson, "Queen Mary." Kingsley and Lyell died.

1876 Victoria proclaimed Empress of India. Bulgarian atrocities. Tennyson, "Harold." Morris, "Sigurd."

1877 The Transvaal re-annexed. Turkish-Russian war. Society for the Protection of Ancient Buildings founded. Meredith, "Idea of Comedy."

1878 Treaty of Berlin decided Anglo-Russian differences in Turkey. Second Afghan War. William Booth founded the Salvation Army. Aesthetic Movement started. Whistler v. Ruskin lawsuit for libel. Hardy, "Return of the Native." Gilbert and Sullivan, "H.M.S. Pinafore."

1879 Zulu War. Irish Land League formed. First Women's Colleges at Oxford, Lady Margaret Hall and Somerville. A. J. Balfour, "A History of Philosophic Doubt." Gladstone, "Gleanings." Meredith, "The Egoist." Rowland Hill died.

1880 Gladstone became Prime Minister again. The Ground Game Act passed. Women admitted to degrees at London University. Compulsory Elementary Education. Tennyson, "Endymion." George Eliot died.

1881 Transvaal revolted and regained self-government. Majuba Hill defeat of British by Boers. Irish Land Act regulated rents. Boycotting introduced in Ireland. The Land League made illegal and Parnell imprisoned. Social Democratic Federation founded by Hyndman. Oscar Wilde, "Poems." Carlyle, "Reminiscences." Carlyle died aged 86. Disraeli, Stanley and Borrow died.

1882 Married Woman's Property Act (2nd). Bombardment of Alexandria. Phoenix Park Murders. Stevenson, "Treasure Island." Charles Darwin died aged 71. Trollope died, aged 67. Rossetti died aged 54. James Joyce and Virgina Woolf born.

1883 Fabian Society formed. Maxim Machine Gun invented. Trollope, Autobiography. Shaw, "Unsocial Socialist." Moore, "A Modern Lover." Bishop Colenso, Karl Marx and Wagner died.

1884 Third Reform Bill gave franchise to workers in agricultural districts. National Socialist League founded. Toynbee, "Industrial Revolution."

1885 Salisbury Prime Minister. Fall of Khartoum and death of

General Gordon. Gilbert and Sullivan, "The Mikado." Burton, "The Arabian Nights." Rider Haggard, "King Solomon's Mines." "The Dictionary of National Biography" published. Victor Hugo died.

1886　Gladstone Prime Minister. Home Rule Bill defeated. Salisbury returned as Prime Minister. Kipling, "Departmental Ditties."

1887　Riots in Trafalgar Square (Bloody Sunday). Victoria's Jubilee. Independent Labour Party formed. Conan Doyle, "A Study in Scarlet." Rider Haggard, "Allan Quartermain." Jenny Lind died.

1888　Deaths of Emperor William and Emperor Frederick of Germany. Parnell Commission. Local Government Board resulted in elected County Councils. Kipling, "Plain Tales from the Hills." Matthew Arnold died.

1889　Charter for British South Africa Company granted to Cecil Rhodes. More Trades Unions formed as a result of Dock Strike. Armenian Atrocities. Stevenson, "Master of Ballantrae." Conan Doyle, "Sign of Four." Tennyson, "Demeter." Swinburne, "Poems and Ballads." Wilkie Collins died.

1890　Collapse of Baring Bank. Parnell Divorce Case. Stanley, "Darkest Africa." John Henry Newman died aged 89. Burton died.

1891　Tranby Croft Scandal. Irish Land Act. Labour Commission. Hardy, "Tess of the d'Urbervilles." Wilde, "The Picture of Dorian Gray." Marshall, "Principles of Economics." Death of Parnell and W. H. Smith.

1892　Gladstone Prime Minister. Second Home Rule Bill rejected by Lords. Wilde, "Lady Windermere's Fan." Kipling, "Barrack Room Ballads." Bicycling became popular and early motor cars introduced. Alfred, Lord Tennyson, died aged 77.

1893　Conan Doyle, "Sherlock Holmes." Yeats, "The Celtic Twilight." Fanny Kemble died. Jowett and Madox Browne died.

1894　Lord Rosebery Prime Minister. Urban and Rural District Councils and Parish Councils introduced. Trial of Dreyfus. Kipling, "The Jungle Book." Shaw, "Arms and The Man." Wilde, "Salome." Walter Pater died aged 55.

1895　Sino-Japanese War. Jameson Raid. Armenian Atrocities. Salisbury Prime Minister. Venezuelan Crisis. Trial and conviction of Wilde. Wells, "The Time Machine." Shaw, "Candida." Wilde, "The Importance of Being Earnest." Death of Huxley, aged 70. Death of Pasteur and Randolph Churchill.

1896　Daily Mail established. A. E. Housman, "A Shropshire Lad." Max Beerbohm, Works. Tom Hughes, William Morris both died.

1897　Diamond Jubilee. Engineers' Strike. Workmen's Cooperation Act passed. Havelock Ellis, "Studies in the Psychology of Sex."

Webb, "Industrial Democracy." Conrad, "The Nigger of the 'Narcissus.' "

1898 Spanish American American War. Kitchener conquered Sudan and expelled the French from Fashoda. South Wales Coal dispute. Wells, "War of the Worlds." Webb, "Problems of Modern Industry." Hardy, "Wessex Poems." Shaw, "Plays Pleasant and Unpleasant." Lewis Carroll, Gladstone, Aubrey Beardsley and Bismarck died.

1899 Boer War broke out. Dreyfus Case. Dispute with the U.S.A. about Venezuela. British Guiana border settled. Somerville and Ross, Experiences of an Irish R.M. Yeats, "The Wind Among the Reeds."

1900 Queen Victoria visited Ireland. The Labour Party formed. The Daily Express established. Conrad, "Lord Jim." Ruskin, Sidgwick and Oscar Wilde died.

1901 Australian Commonwealth formed. Shaw, "Plays for Puritans." Hardy "Poems Past and Present." Stubbs died. Death of Queen Victoria and accession of Edward VII.

1902 Peace in South Africa. Boer War ended with Peace of Vereeniging. Kipling, "Just So Stories." Rhodes died.

1903 Wright Brothers made first powered heavier-than-air, fixed-wing flight.

1910 Death of Edward VII, succeeded by George V.

1914 First World War.

# Introduction

The Victorian age, extending from 1830 to 1901, covering the greater part of Queen Victoria's long life and reign has been the subject of a mass of documentation and literature. There is such a wealth of material, both at first and second hand, that it is difficult, if not impossible, to hack a straight path through the tangled mass of verbiage. Furthermore it was a self-contradictory age, an age of euphemism, inhibition and humbug, when if the truth appeared to offend it was conveniently ignored or transformed into more acceptable form. Thus a gentleman was never drunk, he was disguised; and his limbs, not his legs, kept crossing.

The complex conventions which governed such thinking and social behaviour were merely an armour against insecurity. Above all it was an age of radical change and expansion, both at home and abroad, hence, however complacent a face they might show outwardly to the world, inwardly the Victorians felt insecure. It was a sign of this insecurity that the Victorians as a whole were obsessed with gentility, for it was the ambition of all classes to attain gentlemanly behaviour. This desire to be considered a gentleman was the product of the rigid class system itself and probably the most rigid arbiter of all was the gentleman's gentleman.

Since this is not a history of the period, but is concerned primarily with the Victorian gentleman, there are inevitably many aspects of the age which are not covered at all. As far as possible, however, a picture of the gentleman's life of the day, from his childhood upwards, has been presented in the words of his contemporaries, by quoting from diaries, letters, the comments of visitors to the country, newspapers, journalists, reports of trials and similar documents. Inevitably the result is a patchwork, but most observations of life are a similar patchwork. Wherever possible the reader has been kept informed of the facts to provide a balanced picture and to fill in the gaps.

Queen Victoria's own diaries, Greville's diaries and the diaries of leading statesmen have for the most part been left unquoted since they have been so very much used elsewhere and also because they are more concerned with affairs of state than with the everyday life of the Victorian gentleman. The sources selected have been largely chosen for their ability to provide a fair picture of life as they saw it. Sometimes the circumlocutions used are themselves extremely revealing. It is a pity

Victoria married Albert on 10 February 1840 at St James's Palace. Their austere moral standards were to have a tremendous influence on early Victorians.

that pithy Victorian writers are so rare, but the few exceptions are all the more welcome as a result.

Amongst the material included are a Victorian professional letter-writer's conception of a father's letter to his son at school; an architect's views on the perfect mid-Victorian house; travel in an early locomotive with Stephenson, described by Fanny Kemble, the foremost actress of her day; a Frenchman's views on the various aspects of an English gentleman's life, including his mistresses; some uninhibited descriptions of the officers of a Sepoy regiment prior to the Indian Mutiny; life in an early Swiss chalet described by the wife of a friend of one of the earliest mountaineers; an eyewitness account of the crash of a late Victorian glider pilot by a friend of the gentleman involved. These provide only a part of the picture and of necessity only a very small part. Like the entrée at a Victorian banquet this is only a foretaste.

The Great Exhibition held at the Crystal Palace embodied all the invention, enterprise and energy that were the mainspring of social mobility in Victorian England.

There are inevitably many aspects of the gentleman's life which cannot be sketched in full detail. His politics could obviously vary very considerably and this is after all a social not a political study, although on occasions some of the factors affecting his political viewpoints have been mentioned. This was the age of revolution abroad, of Chartism and Radical thinking at home, of early socialism. It was also the age of Liberalism and of Toryism, of Gladstone and Disraeli. It was the age of emancipation, starting with the rotten boroughs and ending with the third Reform Bill of 1884 which extended the vote to all adult males. Small wonder that nervous gentlemen saw it as the herald of revolution.

The immense change in outlook and thought between gentlemen of the first half of the Victorian age and the latter half must not be overlooked, but nor must the fact be forgotten that this coincided with a massive increase in population. With the death of the Prince Consort in 1861 there was a gradual change of mood from the old, narrow moral outlook to a more permissive, freer attitude of mind near the end of the century. This was mirrored in the attitudes of the Victorian gentleman. But whereas at the start of the period it was possible to refer to the "Upper Ten Thousand," by the end of the Victorian age it would have been very reasonable to refer to the "Upper Hundred Thousand."

The emergent middle classes sent their sons to the old and the new public schools where they were die-cast in the Arnold mould of muscular Christianity. Individualism may not have been completely suppressed, but inevitably the individual learned to live within the rules of society and to understand the general standards of gentlemanly conduct which were expected of him. The result at times was an almost schizophrenic division between the actions of an individual in his private life when following his repressed instincts and desires and his behaviour in public dictated by the rules of society. The ability to equate the two when they were conflicting without disturbing the equilibrium of either was not supreme hypocrisy, but the effect of early training. Whether in the process he developed a guilt complex depended very much upon the individual.

This is not to say that the great majority of the Victorians did not lead full and happy lives. They undoubtedly did, but within the framework of a very rigid society to which they had to adapt themselves. It is as well not to forget that they were our immediate ancestors, the fathers or grandfathers of many people alive today. There is inevitably a generation gap and it is easy to fall into the trap of generalizing and even moralizing. It is important to remember that behind their stiff collars and beneath their beaver hats they were very human and very different from each other, just like their sons and grandsons or third— and fourth— generation descendants today.

From the death of George IV in 1830, which rang down the curtain on the Georgian period to the death of Queen Victoria in 1901 Britain attained unprecedented growth, enormous expansion in trade and industry, as well as a world wide extension of the Empire. It was a period which saw changes never before envisaged, from the horse to the petrol engine, from craftsmanship to mass production, from germ laden medicine and crude surgery to antiseptics and anaesthetics, from the muzzle loader to the breech-loading gun. It was the crucible for the twentieth century and the Victorian gentleman took his share in its shaping.

# CHAPTER ONE
# Birth and Childhood

The births and the obstetrics of the early Victorians were little different from those of their Georgian parents and grandparents. It was not until the late 1840s in Britain that experiments began with the use of ether and chloroform as anaesthetics. It was Professor James Simpson of the Chair of Midwifery at Edinburgh who first experimented successfully with its use in childbirth in 1847. Despite almost inevitable opposition from diehard male colleagues, who maintained that it increased the high rate of mortality in child-birth, Simpson eventually triumphed. Queen Victoria herself used chloroform for the birth of her ninth child, Princess Beatrice, in 1857 and from then onwards it was in general use. In the latter part of the Victorian age, at least, childbirth could be a relatively painless process.

Although their advantages might seem obvious to us today, it would be naive to imagine that discoveries of this kind were immediately adopted by every doctor in the country, or that old fashioned methods were not adhered to as late as the end of the century. For instance, although "bleeding" had already been largely discarded by enlightened physicians, as late as 1861 no less authority than Mrs Beeton gave directions in her famed *Household Management* on "How to Bleed," seasoning her advice with a touch of graveyard humour:

"When a person is bled, he should always be standing, or at any rate in the sitting position: for, if, as is often the case, he should happen to faint he can, in most cases at least, easily be brought to again by the operator placing him flat on his back and stopping the bleeding. *This is of the greatest importance.* It has been recommended, for what supposed advantages we don't know, to bleed people when they are lying down. Should a person under these circumstances faint what can be done to bring him round again? The great treatment of lowering the body of the patient to the flat position cannot be followed here. It is in that position already, and cannot be placed lower than it is — except, as is most likely to be the case, under the ground."

In 1865 Mrs Beeton herself died aged twenty-nine after giving birth to a son and developing puerperal fever, still the scourge of childbirth due to lack of understanding of the need for aseptic precautions. With the work of Joseph Lister, already on the track of antiseptics in his Chair of Surgery in Glasgow, the next two decades saw the development of war on microbes and the end of such unnecessary death by careless infection. By the end of the Victorian age a clear understanding of the need for antiseptic precautions had greatly reduced the mortality in surgery and in hospitals, especially in childbirth.

Despite the very considerable advances in medicine during the latter part of the Victorian age, the treatment of infectious diseases remained primitive. Admittedly smallpox, the bane of the previous century, had been more or less brought under control thanks to inoculation, but such scourges as diphtheria, scarlet fever, typhus and typhoid, then not clearly distinguished, tuberculosis and even cholera, which swept the country on three occasions up to 1850, continued to kill off large numbers of young and old regardless of their social status. Lack of good drainage, impure drinking water and simple lack of hygiene were among the principal causes.

A suppressed report concerning the state of Buckingham Palace in mid-century indicated that a main sewer ran under the courtyard and that newly painted basement rooms turned black overnight from the fumes. The drainage at Windsor was even more antiquated and it was from this source that Prince Albert caught the typhoid from which he died in 1861. If the royal palaces were in such a state it is unlikely that the general public fared much better.

Although matters were improving slowly throughout the latter years of the century it was not until 1902 that the various individual companies supplying water to London were united under the aegis of the Metropolitan Water Board. Comment by *Punch* at the time of the Great Exhibition in 1851 indicated the state of the water supplies then. Referring to the organisation of the Exhibition *Punch* noted scathingly, "The contractor is bound to supply gratis, pure water in glasses to all visitors demanding it; but the Committee must have forgotten, that whoever can produce in London a glass of water fit to drink will contribute the rarest and most universally useful article in the whole Exhibition."

Impure drinking water and contaminated milk were both hazards to the young, but the generally spartan regime of childhood ensured that only the fit survived. Some of the practices suggested for the treatment of babies in Mrs Hemans's *Young Woman's Companion*, published in 1832 and frequently reprinted, show what young Victorian children underwent. On bathing the baby she wrote:

"It would be extremely hazardous to dip the tender body of a new born babe in cold water and keep it there during the necessary operations of washing; but the use of the cold-bath may be safely brought about by degrees in five or six months after the birth, and will then be found not only one of the best means of promoting health and strength, but of preventing also many of the most distressing complaints to which children are subject . . .. At night it will be enough to wash the lower parts; and even for this purpose a little warm water may be added to the cold in severe weather . . . and the habit of personal cleanliness, being rendered familiar in childhood, will be retained through life, and contribute very much to its duration and enjoyment."

At first sight, compared to their grandparents of the Georgian age, who seldom bathed at all, the Victorians appear to have made a fetish of cleanliness. Equating cleanliness with Godliness, however, was really just a typical piece of Victorian face-saving. The reason the soap manufacturers boomed during the period was not that the Victorians were naturally cleaner than their grandparents, for indeed exactly the opposite was the case. Due to the vast increase in industry, resulting in a sooty, fog-laden smoke-filled atmosphere in all the large towns and cities, it became essential for them to wash much more frequently. Instead of admitting the uncomfortable truth that they were dirtier than their grandparents they made a virtue of necessity. Hygiene was another matter altogether, about which they knew remarkably little until towards the end of the century.

From the viewpoint of hygiene Mrs Hemans's comments on the bedding most suitable for a baby's cot are extremely revealing: "Nothing can have a more relaxing tendency, or be at the same time more unfavourable to cleanliness, than beds and pillows stuffed with feathers. These absorb and retain the perspirable matter, as well as every other impurity, so that the child who sleeps upon them must inhale the most noxious vapour, while its action on the surface of the body must destroy the energy of the skin and render his whole frame, both within and without, the ready receiver of disease. Horsehair cushions and mattresses are far preferable; but . . . soft bran . . . would more readily let any moisture pass through them, would never be too much heated and might frequently be changed or renewed without any great trouble or expense."

On the subject of baby's clothes she wrote sensibly enough by the standards of the day, "Excess is generally the fault to be avoided in the clothing of infants, as much injury and many deaths are the effects of and a scarf, edged at both sides with embroidery, terminates the back. Pattern of frock, 2s. 7d.

Figs. 2 and 2A. GIRL OF SIX.—Pink cotton trimmed with cambric, embroidered with scarlet. The Princesse frock is plaited in front, and simulates a waistcoat and paletot. A drapery crosses the

No. 9. CHILD'S CHEMISE AND DRAWERS COMBINED.

front, and is concealed beneath the plait at the back. Round cape on the shoulders, and a pointed collar. For front see Fig. 2A. Pattern of frock, 2s. 7d.

No. 8. BOY'S WAISTCOAT AND SKIRT.

with flot bows. The back is cut *en Princesse* and draped as a tunic, a large collar terminating in front with flot bows. For back see Fig. 3A. Pattern of costume, 3s. 7d.

Figs. 4 and 4A. GIRL OF TWELVE.—Summer serge, with white sateen waistcoat and collar. The fronts simulate a paletot, and the

Extract from an illustrated catalogue of children's clothes typical of the period.

not properly attending to this important precaution .... A thin, light cap, slightly fastened with a bit of tape .... A piece of fine flannel round the navel, a linen or cotton shirt, a flannel petticoat, and a linen or cotton robe, are soon put on; and where fastenings are requisite, they should consist of tape, without any dangerous use of pins."

Even by the rough and ready standards of hygiene prevailing the amount of washing of clothes and bedding involved each day must have been immense. Depending on the size of the gentleman's household, of course, the services of one or more full-time laundresses, or washerwomen, were taken for granted. Labour was cheap and readily available. Thus a nurse in charge of the nursery would generally have at least one nursemaid under her, but even so the bulk of the washing would probably be passed to the washerwoman. Circumstances, of course, varied enormously and in some cases the nursery would be regarded as a self-contained part of the household dealing with its own washing entirely, in which case the nursemaid would be kept very busy.

Thanks to the ready availability of nurses and nursemaids the average Victorian parents saw little of their babies. Indeed it was common practice, though frowned on by Mrs Hemans, to employ a wet nurse to feed the child. As late as 1876 Thomas King Chambers, M.D., F.R.C.P.,

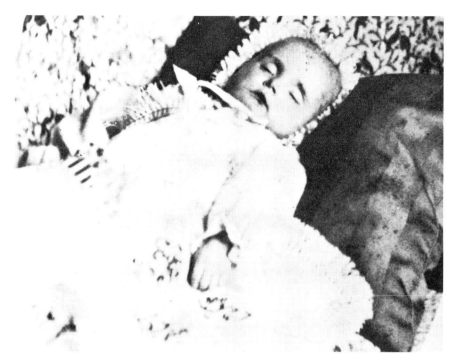

The Victorian baby's clothes made an elaborate outfit with lace generally much in evidence.

in his *Manual of Diet in Health and Disease*, attempting to show all the objections to the practice, merely ended in bathos:

"If a mother, with or without, reasonable cause, deputises her duties to a wet nurse, she ought thoroughly to understand that the expedient is not without its drawbacks. All the best accoucheurs agree that in choosing a woman for the office, observation of the figure, the complexion, the colour, the teeth, or even the shape and development of the breasts, and the analysis of their secretion, are all unimportant compared with a knowledge of the regularity of the catamenis. In this respect it stands to reason we must take the applicants own character of herself, a serious temptation to dishonesty. A married woman may not improbably have a concealed constitutional taint, which is communicated through the milk, and at the best is an unpleasant inmate in the family. A poor married woman, however respectable, is removed from a starving home to sudden abundance, and invariably overeats herself and it is fortunate if she does not over drink herself too. She pines and grows anxious about her child if it is alive, and insists upon having her troublesome husband to see her openly or secretly, on the pretence (a fallacious one) that his visit increases the flow of milk. Moreover, a rich mother cannot but feel some compunction in purchasing for her own offspring what is stolen from another, who is sometimes seriously affected by the fraud and retires disgusted from this false world."

Despite Dr King's book and others of a similar nature, diet was one of the subjects on which the Victorians tended to have somewhat misguided ideas. Surprisingly, in the last two decades of the century one of the diseases common amongst children of the upper classes was scurvy, caused by feeding them on boiled milk, which although less likely to be infected lacked the anti-scorbutic content of plain milk. By the end of the century the advantages of orange juice in the nursery diet as countering this tendency had become appreciated.

Mrs Hemans, more practical and slightly more direct than Dr King, warned against the bad habits of some nurses in the nursery, asking rhetorically, "Is it possible to conceive a more shocking object than an ill-tempered nurse, who . . . in the excess of her folly and brutality endeavours by loud harsh threats and the impetuous rattle of the cradle to drown the infant's cries and to force him into slumber? She may sometimes gain her point, but never till the poor victim's strength is exhausted."

The idealized family nanny of several generations standing was apparently sadly lacking in the early Victorian period for Mrs Hemans also warned against those nurses, who she claimed "are too apt for their own ease, or to gain time for other concerns, to cherish the sleepy dispositions of infants, and to increase it by various things of a stupefactive quality; all these are extremely pernicious. Opiates under the name of cordials, or carminatives, or in any shape or form whatever, should not be given to a child in health."

Despite this warning it was one of the hazards of early Victorian infancy that many nurses contrived to dose their charges with opiates, varying from a measure of port or brandy, if available, to such mixtures as laudanum and treacle. When the children were in good health, either as a punishment or purely as a precaution it was also common practice to dose them with some of the contents of the nursery medicine cupboard, which might vary from brimstone and treacle to castor oil, Gregory's powder, or rhubarb and soda. Nor were such practices always restricted to nurses, for Augustus Hare in his autobiography *The Story of My Life* referred to an occasion about 1840 when his aunt dealt with him in this way. He was about six at the time and recorded subsequently:

"We went to visit the curate, [when] a lady very innocently gave me a lollipop, which I ate. This crime was discovered when I came home by the smell of peppermint and a large dose of rhubarb and soda was at once administered with a forcing spoon, though I was in robust health at the time, to teach me to avoid such carnal indulgences as lollipops for the future. For two years, also, I was obliged to swallow a dose of rhubarb every morning and evening because – according to old fashioned ideas – it was supposed to 'strengthen the stomach.' "

If only a fraction of what he wrote about his childhood was true

Augustus Hare undoubtedly suffered abominable persecution from his sadistic aunt, but the regimen in most early Victorian nurseries was strict. The Victorian ruling "Children should be seen and not heard" was generally firmly applied. The use of cane, strap or even birch was common and such punishments as locking in a room or dark cupboard with only bread and water were widespread. Undoubtedly there was a great deal of sadism and wanton cruelty on occasions and an ill-natured adult, parent, aunt or nurse, could cause children's lives to be a hell. There must have been many unrecognised psychopaths and others with warped natures in such positions with virtually nobody to check them.

One such unrecognised candidate for a psychiatric couch had a considerable effect on the upbringing of many Victorian children more especially in the early part of the period. Mrs Sherwood, who wrote the famous *Life of the Fairchild Family*, a moral novel of family life which was immensely popular throughout a large part of the early Victorian period, described her own childhood in the late Georgian period as follows:

"It was the fashion then for children to wear iron collars round the neck with backboards strapped to the shoulders. To one of these I was subjected from my sixth to my thirteenth year. I generally did all my lessons standing in the stocks with this same collar round my neck; it was put on in the morning and seldom taken off till late in the evening; and it was Latin I had to study. At the same time I had the plainest possible food; dry bread and cold milk were my principal food and I never sat on a chair in my mother's presence. And yet I was a very happy child and when relieved from my collar I not unseldom demonstrated my delight by starting from our own half door and taking a run for half a mile through the woods . . .."

With such a childhood to look back on it is not surprising that the *Life of the Fairchild Family* abounded in moral scenes depicting repressive and sadistic parental behaviour as natural and right. Sins were always visited with condign punishment. God was on the side of Father and the big battalions.

The Fairchild family of the title consisted of Mr Fairchild and Mrs Fairchild, Lucy, Emily and Henry, with the manservant John, and sundry female servants. On one occasion when Henry stole an apple from a tree in the garden, aged about four or five at the time, Mr Fairchild instituted a full-scale inquisition into the theft and Henry was too frightened to tell the truth. Finally John admitted to seeing him eat it. The story continued:

" 'Henry,' said Mr Fairchild, 'is this true? Are you a thief – and a liar too?' And Mr Fairchild's voice was very terrible when he spoke.

"Then Henry fell down upon his knees before his papa and confessed his wickedness.

" 'Go from my sight, bad boy!' said Mr Fairchild: 'if you had told

With lace collar and cuffs, velvet jacket and buttoned knee-breeches, patent leather shoes and silver buckles, the Fauntleroy look dominated late Victorian boy's fashions.

the truth at first I should have forgiven you; but now I will not forgive you.' Then Mr Fairchild ordered John to take Henry and lock him up in a little room at the top of the house, where he could not speak to any person. Poor Henry cried sadly, and Lucy and Emily cried too; but Mr Fairchild would not excuse Henry. 'It is better,' he said, 'that he should be punished in this world whilst he is a little boy, than grow up to be a thief and a liar, and go to hell when he dies: for it is written, "Every liar shall have his portion in the lake which burneth with fire and brimstone." ' "

Mrs Fairchild recounted by way of light relief to the children a "moral tale" on another occasion which almost certainly owed a good deal of autobiographical detail to the authoress. In this story she was left as a child one summer by her aunts with whom she was staying in a cherry orchard with permission to pick any fallen cherries, but not to climb the trees. Along came a neighbouring villager's daughter of poor class who persuaded her to climb a tree. Caught red handed by a servant an interesting social problem arose:

"The person who happened to come to look for me in the cherry-orchard was Mrs Bridget, who was the only one of the servants who would have told of me. . . . and dragged us by the arms into the presence of my aunts, who were exceedingly angry . . . [the other child] was given up to her mother to be flogged; and I was shut up in a

28

dark room, where I was kept several days upon bread and water. At the end of three days my aunts sent for me and talked to me for a long time . . . 'And how many Commandments,' said my Aunt Grace, 'did you break last Sunday?'

" 'You broke the Fourth Commandment,' said Aunt Penelope, 'which is "Remember the Sabbath day to keep it holy": and you broke the Fifth which is "Honour your Parents". We stand in place of parents to you. You broke the Eighth too, which is "Thou Shalt not steal." ' 'Besides,' said my Aunt Grace, 'the shame and disgrace of climbing trees in such low company, after all the care and pains we have taken with you . . .' ' "

On another occasion Mr Fairchild caught the children fighting amongst themselves and the description of the indiscriminate whipping he then inflicted has a distinctly sadistic flavour. Indeed the entire book reeks of repression and regrettable masochistic pleasure in recounting such scenes. For refusing to learn Latin and daring to say he does not want to, Henry is disowned and immured in a room with nothing but bread and water. After catching the children quarrelling, Mr Fairchild, unspeakable tyrant that he is depicted to be, takes the three young children into a dark wood and shows them the corpse of a felon hanging rotting in chains on a gibbet (last practiced in Leicesterhire in 1832). Despite their cries of fear he insists on the shrinking and terrified children remaining there while with evident relish he recounts the history of the wretched man's downfall.

Plainly Mr Fairchild was based on bitter experience and no doubt numerous Victorian parents based their behaviour in turn on his, or at the very least indicated to their offspring how lucky they were to be treated so mildly in comparison. Certainly Augustus Hare managed to find real life as bad, if not worse, than anything conjured up by Mrs Sheridan:

"I had a favourite cat called Selma; which I adored, and which followed me about . . . wherever I went. Aunt Esther saw this, and at once insisted that the cat must be given up to her. I wept over it in agonies of grief but Aunt Esther insisted. My mother was relentless in insisting that I must be taught to give up my own way and pleasure to others . . . soon there came a day when Selma was missing; Aunt Esther had ordered her to be . . . hung."

The conclusion of this affair has an ironic touch: "From this time I never attempted to conceal that I loathed Aunt Esther. I constantly gave her presents for which my mother made me save up all my money — for her birthday, Christmas, New Year, &c. — but I never spoke to her unnecessarily. On these occasions I always received a present from her in return — *The Rudiments of Architecture*, price ninepence, in a red cover. It was always the same, which not only saved expense, but also the trouble of thinking. I have a number of *The*

*Rudiments of Architecture* now, of which I thus became the possessor."

On the other hand, the considerable powers of a sadistic adult over a sensitive child are well depicted by Augustus Hare in another passage: "Aunt Esther resolutely set herself to subdue me . . .. I was a very delicate child and suffered absolute agonies from chilblains, which were often very large open wounds on my feet. Therefore, I was put to sleep in 'the Barracks' — two dismal, unfurnished, uncarpeted north rooms, without fireplaces, looking into a damp courtyard with a well and a howling dog. My only bed was a rough deal trestle. My only bedding a straw palliasse, with a single coarse blanket. The only other furniture in the room was a deal chair, and a washing basin on a tripod. No-one was allowed to bring me any hot water and as the water in my bedroom always froze with the intense cold, I had to break the ice with a brass candlestick, or, if that were taken away, with my wounded hands. If, when I came downstairs in the morning, as was often the case, I was almost speechless from sickness and misery, it was always declared to be 'temper.' I was given 'saur-kraut' to eat because the very smell of it made me sick."

On such a diet and with such treatment it is not surprising that young Augustus Hare was declared to be suffering from curvature of the spine and was forced to wear a heavy metal corset during his childhood days.

Poor diet and lack of care in infancy frequently resulted in undiagnosed cases of rickets or bone malformations which were treated with irons on legs or body. This was by no means uncommon and Walter B. Woodgate in his *Reminiscences* recalled seeing his younger brother, who was born in 1845 suffering in this way:

"He was a very sturdy kid; he could stand with the help of a chair when eleven months old; and could toddle well at his first birthday anniversary. Perhaps the nurses overdid his capacity for pedestrianism . . .. Anyhow by the time he was about two years old, he had to be put into irons to straighten his little legs, which were bowed more than usual for children of that age . . .' "

Despite such handicaps and however stern their upbringing most Victorian children no doubt managed to get some fun out of life, as children will. Even Mrs Sherwood regarded her childhood as happy and one suspects that Augustus Hare's was not quite as bad as he made it out to be. The Woodgate boys certainly seem to have had a perfectly happy childhood. Sons of a clergyman in the Midlands, not far from Birmingham, they were reasonably typical gentleman's sons of their period, the one becoming a barrister and the other a soldier. The grim industrial area near which they lived, however, was well described by Woodgate:

"The Lye Waste, between us and the Black Country, was a savage district, busy with chain-making for the pits . . .. This Lye Waste boasted that coroners' inquests on infanticide were unknown in its area . . .. The solution was simple. Most Lye Wasters kept pigs; if there chanced to be a superfluous baby, the family pig was kept on short commons for a day or so. Then the infant (somehow) 'fell' into the sty! . . . and in half an hour no coroner could have found any remains to sit upon."

In the absence of reliable contraceptives the Victorian gentleman must sometimes have wished that he too could resort to such crude methods of family planning as he watched his family grow yearly in numbers. Fortunately schooling for boys was comparatively cheap and for girls negligible, while income tax was almost non-existent thus it was possible to accept families of nine to twelve children with equanimity. The entire pattern of Victorian life was indeed centred round a large family, but even by such standards one clergyman on record was somewhat excessive.

"I have had twice twenty-four children," he informed a startled Canon's wife soon after his first introduction to her.

"I collect you have been twice married, sir, "she replied icily.

"No, madam," he insisted. "I have but the one wife."

The solution to this seeming impossibility was simply that he had had twenty-four children by this unfortunate woman and on the death of one had sired yet another. He had thus, as he coyly persisted in phrasing it, "had twice twenty four children." Just what his wife thought about it is not reported, but the likelihood is that she would never have dreamed of complaining and accepted her lot with due resignation. It is, of course, even possible that she enjoyed life with her enormous family around her.

It is unwise to assume that because a wife in the Victorian age had a large number of children she was unable to enjoy a full social life, or have time for outside interests. With a large staff to look after her family and household she could readily afford the time to indulge within reason whatever pursuits she wished. That many wives failed to take full advantage of their opportunities due to a limited education, or sheer lack of drive, is another matter. Many of them enjoyed a very full life. Hippolyte Taine, the French philosopher, in his *Notes on England*, written after visits in the 1860s quoted the case of a country gentlewoman with nine children who was also an accomplished Greek scholar and socialite. On the other hand she had two nurses and two governesses, as well as abundant other staff to look after her family and household. In such a case it is also possible that she found time to take an interest in her family as well, but the sad probability is that they saw little of her.

It was part of the Victorian way of life largely induced by having so many servants that the parents generally had a little time with their

Before dinner in the evening, it was common practice for the nursery inhabitants to be paraded downstairs and shown off to the assembled company of guests and relations.

children when they were young. While they were babes in arms they were restricted almost entirely to the nursery save for occasional ceremonial visits to the drawing room. Although exceptionally the parents might visit the nursery it was generally accepted that this was a circumscribed area ruled over by the nurse, or governess. As the family grew in size, so visits became more difficult.

Such large families, of course, had advantages, as well as disadvantages for the young. There would always be brothers or sisters to play with and the family itself became a self-contained unit. With a family possibly spread over twenty years or more, the youngest of the family might have grown-up brothers and sisters. In such circumstances as soon as the youngest had left the nursery and prior to going to school he was often extremely precocious. He would naturally ape his elder brothers and would probably be rather spoiled by everyone. Alternatively he might be both bullied and suppressed. Much, as always, depended on the family and the example set. To judge by the jokes in *Punch*, however, the precocious younger brother making fun of his older brothers, or bullyragging his older sisters was a stock joke from the 1850s onwards.

When the children were considered old enough to come downstairs to meals they were generally served at a separate table with the nurse, or governess, in charge of them for it was the widespread Victorian belief that children should be fed strictly and not overindulged. Breakfast and lunch might be allowed downstairs, but the evening meal at about five would be in the nursery, or schoolroom, with bread and butter, or jam, but seldom both, and only one slice of cake accompanied by milk or cocoa. For girls of fifteen or sixteen, still in the schoolroom, and even for voracious eight-year-old boys, this was simply not enough and it was common practice to sneak downstairs later on as dinner was being served in the hope of obtaining some leftovers from sympathetic servants.

In the nursery to a large extent the children would be expected to amuse themselves and to use their imaginations in doing so, for it was another Victorian axiom that too many toys might spoil the child. In almost every nursery there would, however, be a number of well-worn toys of the solid wooden variety such as cutlasses, cannons, wheel-barrows, trolleys, hobby horse, tops, balls, marbles and similar treasures. Wooden dolls' houses and wooden dolls, succeeded latterly by china-faced dolls made in France and Germany, now prized collectors items, were almost always to be found. Pride of place generally went to a large wooden rocking horse covered in real horsehide and with real mane and tail on which perhaps several generations of the same family would learn their early seat on a horse.

Family prayers each morning and grace before meals were a part of the natural order of things in almost every gentleman's household especially in the early part of the Victorian age. A visit to church on Sunday was generally enforced for all the family and the utmost decorum was expected, however young the child. In a clergyman's family, of course, this was accepted routine twice daily, but in most gentlemen's families it was an understood pattern of life until the general easing of standards in the last three decades. For most of the Victorian age there was a feeling that it was necessary in inculcate a belief in Christianity in the young by example and, if necessary, by force, which scarcely surprisingly was not always successful

The daily routine of the nursery included taking a walk outside when old enough. The baby carriage, or perambulator, was a necessary Victorian invention in the circumstances. E. B. Ellman in his *Recollections* recalled seeing his first "child's carriage" sometime in the 1840s, which he described as "a sort of big basket on wheels in which two children could sit and which was drawn by a handle in the front." It was not long before perambulators were being manufactured and sold in considerable numbers. Although a basketwork type was made and also a full-bodied, deep "carriage" the commonest variety was undoubtedly a three-wheeled type, with two large wheels behind and one in front, which was pushed from behind. By the 1860s and 1870s the "prams" were a familiar sight in London parks, being pushed by nurses and frequently escorted by a red-coated soldier. The idealized picture of family nursery life was in the making and it is not surprising that the conception of *Peter Pan* came to J. M. Barrie in the 1890s.

Although there was little interchange between families of gentlemen in the early Victorian era, the daily outings in the parks soon resulted in nurses and children getting to know each other in London. This in turn led to childrens' parties becoming quite a common feature of London life in the 1880s and 1890s. In the country, however, though children of friends or relations might sometimes come to stay there was seldom the same social intercourse at the nursery stage. With large families this was perhaps not important, although the unfortunate only child suffered considerably, but even so shyness in the presence of strangers was a common Victorian failing, especially amongst the early Victorians.

Life in the nursery, or under a governess, had its compensations for the son of a gentleman in a good hunting country like Warwickshire. It would not be long before he was introduced to his first pony and from then onwards, regardless of the discipline at home, he would always have an escape. Yet this was not without its hazards.

"Among our live stock" Woodgate recorded, "were two Welsh ponies; in summer they ran at grass. One of these was reputed vicious when at pasture, though quiet as a lamb to ride. It may have

TAKING IT MANFULLY.

been only play — it was rough horse-play anyhow — the pony would run at women or children — though not at men. Once he chased my elder sister and myself and jumped a ha-ha to follow us into the garden. It was understood that no-one in petticoats went unprotected into his pasture.

"My brother Edward had a tiny child's wheelbarrow; somehow he had slipped his nurse and wandered . . . in the glebe field where Welsh 'Taff' grazed . . .. There in the middle of the field stood the child, facing the pony, which was prancing at him. The little wheelbarrow was the only barrier. As the pony worked to right or left, as if to reach the child — the latter, cool as a cucumber, swung round also, keeping the wheelbarrow as a pivot and never taking his gaze off the pony . . .. When the kid was brought back safe all he said was that he had a long talk with the pony, who at last had promised not to hurt him."

The mention of petticoats, of course, demonstrates the continuance throughout almost the entire Victorian era of the age-old habit of dressing all the children in the nursery alike up to about the age of four or even older. This could be equated with the primitive custom of allowing the children of the tribe to mingle freely until the age of puberty, but more commonly has been ascribed in origin to the ancient belief that the fairies or "little people" might make away with the heir, or first born, hence to confuse them all the children were dressed alike until safely grown beyond harm. A more probable explanation is simply that of economy. When clothes were expensive and it was desirable to pass them down through a family the obvious convenience of having them of one sex was not to be ignored.

When "breeched," the young Victorian male was frequently dressed in sailor suits, or sometimes in the latter part of the century, in knickerbockers and Norfolk jacket imitating the male fashions of the times. A particularly obnoxious dress for the young nursery bound male in the latter part of the century was the "Little Lord Fauntleroy" velvet knickerbocker suit with lace collar. This unlikely garb was popularised by Mrs Hodgson Burnett's very tedious moral tale entitled *Little Lord Fauntleroy*, which met with a highly undeserved success amongst the Victorian gentleman's wives in England and the matrons in America. This absurd fancy dress was also popularised by none other than Oscar Wilde, who believed in the "life beautiful" and actually appeared in a similar suit himself. Numerous young Victorians forced to wear such clothes no doubt failed to appreciate their beauty.

Inevitably since he was brought up largely outside their immediate influence, the young Victorian's parents were somewhat distant figures. They were to be addressed dutifully as "Mama" and "Papa" and worshipped from a distance. "Papa" especially was regarded as the fount of all wisdom and the source of all power. This myth was carefully cultivated by the entire Victorian household, but children

The sailor suit was another of the popular forms of children's dress throughout most of the Victorian era.

The Viscount Ansen (later Second Earl Lichfield) with his brother and sister. Note that the clothes of the brother and sister are indistinguishable.

have a disconcerting habit of penetrating to the root of such matters when given opportunity to do so. In most cases the parents were not seen sufficiently often for the truth to be discovered.

W. P. Frith, the great Victorian painter, whose masterpiece was probably that much reproduced picture entitled "Derby Day" hung in the National Gallery in 1858, gives a revealing vignette of the differences between classes in his *Autobiography*. The principal figure in the crowded canvas is the acrobat encouraging his son, who is standing in the foreground hungrily eyeing an enormous pie which is part of a nearby picnic. When painting this picture with an acrobat and his son as models, Frith recorded:

"One of my children came into the studio with a message: 'Mamma, says papa, will the models want luncheon?'

" 'Mamma – papa!' said the little acrobat with contempt: 'Why don't you say father and mother, young 'un?'

" 'Don't you be cheeky!' said the parent."

Frith, of course, as an artist and somewhat Bohemian did not qualify as a Victorian gentleman except in the eyes of fellow artists but even so the clear-cut differences between classes and "stations in life" is very obvious. The sons and daughters of the wealthy Victorian gentleman were often subconsciously much more influenced by the actions of the members of the servants hall, which was usually adjacent to the nursery wing, than by their parents. The various personalities such as the butler, housekeeper, footmen, maids and others in this sphere, including nurse, or governess, were often much more real and important than the distant "Mamma" and "Papa."

Once he was out of petticoats the young Victorian male's horizons broadened considerably. He would then be able to roam more freely, making the acquaintance of the grooms and stableboys at first and then graduating to the gamekeepers and outside staff if his father's establishment stretched to such employees. He would soon be astride his first pony and out hunting. Having been taught the rules of safe gun-handling he would be taking his first shots at game. In season he might be fishing or bird-nesting. For the son of the gentleman with an estate in the country, the years from four or five to about eight when he was finally regarded as old enough to go to school were a halcyon period.

Admittedly this was the period when the youngster usually graduated from the care of his nurse to that of a governess. For the first time he was subjected to the disciplines of the schoolroom, but his early lessons in reading, writing and arithmetic, the "three Rs" beloved of the Victorians, were not usually very arduous. He would generally have most of the afternoon at least free for his own pursuits and few of the governesses employed were very effective at disciplining their young male charges.

POOR LITTLE FELLOW!

*Emily.* "WANT SOMETHING TO AMUSE YOU! WHY, I HAVE GIVEN YOU BOOK AFTER BOOK, AND LENT YOU MY PAINT-BOX, AND I'VE OFFERED TO TEACH YOU YOUR NOTES. WHAT MORE DO YOU WANT?"

*Augustus.* "OH, AH! I DON'T CALL THAT AMUSEMENT. I WANT SOME FIGS! OR SOME GINGER-BREAD NUTS! OR A GOOD LOT OF TOFFEE!! THAT'S WHAT I CALL AMUSEMENT."

This was, however, not always the governesses' fault, as Charlotte Brontë, then governess to Mr John Sidgwick's children, made clear in a letter to her sister Emily:

"8 June 1839: I have striven hard to be pleased with my new situation. The country, the house, and the grounds are as I have said, divine; but, alack-a-day, there is such a thing as seeing all beautiful around you – pleasant woods, white paths, green lawns, and blue sunshiny sky – and not having a free moment or a free thought left to enjoy them. The children are constantly with me. As for correcting them, I quickly found that was out of the question; they are to do as they like. A complaint to the mother only brings black looks on myself and unjust partial excuses to screen the children . . .."

Charlotte Brontë went on to emphasize the drudgery involved in her job:

"I said in my last letter that Mrs Sidgwick did not know me. I now begin to find she does not intend to know me; that she cares nothing about me except to contrive how the greatest possible quantity of labour may be got out of me, and to that end she overwhelms me with oceans of needlework; yards of cambric to hem, muslin nightcaps to make, and above all things, dolls to dress . . . . I see more clearly than I have ever done before that a private governess has no existence, is not considered as a living rational being, except as connected with the wearisome duties she has to fulfil."

The position of governess was undoubtedly a very invidious one. Often the daughters of professors, or clergymen, from impecunious middle class homes, they were usually forced to become governesses for lack of any better alternative. Since they were seldom fully accepted as members of the family in most houses, yet were clearly not servants, they fell between two stools, being treated as neither one thing nor the other. While dinner was being served in the dining room, they were usually served with a tray in their own rooms in solitary and unhappy state. It is not surprising that a number turned to authorship.

Charlotte Bronte's employer, Mrs Sidgwick, sounds the sort of person catered for in *Beeton's Complete Letter-Writer* of the 1860s, which contained a suggested draft for "An Unfavourable Answer to an Enquiry Respecting a Governess's Abilities, etc." This proposed draft ran:

Address . . . . . . .
Date in full. . . . .

Madam,

You were pleased to send me a polite note asking for my opinion of Miss . . . . . 's character and capabilities, and in answer I regret exceedingly to say that it is not so favourable as I could wish. She lived in my family nearly . . . . . . and during that time she displayed no interest in her duties, and allowed my daughters to fall considerably behind in their education and deportment. I had frequently the disagreeable duty imposed upon me of reprimanding Miss . . . . . . and on such occasions I hoped that it might be the last, but the necessity continued to arise up to the time of her dismissal. I found her deficient in music and French, and by no means a good English grammarian. It pains me to write so unfavourably of my daughters' late governess, but were I to conceal the truth it would do her no permanent service, unless she seriously took herself to task.

Believe me,
Madam,
Your obedient servant,
( . . . . . . . . . . . . . . . . . . . . )

Standards amongst governesses, as amongst nurses, of course varied enormously. Lord Curzon, amongst others, found himself as a child in

AN INJURED BROTHER.

Mamma. "DEAR! DEAR! DEAR!—WHAT A PITY IT IS YOU CAN'T AGREE!"

Small Boy. "WELL, MAMMA, WE SHOULD AGREE, ONLY SHE'S SO UNKIND!—SHE WON'T BE A PIG, AND LET ME DRIVE HER ABOUT BY THE LEG!"

A TERRIBLE THREAT.

Master Jack. "NOW THEN, CHARLOTTE, ARE YOU GOING TO LEND ME YOUR PAINT BOX?"

Charlotte. "NO, SIR. YOU KNOW WHAT A MESS YOU MADE OF IT LAST TIME!"

Master Jack. "VERY WELL. THEN I'LL PUT MY GUINEA PIG ON YOUR NECK!"

the control of a twisted female, who made his life a misery. W. B. Woodgate, on the other hand, referred to his governess, a Miss Sugden, as one "to whom I owe an infinite debt for sound grounding in history, geography, arithmetic, French and tables of dates." There were undoubtedly some honourable exceptions capable of teaching a wide range of subjects and imbuing rebellious young males and their dumpy teenage sisters with an interest in their subjects. Not surprisingly, however, the majority found that their young male charges much preferred the tuition of grooms and gamekeepers.

In the 1860s Hippolyte Taine was particularly impressed by the greed and savagery of the English boys he met. Accepting their portrayal in *Punch* as the true picture, he saw him as a pugnacious, savage minded child, ready to threaten his sister with a guinea pig down her neck if she did not agree to his wishes, prepared to show his elders the way in the hunting field, willing to protect his uncle against footpads at night. That these were caricatures rather than an accurate picture seems to have escaped him, but Taine found the English, as a whole, gross in many ways and one suspects he neither liked nor fully understood children, especially English children.

From his nursery days onwards the importance of "being a man" was always being rammed home to the average Victorian youngster. Even when breaking the ice on the morning washing bowl, they were not expected to complain and would have got short shrift had they done so. A beating was expected to be taken "manfully" and a fall from a horse treated as lightly. This was the "manliness" on which the Victorians prided themselves and which Taine found somewhat irksome. These were lessons not generally learned from a governess, but from elder brothers, stableboys, grooms and gamekeepers.

As Siegfried Sassoon showed so delightfully in his *Memoirs of a Foxhunting Man* an intelligent groom could do enormous service even for a solitary, shy youngster brought up by a maiden aunt. Only when Tom Dixon finally got the eight-year-old Sassoon mounted on his first pony did he accord him the repectful title "Sir," thus emphasising the great importance of the event in the boy's mind. Only by his careful encouragement and tactfully offered advice could the sensitive, introverted child have ever taken up hunting and developed into a keen sportsman.

It is significant also that Sassoon as a youngster in the 1890s read a great deal of Surtees and felt he had learned a lot from him, although totally missing the satire. The literature of the Victorian age undoubtedly mirrored the changes in the decades. Thus Dickens and Thackeray were followed by Surtees, with his wonderful range of satirical characters from Jorrocks, the epitome of the sporting City man, to the Duke of Donkeyton, the archetypal aristocratic ass and his winsome son the Marquis of Bray, despair of debutante daughters, all larger than life, but based on reality. Then there was Lewis Carroll's *Alice in Wonderland* and *Through the Looking Glass* and Edward Lear's *Book of Nonsense* first published in 1846, anonymously, with limericks only, it began:

> There was an old Derry down Derry,
> Who loved to see little folks merry;
> So he made them a book
> And with laughter they shook,
> At the fun of the Derry down Derry."

The early sales were slow, but it was republished in 1856 and under his own name with his drawings in 1861. Thereafter it sold thirty editions in his own lifetime. The last decades of the century also saw such popular boys' writers as G. A. Henty, Ballantyne and the American Fenimore Cooper, as well as widely read authors such as Conan Doyle and H. G. Wells.

From the 1870s onwards after Prince Albert's death, young Victorians enjoyed a steadily increasing freedom and enjoyment compared with earlier generations. By the late 1880s Victoria had become little more than a figurehead and Edward's free and easy ways set the tone for the upper classes, despite the frowns of older generations. The swing away from early Victorian austerity had begun. Towards the end of the century the attitude to children was more enlightened and easier than in the early decades of the reign.

There can be little doubt that the repressive early Victorian upbringing was responsible for many a strange neurosis in later years. Such unfortunate quirks as that of A. J. Munby, who became fixated at an early age on dirty serving wenches and eventually married one, thereafter continuing to live a double life for the next forty years, is but one example of a life twisted in childhood. Many more Victorians developed a neurosis about flagellation sometimes indeed known as the "English disease" amongst flagellationists. Even an otherwise blameless and respectable clergyman such as Francis Kilvert made a habit of noting in his diary whenever he saw a young girl's bottom suitable for beating. On the whole it is only surprising how many apparently normal people survived such repressive childhood, but it must be remembered that above all the Victorians were trained to avoid showing their feelings in public. Neurosis and dirty linen were simply kept out of sight. They did not even admit that they existed.

By the end of the century boys' clothes had to some extent come to be an imitation of their parents'.

# CHAPTER TWO

# Preparatory and Public Schools

During the Victorian age the educational system of Britain underwent a dramatic expansion, to keep pace with the population explosion and to provide leaders for the ever increasing British Empire. Throughout the period new public schools proliferated and the old public schools expanded and altered until in some cases they were changed almost beyond recognition. The sons of stockbrokers and other city business men, of brewers and industrial magnates, of lawyers and doctors even of wealthy tradesmen, none of whom could themselves have qualified as gentlemen in the Georgian era, or even in the early part of the Victorian period, all went to public schools and after undergoing the process misleadingly referred to as "education" emerged as embryo Victorian gentlemen.

At the start of Victoria's reign Winchester, Eton, Harrow, Rugby and Westminster were perhaps the best known and oldest established public schools in the country. As the century progressed new schools were developed on similar lines and old foundations revitalised. Some had a particular bias as in the case of Wellington founded in 1859 and backed by Prince Albert with the object of assisting the widows of army officers to educate their sons. Haileybury, the old East India Company College, closed with the ending of the John Company influence in India after the Mutiny, was re-opened as a public school with a bias towards the army, the church and India. To name only a few others in the south Radley was one of the first of the new public schools to be founded in the late 1840s, while Charterhouse and Uppingham were both examples of old foundations extensively redeveloped. In Scotland,

43

Rugby School at the end of the 1880s.

Edinburgh Academy, Fettes, Glenalmond, Loretto, Merchiston and
Watsons were all products of the 19th century. In effect all had the
same purpose and were conducted on roughly similar lines.

Each might, and indeed did, develop its own distinctive features.
Each, for instance, almost inevitably, developed its own vocabulary of
slang terms generally completely unintelligible to strangers and frequently changing with the generations. Many continued a form of
fagging system and some degree of bullying was common, although
much depended on the degree of control exercised by the masters. Each
had its own system of houses and internal control, even if some were
almost carbon-copies of others.

Some had their own games peculiar to themselves and played by
no-one else, but as the century progressed uniformity of games and
rules became recognised as of importance for competition. There was
small point in fostering the team spirit if there were no other teams
playing the same game with the same rules. All the schools encouraged
the team spirit, at least towards the end of the century. All had some
form of corporal punishment of varying degrees of severity. All utilised

in some form the prefect system first introduced by Thomas Arnold at Rugby in the 1830s.

Thomas Arnold, the central figure of *Tom Brown's Schooldays*, was recognised as the great educational innovator of the first half of the 19th century. When he was appointed headmaster of Rugby in 1827 he set about revolutionizing the old educational ideas. His greatest success was the introduction of the prefect system, whereby control was passed in some measure to the senior boys and this was extensively copied throughout the country. His greatest concern was always for the "moral tone" of his pupils. By the time of his death in 1842 it was acknowledged that he had radically altered the public school system. Yet, although he had numerous imitators, he was also not without his critics, not least his son Matthew Arnold.

Hippolyte Taine, who visited Westminster and Harrow, was appalled by almost everything, but particularly the system of fagging. He also noted that the bullying at Westminster was extremely bad, but he concluded that the young English were naturally more pugnacious than the young French. He quoted Thomas Arnold's somewhat insular but revealing comments on a visit made to France.

"We see few here whose looks and manners are what we should call those of a thorough gentleman . . .. A thorough English gentleman – Christian, manly and enlightened – is more, I believe, than Guizot or Sismondi could comprehend; it is a finer specimen of human nature than any other country, I believe, could furnish."

In 1839 Arnold was obviously concerned with the general disrepute connected in so many gentleman's minds with the status of the schoolmaster. He pointed out the advantages of schoolmasters also being clergymen:

"The position of the schoolmaster in society . . . has not yet obtained that respect in England, as to be able to stand by itself in public opinion as a liberal profession; it owes the rank which it holds to its connexion with the profession of clergyman, for that is acknowledged universally in England to be the profession of a gentleman. Mere teaching, like mere literature, places a man, I think, in rather an equivocal position; he holds no undoubted station in society by these alone; for neither education nor literature have ever enjoyed that consideration and general respect in England which they enjoy in France and in Germany. But a far higher consideration is this, that he who is to educate boys, if he is fully sensible of the importance of his business, must be unwilling to lose such a great opportunity as the clerical character gives him, by enabling him to address them continually from the pulpit, and to administer the Communion to them as they become old enough to receive it."

In the same year, 1839, he also wrote condemning such popular authors as Dickens for distracting his pupils:

"Childishness in boys, even of good abilities, seems to me a growing fault, and I do not know to what to ascribe it, except to the great number of exciting books of amusement, like Pickwick, and Nickleby, Bentley's Magazine, etc. etc. These completely satisfy all the intellectual appetite of a boy which is rarely very voracious, and leave him totally palled not only for his regular work . . . but for good literature of all sorts, even for history and poetry."

In the Georgian period it had been common for the country gentleman, if he did not employ a tutor for his sons, to send them initially to the local village school or grammar school if one was available close at hand, or else arrange for the local parson to tutor them along with some of the brighter village lads. They would then customarily go on to their public school at around the age of ten. The standard of education they had attained, of course, varied very considerably, but in most cases it was probably a good enough grounding, since in any event the public school did not expect much, or, it must be added, teach much beyond Latin, at least initially.

With the vast expansion of the public schools this system became outdated largely through weight of numbers. The public schools began to expect their pupils older, between the ages of twelve and thirteen normally, and with some sound preparation behind them. Private tutors

A typical schoolroom towards the end of the Victorian era; discipline was still rigid by modern standards, but the brow-beaten look was beginning to disappear.

were still employed in rare cases, even as late as the 1890s, when Siegfried Sassoon recalled being inefficiently tutored by an elderly retired elementary schoolmaster named Mr Star. The sheer difficulty of finding a tutor in most cases, as much as the cost involved, was insurmountable. If there was what seemed to be a good elementary or preparatory school within reasonable distance this must have appeared a much more sensible alternative as few boys learned much at the hands of their governesses, however suitable they might be for girls.

The unfortunate fact was that there were no restrictions on, or qualifications required for setting up a preparatory school and many remarkably inefficient, indeed downright appalling, establishments were opened during Victoria's reign. As there were no inspections there were no standards which required to be met. The masters were generally unqualified and badly paid. Food was almost invariably poor or insufficient and punishments often sadistic. The recollections of many Victorians looking back on their childhood days are filled with indignation as they recall their preparatory schooldays.

Augustus Hare, aged nine in 1843, was sent to a school opened by the Rev. Robert Kilvert, the father of the Rev. Francis Kilvert, near Chippenham. Hare later recorded:

"The greater portion of Mr Kilvert's scholars — his 'little flock of lambs in Christ's fold' — were a set of little monsters. All infantine immoralities were highly popular — and in such close quarters it would have been difficult for the most pure and high minded boy to escape from them. The first evening I was there, at nine years old, I was compelled to eat Eve's apple right up — indeed the Tree of Knowledge of Good and Evil was stripped absolutely bare: there was no fruit left to gather."

Augustus Hare may well have been exaggerating a little, since he did not give this impression to Francis Kilvert when they met subsequently, although it is possible he was being polite at the time. On the other hand, the recollections of a very great many Victorians all bear witness to much the same thing. The experiences of Sir Francis Burnand, son of a stockbroker in London, who was sent to a private school at Stamford Hill in the 1840s, prior to going to Eton in 1850 aged 14, were fairly typical. At six years old they were beaten on the hand with a ruler. A regular punishment consisted of having a leather stock strapped round their neck with a stick under their armpits and their wrists bound together behind their back, then being placed in a corner during tea and being fed on dry bread, milk and water.

Lord Knutsford, who was sent off to his preparatory school in the 1860s at the age of eight considered it a very good one by the standards of the day and noted that it had been carefully chosen by his father. They were fed giant helpings of Yorkshire pudding which had to be eaten before they received any meat and "were tubbed once a week – all twenty-one of us – in the same water by the old house-maid." He also recorded:

"Dr Huntingford had a very scientific method of caning – far too severe for little boys. We had to kneel down before him, put our heads between his ankles, and then from his full height (he stood six feet four inches) down came the cane with a tremendous swish."

In the 1870s George Cornwallis-West admitted that the boys were well taught at his preparatory school, but since they only were given bread and butter for breakfast and tea and indifferent beef or mutton at midday they would have been very underfed had it not been for food sent from home, which they were expected to share round. He noted that bullying was atrocious and included the refinement of forcing small boys to eat flies. "The Headmaster himself was, I honestly believe, a sadist; I am certain it afforded him intense pleasure to administer the severest thrashings, having first deprived the boy of any form of protection. He once, when I was there, thrashed a boy until he fainted."

It is, of course, easy to colour the picture and exaggerate the horrors of childhood in after years. Yet even the literature of the day bears out the same story. For instance F. Anstey's humorous *Vice Versa*, written in 1882 depicts the headmaster as a sadistic lout and the school appallingly badly run as the father, Mr Bultitude, finds out when by a magic eastern talisman he and his son change places.

No doubt there were exceptions, but they seem to have been remarkably rare. Presumably some Victorian boys enjoyed their preparatory schooldays, but few of them seem to have bothered to place the fact on record. Unfortunately cruelty and perversion, even downright sadism, seem to have been commonplace and bullying and underfeeding were also frequent. Just what degree of real vice existed it is hard to say. Certainly there was some homosexuality at public schools, but by mere virtue of age it was presumably not common at preparatory schools. Even at public school it does not seem to have been so very prevalent, as has sometimes been suggested. Taine, who was admittedly more interested in heterosexual relationships, never mentioned the subject although he expressed his revulsion at the idea of sending boys away from home so young. Augustus Hare, who was at Harrow for a short time, recorded, "I have often heard since much of the immoralities of public-school, but I can truly say when I was there, I saw nothing of them."

Unfortunately the Victorians so often talked in euphemisms and employed such circuitous language on occasions that it is very difficult sometimes to be certain exactly what they intended to convey. A good example of this is to be found in a letter written by Benjamin Jowett, Master of Balliol from 1870–1893, to a young relation, who was about to go to school as a boarder for the first time. One wonders if after

Boys at Christs Hospital in their traditional monastic uniform. Here in the 1870s the brow-beaten look was deliberately cultivated.

reading it the boy was any the wiser, although it is certainly an impressive warning:

"I need not warn you about lying or falsehood. But there is another matter about which I ought to warn you because you have been brought up at home and are thus happily innocent about it. It is one of the great trials of life at school. Boys about your age, or a little older, are sometimes very vicious and indecent, both in word and also sometimes in action; indeed, it happens occasionally that there are one or two boys in a school horribly wicked about these things. Now, if you come across anything of this sort take no part in it."

This "horribly wicked" action against which Jowett was warning his young relative was not homosexuality, but masturbation. The Victorians regarded masturbation as the most "vicious form of incontinence." It was described in these words by Dr William Acton in his book published in 1857, which went into a second edition within a year, entitled *The Function and Disorders of the Reproductive Organs in Childhood, Youth, Adult Age and Advanced Life, Considered in their Physiological, Social and Moral Relations*. This work is remarkable in having only two short references to females in it, but otherwise being totally concerned with the human male. With reference to a boy who habitually masturbates Dr Acton draws a sombre picure:

"The frame is stunted and weak, the muscles undeveloped, the eye is sunken and heavy, the complexion is sallow, pasty, or covered with spots of acne, the hands are damp and cold and the skin moist. The boy shuns the society of others, creeps about alone, joins with repugnance in the amusements of his schoolfellows. He cannot look anyone in the face, and becomes careless in dress and uncleanly in person. His intellect has become sluggish and enfeebled, and if his evil habits are persisted in, he may end in becoming a drivelling idiot or a peevish valetudinarian . . .."

Read in conjunction with this appalling description of Dr Acton's, Jowett's advice to his young relation becomes clear. A further letter to a schoolboy which Jowett wrote in 1861 also makes the same point, though in this instance rather more indirectly. He wrote on this occasion:

"Shall I give you some good advice? It is only this – to make yourself a good cricketer, football player etc., and not to sit 'sapping' too much while other boys are at play. It does not answer in the long run. You want to improve your mind as well as do a certain number of lines, sums, etc. But you cannot do this unless you improve your health. the boys are not far wrong in respecting a boy who is 'good at games' and I would advise you to try and gain their respect in this way as well as in books."

Despite Jowett's paternal, or avuncular, tone, he once again takes refuge in euphemism, so that the young recipient is no wiser as to the real reasons for his advice. Of course frankness on such matters was unheard of at this time, especially between different generations. Nevertheless it is rather surprising to find a sample letter "from a father to his son at school," included in Beeton's *Complete Letter Writer*, published in the 1860s. The moral sentiments expressed in it appear to belong to an earlier generation and perhaps the hack writer who produced the letter for Beeton was elderly. Despite this it gives an idea of the stilted phraseology often employed between Victorian father and son, which Taine also commented on at the same period:

Address . . . .
Date in full . . . .

My dear . . . .
While satisfied that you will cause us no disappointment as regards your conduct and studies at school, I think that perhaps a line from me now will serve to impress upon you still more distinctly the necessity of being prudent and diligent. You are still very young  and know nothing of the temptations which come across the way of youth, nor of the evils which arise in

after life from habits contracted at school under the influence of unprincipled associates. I am desirous that you should choose for your companions clever boys, from whom you may learn how to combine accuracy and expedition in performing your tasks; but I would rather that your associates were dull, and unable to be of any service to you, than that they should be clever and ill-disposed. Avoid every thing that your conscience and your Bible tell you is wrong, even in the most trifling matters, as it is of the utmost importance for you to begin life with no bias in favour of the airy pleasures of the world. Read your Bible earnestly morning and night; regard it as your best friend, and when you are in doubt or difficulty, always turn to it for counsel. Next to the duty you owe to God is that which you owe to your parents, and you cannot perform that duty better than by diligently studying your books and bearing your father and mother always in mind. By remembering how grieved they would be were your teachers to report unfavourably of your progress, you will be less liable to fall into indolent habits, or that which is equally pernicious, namely, the reading of books of fiction of a low class. It would be a good plan to avoid fiction altogether until you are older and read history both for instruction and amusement. You cannot read too much history and biography, only let your reading be attentive and methodical. Do not turn over a leaf until you have thoroughly mastered the page, otherwise you will never be able to turn what you have read to useful account. And now my dear . . . . . . . . I think I have said all that is needful at present. What I have omitted your own good sense ought to supply, and will supply if only you will consult it. Write home often and unreservedly. Always regard us as your best friends, and hide nothing from us.

With kindest love from your mother,

Believe me,

Ever your affectionate father

( . . . . . . . . . . . . )

Whether this moralising epistle was intended for a son at a preparatory or public school is not clear. All that is clear from the records of the period is that very few Victorians remembered their preparatory school days with any pleasure. Lord Randolph Churchill must be one of the very few exceptions who was happy at his. The seven year old Winston, however, had to be removed from his which was run by a confirmed sadist and numerous contemporaries repeat the same familiar story, Sir Osbert Sitwell and Lord Curzon amongst them.

When it came to their public schooldays the Victorians had rather more conflicting opinions. To many they were, if only perhaps in retrospect, "the happiest days of their lives." The image presented by *Tom Brown's Schooldays*, in which the headmaster was modelled on Thomas Arnold remained the ideal of life at the Victorian public school. Here there was bullying admittedly. Flashman was the prototype of the school bully and in the best traditions of drama was discovered and foiled by the hero. Brook, the head of the school was the portrait of all that was considered desirable in the manly, muscular Christian Victorian leader of men. Yet idealised or not it presented a fair enough portrayal of life at a public school. Like the Victorian childhood inevitably it varied and although much was unpleasant and even by modern standards positively appalling it was of a piece with the standards of the day and was accepted as such. Floggings were an accepted fact of life as were fagging and bullying to some extent. As always there were those who loathed every moment of it and those who enjoyed life to the full. In general it was probably those who loathed it who tended to write most about it subsequently. The noisy minority in any day and age can give a very misleading impression of the feelings of the majority.

Augustus Hare, accustomed to present a fairly dire picture of his youth was quite restrained on the subject of Harrow, where he spent a year before being removed for health reasons. His attitude to his education there was scathing enough:

"I may truly say that I learned nothing useful at Harrow and had little chance of learning anything. Hours and hours were wasted daily on useless Latin verses with sickening monotony. A boy's school education at this time, except in the highest forms, was hopelessly inane."

He was still wearing his metal corset due to curvature of his spine, "a terrible iron frame, into which my shoulders were fastened as into a vice ... stooping being almost impossible." Yet despite this he does not seem to have been unduly worried by bullying, or perhaps it was merely that he was accustomed to far greater sadism at home than he ever experienced at school.

"The constant cruelty at Harris's where the little boys were always made to come down and box in the evening for the delectation of the fifth form — of how little boys were constantly sent in the evening to Famish's — half way to the cricket ground, to bring back porter under their greatcoats, certain to be flogged by the headmaster if they were caught, and to be 'wrapped' by the sixth form boys if they did not go out and infinitely preferring the former — of how if the boys did not 'keep up' at football, they were made to cut large thorn sticks out of the hedges and flogged with them till blood poured down outside their jerseys."

This, of course, was in the 1840s and public schools were still developing on the lines Arnold had pioneered at Rugby in the previous decade. In the 1870s George Cornwallis-West was commenting on the freedom he found at Eton after his preparatory school and recorded, "Life at Eton was a joy to me at all times."

W. A. Fearon noted in *The Passing of Old Winchester* around mid-century: "Our life was certainly a narrow one in every way. We were shut off from the outside world. We were shut off from one another. We were shut off from the Masters. Masters and boys lived in different worlds. I never spoke to a Master except officially, on school business . . . nor did it ever occur to me that there could be any other relation. The Masters were simply another creation.

"But the first real change in the relation began with the establishment of the first House in 1859. Still even then the Wykehamical tradition was so strong that I am assured that the first housemaster . . . never went at night into his own boys' bedrooms without putting on his tall hat and overcoat."

Sir Francis Burnand, who went to Eton in 1850, viewed his schooldays there fairly dispassionately afterwards. His new boy routine consisted of rising at six by the light of a tallow candle. Until he had prepared his fagmaster's breakfast of tea or coffee, boiled eggs, buttered toast and grilled chicken he was unable to breakfast himself. By the time he left he knew how to grill chickens to perfection, make delicious buttered eggs and excellent coffee. There may be worse things to learn, but no doubt his father, who was paying £250 a year for the privilege, might have had other views on the matter. It hardly seems necessary to have had to dress in white turn down collars, black ties, waistcoats and jackets and top hats to perform such menial tasks, but that was part of the "system."

On the other hand W. B. Woodgate, who was sent to Radley in 1850, when it was still one of the newest public schools to be opened, recollected his schooldays with unmixed pleasure. He was obviously happy there and certainly appears to have made the most of it. By the standards of the day it is clear that it was particularly well organised with innovations which were well ahead of its time, even if they were inevitably soon to be copied elsewhere. He recollected:

"Compared to other public schools, this foundation was then reported to be almost Sybaritic. Separate cubicles for each boy; shoes blacked for us by servants, not a task for fags; fresh joints at dinner – (no 'resurrection pies') – and matrons to look after us if we even cut our fingers and needed plaster. Hot baths twice a week; and casual invitations from masters to boys to spend spare evenings in their rooms."

Yet looking back on his schooldays sixty years later he was compelled to admit that schools had very greatly improved in the interval. Even in an enlightened school of the period it seems they did not insist on the boys changing their clothes for games, or bother about elementary hygiene. The point was not even considered important. He

A dormitory at Christs Hospital in the 1880s.

recorded:

"When I first began school life, there was no flannelising for games; we rolled in the mud in our everyday linen shirts and cloth trousers, ignored rain, and then sat at school hours after play in our sodden attire. Yet I never knew of any pneumonia resulting; we were used to it . . . the fittest survived."

It may be that being nearly eighty when he wrote his *Reminiscences* Woodgate's memory was failing him and tingeing his schooldays with a more roseate hue than they merited. According to another source, boys at Radley at this period were perpetually half starved and roasted acorns over candles as well as eating bulbs of crocuses and other flowers to supplement their diet. Woodgate himself admitted to poaching game with snares on a neighbouring estate. He would then intercept the carrier's cart delivering each day to the college and consign the game to himself as if a present from a relation. He would later collect it for dinner the next day.

Such additions to their foods were very necessary when it is appreciated that their breakfast consisted of nothing more than bread and butter at eight in the morning. On whole and half holidays they only had a chunk of dry bread for lunch until their principal meal at four p.m. Only the rowing eights, who usually ran most of the one and a half miles between the school and the river were allowed the indulgence of buying biscuits and a glass of beer at the public house there. Small wonder that they were perpetually hungry.

To be fair to him Woodgate admitted as much but in his detailed account of his schooldays his principal complaint was lack of sleep rather than lack of food. He noted:

". . . our hours were much the same as at other public schools of the period. Nine o'clock was the general dormitory hour. 'Reveille' bell sounded at 5.45, and by 6.30 we had attired, reached the school-room, had prayers and roll call, and were ready for an hour and a half study on empty stomachs, till breakfast time at 8 a.m. Now this gave only a few minutes over eight hours in bed even for those who went to roost at nine.

"When studies were built and awarded to seniors, matters became even worse for those thus privileged. Study-boys who were not prefects were allowed to sit up till 10 p.m. Their dormitory lights to be out by 10.30 p.m., while prefects were allowed a further half hour. Naturally all those privileged usually sat up to their full tether – even if not working.

"I myself got a study when short of fourteen, having reached the fifth form. Result at that tender age I averaged well under eight hours sleep nightly. Meantime, apart from lessons, our average physical tax had been in play hours, two and a half hours of football or fives in winter, and in summer three miles on foot to the river and back and some miles of rowing as well. All this performance on one meat meal and two farinaceous ones; prefects got supper, others did not."

He commented on the improvements in the 1890s by which time cocoa was provided on getting up, "animal food" was provided with breakfast and there was afternoon tea as well as the final evening meal, making nearly twice as much food. Along with this he noted they had nearly an hour's more sleep. He pointed to the results in the increased average weights of school crews rowing at Henley at that time as compared with the 1860s when schools first competed there.

Writing in 1890 in his *Leaves of a Life*, Montagu Williams, Q.C., who was at Eton at much the same time as Burnand and as Woodgate at Radley, looked back on his schooldays forty years earlier as the happiest days of his life. He admitted that Eton had changed immensely during that period and indicated that considerable changes were taking place about the time he was there. Bullying he mentioned included making new boys dance in the middle of a paper bonfire, or tying them up in their gowns and dumping them in a remote spot. Since he had an elder brother at the school, he knew what to expect and how to prepare for it. In the first case by wearing two pairs of thick trousers and heavy coat and in the second by carrying a small knife in a pocket. Thus no doubt he did not suffer greatly. Nor did he receive more than one flogging during his school career, which was also by no means typical.

He recorded the method of administering a flogging by Dr Hawtrey the head master of the time: "When any member of the Upper School was punished, the punishment took place in the head master's room, where the block was kept. The Sixth Form praeposter kept the key of the birch cupboard and superintended the execution. If the culprit were a friend of his, he busied himself, while Hawtrey was giving a preliminary lecture, in picking the buds off the birch. The sufferer was in the hands of two holders-down while the punishment was being inflicted, and the number of cuts was regulated by the gravity of his offence."

In his reminiscences of his schooldays, entitled *Seven Years at Eton, 1857–1864*, J. Brinsley Richards was rather more specific about beatings in the Lower School. He arrived at Eton in 1857 as a sensitive ten year old:

"I had never been chastised since I was in the nursery after the manner in use at Eton. When I first came to the school, and was told how culprits were dealt with . . . I fancied I was being hoaxed. I never quite believed the stories until I actually saw a boy flogged . . . the victim . . . was a . . . boy called Neville . . .. In the Lower School floggings were public . . .. [The birch] was nearly five feet long, having three feet of handle and nearly two of bush. As Mr Carter grasped it and poised it in the air, addressing a few words of rebuke to Neville, it appeared a horrible instrument for whipping so small a boy with, Neville was unbracing his nether garments – next moment when he knelt on the step of the block, and when the Lower Master inflicted upon his person six cuts that sounded like splashings of so many buckets of water, I turned almost faint."

Montagu Williams instanced one typical example of schoolboy abhorrence of telling tales, or sneaking, which could have happened in many public schools of the time and earned the boy concerned a flogging and honourable recognition afterwards:

"On one occasion a fag named Fursden was ordered . . . to fetch half a dozen bottles of beer, secreting them in his gown pockets; but he was caught in the act . . . and . . . told that unless he confessed who sent him on this errand he would have to go before the headmaster for execution. Nevertheless . . . he maintained a dogged silence, and . . . took his punishment like a man. That night he was asked to supper at Sixth Form table."

There seems to have been a good deal of drinking at Eton at this time, although nothing like what there had been in Georgian times. After school cricket and football matches between Collegers and Oppidans, the two main divisions within Eton, there was considerable revelry. Williams wrote:

"Something like an orgie . . . prevailed . . .. All the jugs and basins were called into requisition and the Lower boys were set to work preparing these vessels for the brewing of 'gin-twirley,' an innocent kind of gin punch. Recourse was also had to a barrel of strong ale, which had been secretly imported . . .. Lights were supposed to be extinguished by ten o'clock, and at that hour Dr Hawtrey . . . visited Long Chamber to see that all was quiet . . .. When Dr Hawtrey entered Long Chamber all were snoring and apparently asleep. He went away satisfied little dreaming that five minutes later the candles would be brightly burning and a merry festival in progress."

A great deal at every school depended on the headmaster. Arnold had set the tone for Rugby and indeed for public school education in the first decades of the Victorian age. Sewell, who took over Radley shortly before Woodgate went there, introduced the prefect system and brought the school into considerable repute. In 1859 E. W. Benson, afterwards to become Archbishop of Canterbury, was appointed the first headmaster of Wellington. With the backing of Prince Albert he developed it into a notable school, even if he resolutely conducted it on British lines rather than the Germanic ones favoured by the Prince.

The development of Harrow on modern lines began in 1845 with the headmastership of C. J. Vaughan, a disciple of Arnold, who reformed the school radically. Amongst his staff he included such men as E. H. Bradby, subsequently headmaster of Haileybury, S. A. Pears, subsequently headmaster of Repton, and F. W. Farrar, subsequently headmaster of Marlborough and Dean of Canterbury. Farrar was also notable as the author of the revoltingly moral tale of *Eric, or Little by Little* and other books, especially *Julian Home*, subtitled *A Tale of College Life*, a thinly disguised account of Harrow life published in 1862.

In 1860 Vaughan was succeeded by H. M. Butler, the first old Harrovian to fill the post. A stern disciplinarian he still had tact and understanding, as instanced by the occasion when a young Scots Highlander appeared at the school wearing the kilt, having travelled south entirely by himself and not possessing a pair of trousers to his name. Butler kept him in his study until a local tailor had been summoned to fit him out with breeches on the spot.

The return of graduates to their old schools as masters helped to perpetuate the public school traditions, which were so much a part of the public school system as it developed during the nineteenth century. Some were gifted masters, able to teach well, while others were indifferent or downright bad, but all provided inevitably a spirit of continuity in the school life. In due course they saw the sons of boys who had been at school with them appear as pupils and sometimes even the grandsons as well. Each public school tended to develop family traditions, or school names, which were to be found appearing generation after generation. All helped to entrench the public school system and standardise the product. Indeed the public schools developed into factories producing every bit as much a standardised

The June 4th celebrations at Eton College in the 1840s.

product as the industrial factories spreading throughout the Midlands.

Prior to the 1850s there had been no organised games as such. For instance in football there were no set numbers for sides and rules had not yet been devised. It was a free for all scrimmage with one half of the school playing the other half. It was only in the second half of the century that a clear division arose between Rugby football and Association football, or that "Athletics" as such began to be taken seriously. Prior to that cross country running of the "hare and hounds" style with a paper-chase trial had been amongst the most organised sport. During the latter half of the century organised "manly" sport became an important part of the school curriculum.

Woodgate's younger brother Edward joined the school in 1855, having been coached in boxing by his elder brother beforehand. Woodgate senior noted:

"He turned his science to practical use by never allowing a bigger boy to lay hands on him (if there was any mutual misunderstanding) without at once calling for a 'ring.' This done, etiquette at once forbade any irregular assault such as a twisted arm or kick, which otherwise might be legitimate punishment for a saucy and defiant youngster: the challenge to fight it out by P.R. rules could not be declined, however absurd the odds in size might be. In such rencontres naturally all popular favour went with the little one; and when the boy's resource

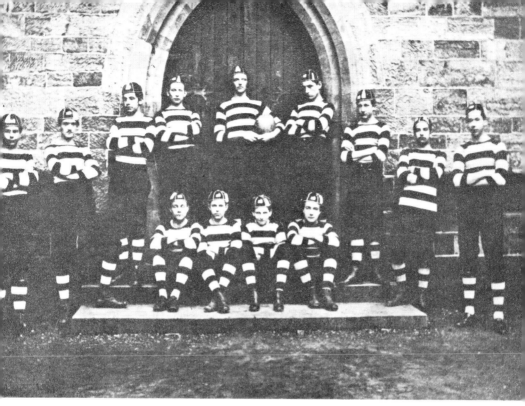

The Tonbridge School rugby team in 1865.

became known, he was generally left alone even when there would have been no moral doubt as to the result had it been fought out. Bigger boys would not face the ridicule and odium of any one-sided fight of this sort."

Boxing and fencing, the former with gloves and under the Marquis of Queensberry's rules, were manly sports, approved in all public schools. Singlesticks, gymnastics and swimming were also taught in many schools towards the end of the century, but it was team games which were regarded as most important in forming the character of the future leaders of the Empire. Rowing, with the introduction of the Oxford and Cambridge boat race was also regarded as a sound character-forming sport, but the old careless ways of the Georgians, hunting, fishing, or casually "lounging" as the fancy willed had long passed. Eton fives, or cross country running, were about the only sports which changed little from the start of the century.

The basic strength and courage, or "Bottom," which the Georgians had admired and cultivated in their bare fist fighting and savage sports such as bull-baiting and cock-fighting were channelled by the Victorians into more civilised lines. Team games were expressive of the parochial patriotism of house or school forming a basis for a fervent patriotism for Queen and Country. It was thus that individualism was suppressed, such as that of Mytton, Shelley, Byron and many other Georgians, and a different thought pattern formed.

The Tonbridge School cricket team in 1865.

Chapel was a central feature of every school's daily routine. In schools where "muscular Christianity" was fashionable, it assumed still greater importance.

As countless books such as Farrar's *Julian Home* stressed, it was a matter of importance never to "let the school down" and this attitude continued into after life. The basic standards of behaviour the suppression of individualism and emotion, conformity with understood levels of gentlemanly behaviour, were all set by five years at public school. The training was in effect a form of brain-washing and those who did not at first conform were soon beaten, literally, into shape. Eccentricity, or individuality, were generally frowned on and suppressed and hard attitudes had at least outwardly to be adopted to survive.

"Pluck and manliness" were what the Victorians admired and desired in their future leaders. Their moral tone was also very important in the eyes of Arnold's followers. Muscular Christianity was the order of the day. Taught by masters who were often clergymen and frequently destined for high office in the church anything else would have been surprising. At Wellington for instance, Benson decreed chapel at nine on Sundays, followed by Bible verse repetition at ten, chapel again at eleven forty-five and lunch at one thirty. Thereafter came Bible study and a school Bible class at three thirty, with another chapel service at six thirty and finally prayers at nine in dormitories. Small wonder that even Prince Albert was driven to enquire if this was not a little excessive.

The fact was, however, that the public schools were not primarily interested in education. They were concentrating on character formation, on the production of future leaders for the Empire, rather than on developing the minds of their pupils. To a very large extent indeed a public-school education stultified the mind and produced a blinkered, narrow outlook. "Gentlemanly" standards of behaviour, unthinking patriotism, pluck, or reliability, were the factors inculcated, as well, above all, as the ability to lead and command others. During the five years or so of schooling, as he rose from the humble position of fag in the lower school to that of a lordly prefect in the sixth form, the average boy learned both to control himself and to control others. His experiences in dealing with other boys at all levels, as well as with his schoolmasters, both in the playing fields and within the school itself, fitted him above all to command men.

Cleverness, ability at any form of school work, was generally regarded as slightly suspect. Bookishness was considered in many schools as almost a form of eccentricity to be condemned rather than admired. The narrow outlook which the public-school system inspired was one of its obvious failings, but it suited the Victorian age which fostered it. Leadership in itself was all very well as long as there was someone to lead and the Victorians had openings for leaders in plenty, in the Empire, in the army and the church, where the very qualities the public schools provided were important.

In the world of commerce or trade, a public-school education was a positive handicap, for a sound knowledge of commercial mathematics, or an understanding of elementary business methods was not only beyond the ken of the schoolmasters and completely outside their sphere of training, but was positively deplored. The fact that the Empire had been built on trading and commerce was happily ignored by all. Only "cads" were in trade and if one's family were in any way connected with such matters a "gentleman" kept it a dark secret and avoided talking about it.

The very uncertainty of their own social background in many cases ensured that the Victorian public schoolboy with middle class antecedents accepted an entire set of prejudices and patterns of behaviour which he could never afterwards entirely dismiss. His own thought processes over a five-year period had been effectively formed according to the standards laid down for him. The products of the different public schools differed only slightly on a social level rather than on an intellectual level.

In general their social ideas were firmly fixed by their education. That any one who had not been educated at a public school might consider himself a gentleman with any justification was to them a laughable piece of pretension. That a city clerk at his desk might reasonably do so was outside their comprehension. Yet their snobbishness and rigidity of mind on this side of the social scale were only equalled by their respect and veneration for the aristocracy on the other. Taine noted this common English characteristic with all the distaste of a born Republican in the 1860s. By the turn of the century this attitude of mind had not changed greatly, if at all. The boy had to grow to manhood before lessons regarding the real worth of social values were learned, if then.

As late as the 1870s, however, Kipling's *Stalky & Co*, his thinly disguised autobiographical novel of his schooldays, shows that in some cases there was still scope for individual enterprise and initiative at a public school. Those who thereafter entered Sandhurst or Woolwich, the recently created army officer training centres, went through a second indoctrination of a similar sort to their public school, where initiative was not encouraged but leadership and obedience to orders were. Inevitably the products of this system developed a brilliance at any task entailing straightforward leadership, or management of men, but where individuality, initiative and above all intellect were required it was a very different matter as the Boer War demonstrated only too clearly.

There were, of course, always individual exceptions to every rule. The public schoolboy who did not go to the University was faced with the alternative of teaching, the army, or an outpost of the Empire. The law and latterly medicine, or business, were other possibilities, although generally only if he had family connections of some sort. Other more Bohemian occupations were journalism or the stage. These were regarded as declassé, unsuitable as a gentleman's occupation, the ultimate sin in the eyes of Victorian society, not that this necessarily weighed greatly with young men who enjoyed the life. Finally there were those who went to the Colonies to make their fortunes and either returned in due course having done so, or settled there, or were never heard of again.

A good example of a chequered start in life was that of Montagu Williams in the 1850s, who, after failing to get a scholarship from Eton to Cambridge gravitated into teaching at Ipswich Grammar School, a job he detested. On the outbreak of the Crimean War he used his father's influence to obtain a commission in the army, but was not posted abroad. When this palled he took temporarily to the stage, meeting Henry Irving and marrying an actress. This seems to have brought him to his senses and he became a student at the Inner Temple for the next three years. Here he fell in with his old school-fellow Francis Burnand and they formed a playwright partnership with some success. They were called to the bar within three months of each other, but whereas Burnand soon returned to full-time literature Montagu Williams went on to a successful career in criminal law.

In the latter part of the century there can be little doubt that the freemasonry of the public school helped greatly in any chosen career. The Victorian ruling classes were aware that in a public schoolboy they were obtaining a reliable standardised product. The public school system might have its faults. Even by the end of the century, although greatly advanced on the restricted Georgian curriculum, the education provided was still very limited and facilities at most public schools were still extremely indifferent. In most cases hygiene remained poor and plumbing inadequate, but it is only fair to admit that this was still the case in most private houses as well. Yet the public schools had achieved every bit as much perfection in turning out boys to a regular pattern as the factories in turning out die stamped goods for consumption at home or overseas. If they were not actually industrial products, the Victorian public schoolboys were undoubtedly products of the industrial age.

By the end of the Victorian era the indefinitely duplicated "assembly line" public-school product was taken as the norm.

The Grenadier Guards. Gentlemen in search of adventure — often of uncertain means — found a respectable occupation in the army.

Signing up for the Horse Guards. Gentlemen were often quite young when they were launched on military careers.

Queen Victoria's drawing room. During the course of Victoria's reign the Court acquired a dominating influence on gentlemanly life.

*(above)* The Hall of the Athenaeum Club. It was during the Victorian era that the London club found an indispensable place in every respectable gentleman's life.

*(below)* The United Service Club, the London club of military gentlemen.

A caricature of gentlemen gathered
to discuss hare hunting. The
satirical image of the gentleman
as a mindless layabout emerged
in cartoons of this sort throughout
the Victorian era.

Gentlemen at dinner at a meeting of the Dilettante Society.

Riding to hounds became a gentlemanly sport in the Victorian era.

Cricket as an organized sport was played and attended by gentlemen.

*(above)* Madam Tussaud's waxworks was a popular outing.

*(below)* The Lord Mayor's Table at the Guildhall. Business began to acquire gentlemanly status during the Victorian era.

*(above)* The Great Exhibition help to foster the imperialist consciousness among Victorians. It brought together all the great achievements of Victorian technology.

*(below)* Lord's cricket ground in 1837, the year of Victoria's accession.

# CHAPTER THREE

# Cambridge and Elsewhere

In Taine's view, life at university for the young Englishman was little more than an extension of his schooldays. Contrasting education in England and France he felt that the English schoolboy had much greater freedom, but that the undergraduate had less. However, observant as he was, he inevitably failed fully to understand the position in England. Whereas undoubtedly the schoolboy on the continent worked harder and probably to more useful effect than in England, the amount of time spent on organised games by the English schoolboy was not quite the freedom Taine may have thought it.

It is true that there were not the same opportunities for vice in the University towns as there had been in the previous century, or as there were in the continent. In this respect, certainly, the young Englishman was much more restricted than his forebears or the continental student. Yet, although apparently hedged in by rules the undergraduates who knew the form could readily ignore most of them and did so.

J. Willmott Dixon in 1911 recalled his memories of life as a Cambridge undergraduate in the 1860s under his pen name "Thormanby" in *The Spice of Life*. He put the undergraduate's position very clearly and his comments applied to the greater part of the nineteenth century:

"Each pupil on his arrival at the commencement of the term paid his tutor a complimentary visit and at the close of each term made another formal call to obtain the necessary 'exeat.' During the interval, provided the pupil attended lectures, chapel and hall a certain number of times in the week and he was in his rooms every night before the stroke of midnight he might go his own way and do whatever he pleased wi his tutor's troubling his head about him."

As with the public schools there was a general broadening of the educational base throughout the nineteenth century, particularly noticeable after the 1850s in the universities. In other ways also the universities became steadily more modern in outlook. Undergraduates from the nobility, who had previously been entitled to wear distinctive gowns and had been afforded considerable licence, by mid-century had lost such privileges. The dons who had previously been enforcedly celibate by the latter half of the century were allowed to marry. Possession of a doctorate of divinity, however, remained desirable qualification for a don at the older universities until close to the end of the century. Some idea of university life in the early part of the period is obtained from the diaries between 1832 and 1842 of Joseph Rommilly, a senior Fellow of Trinity, Cambridge:

"Friday 14th April 1837: All the morning at the Vice Chancellor's Court. Two Causes – viz. 4 men for being in a Billiards Room suspended for 2 terms. The 2nd Cause was James Hore and another for being disorderly in the streets; Hore was very little to blame and was privately admonished by the V.C. The other man (Cooke of Peterhouse) was very riotous and struck the police; he was rusticated one term . . ..

"Thursday 15th March 1838: Last Monday a young man of Trinity (named Joseph Lang) was expelled by Master and Seniors for circulating a blasphemous parody on the Litany; he was caught by Perry's servant just after dropping one of these parodies into P's letterbox. There was no talent in it; The Petitions were such as these 'That the Master may not disturb the devotion of the Congregation by his loud responses' – 'That Mr Whewell may learn the manners of a Gentleman' – There has lately been a feud between the Society and the young men as a consequence of some New Chapel Regulations . . . the most obnoxious of these was instituting 9 reprimands after which a person became ipso facto removed from College. . . . The young men in consequence published Chapel Lists in which they marked the Master and Fellows; at the foot of each List there were remarks on the attendance of the Fellows . . .."

Of some interest is Rommilly's account of the celebrations in Cambridge on Thursday, 28th June 1838, for Queen Victoria's coronation. An enormous feast at midday was prepared for 3,000 Sunday scholars and 12,000 poor. £1,758 were subscribed for the food and 8,120 lbs of meat, 1,650 plum puddings and 99 barrels of beer were provided for them. The entire affair seems to have been organised by the Cambridge University authorities combining with the Town Council and over sixty tables were laid out in Parker's Piece, a convenient open space close to the centre of the town. An orchestra

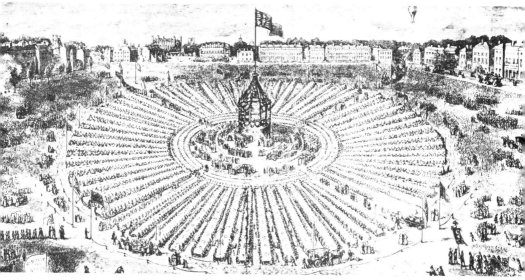

The Grand Coronation Fête held on Parker's Piece at Cambridge on 28 June 1838. (*Radio Times Hulton Picture Library*).

was provided and the meal seems to have gone off very well. Rommilly's part in the proceedings was to carve at the head of one of the tables at which he presided.

In the evening Rommilly went to Jesus Piece, another open space, beside Midsummer Common "to see the 'Rustic Sports' — they were said to be under the direction of Dr Woodhouse — they consisted of donkey races, grinning thro' horse collars, hunting soap tailed pigs, climbing greased poles, eating biscuits against time, bobbing for cakes in treacle and sixpence in meal &c &c. — they were rather a failure. — They concluded with Green and his wife going up in the Nassau balloon."

A fuller version of this last event is given in the *Cambridge Chronicle* of 30th June.

"At half past six, all being ready, Mrs Green was handed into the car, and with her intrepid husband, started in a most majestic manner on their aerial voyage amidst the deafening plaudits of thousands of spectators. They landed at Fulbourn on this 251st ascent of this distinguished aeronaut."

As all this took place out of term time it was intended for the benefit of the people of Cambridge, not the "young men," although no doubt any undergraduates in the neighbourhood were present. The early Victorians were not far removed from their Georgian parents at this stage and as early as 1838 there was no such thing as organised sport, or athletics. They were still to come. The balloon ascent, often accompanied by fire works was a typical finale to a day of celebration.

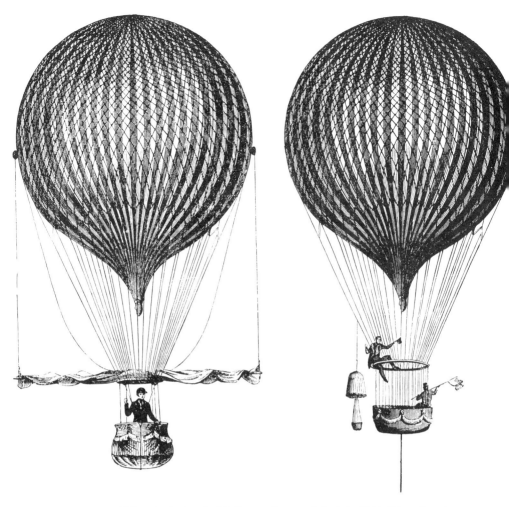

The celebrated Victorian balloonist Mr George Green at Leipzig in 1846. (*Mary Evans*)

Much preferable to Rommilly's taste was the occasion in March 1842 when a deputation from Cambridge was presented to the Queen. How very dearly the dons loved the aristocracy is only too clearly illustrated by Rommilly's account of the event:

"Two of our young noblemen (Ld. Nelson and Ld. Fielding) appeared in their undergraduate gowns; they wore Court Dresses with Swords & added much to the effect. They unfortunately did not join us in the Presence Chamber & were therefore not presented to the Queen; they were afterwards presented to Prince Albert & Duchess of Kent by the Vice Chancellor."

Neither Cambridge, nor for that matter Oxford, were at this stage greatly altered from the eighteenth century. Progress in academic circles is notoriously slow and in matters of simple hygiene and plumbing they were still far behind the not very advanced standards of the day. Sanitation was bad enough in the colleges, but in the towns it was even worse. As a result epidemics were not infrequent. Some idea of how bad it could be is afforded by a record of the events in 1854 written by Augustus Hare to his mother from Oxford, where by this time he was an undergraduate at Balliol:

"October 23rd: There was a special cholera service last night. It is still very bad and the cases very rapid. Those taken ill at five die at seven and for fear of infection are buried at seven next morning.

"October 24th: Typhus fever has broken out in the lower town in addition to everything else and there are 1,000 cases of smallpox besides cholera.

"November 1st. The usual Oxford rain is now varied by a yellow fog and stifling closeness, the consequence of which is that cholera has returned in all its force to the lower town and in the upper almost everyone is ill in one way or another . . . .

December 11th. Yesterday I went to the service at St Thomas's where three fourths of the congregation were in mourning owing to the cholera."

A more cheerful reminiscence of Oxford only two years later is provided in G. V. Cox's *Recollections*. Although organised games had already been introduced in the public schools this is amongst the first references to the fact that they had now begun to take a hold on the universities as well. Nevertheless it was inevitable that healthy young men who had enoyed themselves playing football, rugby, cricket and fives as well as competing at athletics in their public schools would wish to continue with these sports when they reached the university. They may have suffered a good deal of chaff from their less energetic fellow undergraduates and no doubt some critical lectures from die-hard dons opposed to any such innovations, but these do not seem to have deterred them. Cox recorded:

"The month of November was marked by increased energy among our young men in what they denominate 'Athletic Sports.' Not only has football been borrowed from Tom Browns at Rugby by Tom Browns at Oxford, but in addition to foot-races, hurdle leaping, and the like, the absurd exhibition was introduced of *men* (and *gentlemen*) jumping (or attempting to jump) 'in sacks *sewed up to the shoulder* 40 yards out and 40 yards in, round a flag!' In comparison with this, which of course 'convulsed the spectators with laughter' the wheel-barrow race and the donkey races were quite legitimate and classical."

It is eminently clear from his comments that Cox was a typical donnish reactionary, who preferred the donkey races and "Rustic Sports" to these newfangled "Athletics." His donnish sarcasm on the subject, however, was a trifle misplaced, for compared with the "sports" at Victoria's coronation celebrations in Cambridge those he described represented a considerable advance, even if it was another two decades (1880) before the Amateur Athletic Association was formed at Oxford. Already the inter-university competitive element was

Oxford University undergraduates in rooms in college. A scene which might have been repeated any time between 1842 and 1892 with little change. (*Mary Evans*)

growing, however, for 1856 was also the year of the first Oxford versus Cambridge boat race. It is not therefore surprising to find that within three years Cox was attributing the increased number of boating accidents on the river to the more dangerous kinds of boats which had been introduced. He noted:

"November 25th: 1859. A large meeting of University *boating-men* was held in the Radcliffe Library (Dr Acland in the Chair) called by the President of the Boat Club to consider the best manner of preventing *boat accidents* – nine (lives) had been lost in the last nine years."

With drownings and epidemics Oxford appears at first sight to have been a dangerous place, but few Victorians in mid-century were able to swim well and due to the limited standards of medical knowledge then available epidemics were liable to run their course unchecked. Yet medical science was steadily developing and considerable changes were taking place in the fields of medicine and surgery. They were becoming respectable and respected professions. The early Victorian attitude, that a successful doctor should not accept a peerage because he had received fees for his services, was no longer tenable. The lot of a medical student in mid-century, however, was still very different from that of an ordinary university student.

S. T. Tayler, who kept a diary of his experiences as a medical student, while studying at Norwich Hospital and King's College in London University, although a somewhat pompous young man, had some interesting comments about this period. On 16th January 1860, while still at Norwich, he wrote:

"Mr Peter Nichols, senior surgeon of the Hospital is said to be not too well up in his knowledge of human anatomy, but for all that his operations are successful as a rule. It must be remembered that the education of the medical men was very defective in bygone years. Seven years apprenticeship to a doctor qualified a man to practice medicine and surgery without passing any exam. Even when examinations were instituted a man must have been intolerably stupid not to get through the very easy cross questioning. In recent years, however, the reign of severity has wet in the pluckings have become more frequent. The University of London has set a good example in this respect."

As part of his training at Norwich Hospital Tayler was expected to attend operations, assist with dispensing medicine and generally make himself useful as well as he could. By this method of actually assisting the doctors in the hospital he naturally learned a good deal. In his final year before going to King's College he settled down to working out some figures and concluded:

"February 9th 1860. Judging from my statistics just completed I have dispensed about 4,000 bottles of medicine containing according to my calculations 122 gallons. It strikes me patients have a good deal to put up with under the modern system of medicine, when we consider that most medicines are as bitter as gall, to say nothing of their after effects."

He seems to have taken his studies extremely seriously and to have become a very competent dispenser, even to the extent of making his own suggestions to the doctor on occasions. On 3rd June he began to have doubts about a suggestion he had recently made for the treatment of one patient when a different patient taking the same medicine suddenly died. He was able to convince himself that the medicine was not at fault, but the reasons he reveals for his suggestion are of interest:

"Dr Eade's hysteria case for which he had prescribed oxalate of cerium died yesterday. Miss Mason, a patient of Messrs Gibson and Bateman, has been for some years past taking regularly every day oxide of cerium pills, prescribed for her by the late Dr Lubbock. She pays a lump sum of £50 a year for medical attendance but oxide of cerium is rather a costly remedy and leaves little profit to the doctors. I suggested to the firm substituting oxalate of cerium for oxide of cerium, as the former, being the refuse of some manufacture is a very cheap remedy, but the death of Dr Eade's patient is rather a bad omen; although in all human probability the oxalate of cerium had no hand in the business."

In September 1860 Tayler left Norwich for London University, which had only been incorporated twenty-four years previously in 1836. He took lodgings at Holborn and entered King's College. Here he studied under, amongst others, Professor Richard Partridge, who had been in great part responsible for the passing of the Anatomy Bill in 1832 to increase supplies of bodies so necessary for anatomical dissection. The Bill had passed the Commons in 1829, but was rejected by the Lords. At that time in his early days as an anatomy lecturer, Partridge was offered the body of a murdered fourteen year old boy by two London criminals, Bishop and Williams. Very courageously in the circumstances, since public feeling was strong against grave robbers and anatomists, he had them arrested and gave evidence at their trial which aroused enormous public interest. Their execution on 5th December 1831 was attended by a crowd of 40,000. Within ten days the Bill was introduced again and by 1832 had passed both houses and received the Royal Assent.

Like many anatomy lecturers Partridge was famed for his wit and at first the young student from East Anglia was rather shocked, but this soon passed.

"November 10th, 1860: One or two of Mr Partridge's stories this morning, decidedly improper.

"March 14th, 1861: Lecture on the Testicle. Professor Partridge's remarks not so spicy as might have been expected from the subject of his lecture.

"March 16th: Lecture by Professor Partridge on Female Generative Organs. Of course, sundry facetious remarks on rather a delicate subject one particularly laughable on the nice old ladies of Cambridge University."

It was not all lectures, however, even for an earnest young mid-Victorian like Tayler, but his idea of interesting relaxation was not particularly exciting. Yet he was typical of his kind and the topics he chose to discuss were inevitably the popular subjects for conversation amongst any young Victorians of the middle classes. For instance on March 6th 1861 he noted:

"Called on Augustus Dewing, whom I found with a bad headache, which, however, a debate we had on the gentility, or non-gentility, of swearing, seemed to relieve considerably."

Compared with the Georgian medical student, or the early Victorian medical student so ably portrayed by Dickens in such figures as Bob Sawyer in Pickwick Papers, this was all dull stuff, but it may be argued that the medical student in the second half of the nineteenth century had much more to learn. Tayler was wrong in thinking that mere time-serving and answering a few simple questions automatically ensured qualifying even in Georgian times, but certainly the examinations had become much stiffer. Not only that, but the number of subjects themselves were steadily increasing. Whereas there had once only been anatomy, surgery of a primitive order, dispensing and some theoretical knowledge, the scope of medicine had vastly expanded in the latter half of the nineteenth century. Anaesthetics had provided opportunities for major surgery never previously contemplated. New operations and new discoveries concerning the human body were constantly being made. Pasteur's experiments and Lister's revelations in the field of antiseptics opened up entirely new and exciting horizons in the latter half of the century.

Yet even when Tayler decided to experiment with tobacco, he managed to make it sound excessively dull. On May 15th 1861, he wrote:

"Smoked a cigar in the evening for the second time in my life, just by way of observing the physiological effects of tobacco smoking. Experienced no symptoms of 'casting up my accounts' as they say, which rather surprised me, but I felt, I must confess, a bit drowsy and stupid."

About the most dashing entry is for 19th October 1861, when he recorded:

"Paid off my tailor, Garret of Cornhill, his charge of thirty shillings for a pair of trousers appearing exorbitant in my eyes. Beverley and I invested in opera hats this afternoon."

One of the few things the young mid-Victorian medical student appears to have had in common with his Georgian predecessors was seeing a number of public hangings. His comments in his diaries indicate both what he felt he should have experienced and what his real and more human feelings were. He wrote on 19th November 1860, "Saw Mullins the murderer of Mrs Earnsley hanged at the Old Bailey at 8 a.m. this morning. The punishment was certainly richly deserved as for the sake of filthy lucre he did his best to bring about the conviction of an innocent man who had no hand in the business. Still it must be confessed that it is hardly possible to conceive a more awful spectacle than a public execution or one more revolting to human nature. Got terribly squeezed by the ruffianly crowd, so that it is a wonder some of my ribs did not get broken . . . ."

This did not prevent him repeating the performance on a number of occasions and on 20th October 1862 he recorded, "Saw Mrs Catherine Wilson, a nurse, hanged at the Old Bailey for poisoning her friend Mrs Soames seven years ago. It was certainly a very gruesome spectacle. Mrs Catherine Wilson, however, behaved very coolly and being a stoutish woman 'fell beautiful' to use the words of an illiterate bystander."

No doubt most London Universtiy students of the time attended public hangings at least once. The undergraduates at Oxford and Cambridge would normally have only been able to see a hanging out of term time, although no doubt there were ways of arranging a brief absence in London when required. Walter B. Woodgate, after leaving Radley, went on to Oxford in 1859 and although he had always intended to see a public hanging he failed to do so before they were banned in 1868. Thereafter they took place inside the prisons and only those specially invited could attend them. His curiosity made him accept an invitation to watch one in the 1880s when he was practising as a barrister, but he had no desire to witness another.

At the same time Woodgate was an undergraduate at Brasenose

College, Oxford, Willmott Dixon was at Trinity College, Cambridge. Each was of a sporting bent and each went on to become a barrister and also to write. Their descriptions of their times at the older universities combine to give a picture of how an undergraduate lived. Then as now, however, or at any time, University life was very much what each person made it and there was a strong tendency to form cliques, or "sets," both within a college and within the university itself. These might be "sets" of rowing men, athletes, hunting men, scholars, or drinkers, to name only a few of the manifold interests of the average undergraduate. An individual might well be a member of various "sets," sometimes with conflicting interests and it is thus difficult to say of any individual that he was a typical example of his time. Even the colleges within the universities differed greatly from each other. Nevertheless Woodgate and Dixon between them indicate very clearly the popular attitudes of the day.

Woodgate, as suited his country and Radley background, was a keen sportsman and athlete, making his name quickly as a good oarsman and

Undergraduate taste in sports was unchanging.

eventually graduating to the Oxford rowing eight. He was also interested in acting, taking part in college plays, as well as indulging in various wild drinking parties and sporting wagers. He appears to have been a popular character, not easily defeated, with an attractive social manner. His attitude to the dons of his college is therefore of some interest. The normal state of affairs between dons and undergraduates in Oxford at this time seems to have been one of armed neutrality with sporadic outbreaks of open warfare, when dons might find themselves nailed up in their rooms with six inch nails fastening their oaks, or outer doors, firmly shut. Woodgate recorded:

"B.N.C was a comparatively quiet college in these days; we did not fall foul of our dons, as in some other colleges . . . . Weldon Champneys (son of the Dean of Lichfield), who succeded to the boat captaincy . . . used to preach that it was our duty to treat every don as a gentleman until he proved himself to be the contrary. A sound principle. None the less I can recall the look of astonishment on the faces of my tutor and the Vice-Principal, Menzies, when one day I stopped them in the quad, and asked if they would lunch with me! Said my tutor, 'Is this a jest, Mr Woodgate?' 'No, sir,' said I, unabashed, 'but my mother and sisters are with me, and they would like to meet you.' Such a daring invitation had never before been given by junior to don. But the two authorities at once smiled and accepted warmly, and the family rencontre did good, not only between myself and my masters, but also generally in the college."

In Cambridge Willmott Dixon was much the same type as Woodgate. Perhaps less of an athlete and more of a horse racing, sporting bent, he seems to have been ever eager for a vist to Newmarket or a wild escapade with a friend. He unwittingly underlined one of the reasons for the antipathy between undergraduates and dons when he revealed the iniquitous system of credit allowed by local tradesmen to the students, calculated to cause them to run up large bills and ignored by tutors whose duty should have been to look after their pupils' interests.

By this system recognised tradesmen such as tailors, grocers, barbers and so on kept "Tutors' books," in which each undergraduate's account was kept with his signature against the amounts involved and no other record of the transactions. The tutor would transfer these accounts to his own bill, which went at the end of the term to the parent and had to be paid before the son could return the following term. Naturally the father assumed the sums concerned had the tutor's sanction, not realising the procedure was purely automatic. As Willmott Dixon pointed out these moneys were then paid into the tutor's private banking account where they might remain for as much as a year before being disbursed to the tradesmen concerned, thus earning considerable amounts in interest for the tutor:

"But the worst evil about 'tutor's books' was this. It was common practice in my time for even the most respectable tradesmen to bring their 'tutor's books' for one's signature with the amount faintly set down in *pencil*, and if you thought the amount looked too big, the accomodating tailor, or whatever he might be, suggested that he should rub out the pencil figures and insert half or two-thirds of the whole amount to which falsified account you attached your signature. In this way both Paterfamilias and the tutor were hoodwinked, for each thought that the sum signed for was the *whole* amount due! And they were not undeceived till the final account was sent in at the end of the laster term."

The 1850s and 1860s were very much a transitional period at both Oxford and Cambridge, marking the end of the old style and the start of the new. The dons and fellows were gradually allowed to break their celibate habits which had been enforced on them. The increasing concentration on athletics and competitive games such as football and cricket, both inter-college and inter-university, became a much larger part of the undergraduate's life. The changes in the public schools, the broadening of the educational system, were mirrored in the universities. The dons, fellows and undergraduates began to grow more integrated with the new form of university life, until finally the breakthrough came and women's colleges were formed. Not all approved of such changes. G. V. Cox recorded:

A typical view of the Henley Regatta, which became an annual event in the Victorian era.

"November 1859. In chronicling the striking incidents and varying shades of Oxford life, it is but fair to mention the following notice, by the Vice Chancellor and Proctors, as a proof of a growing neglect of manners, the natural accompaniment of a rougher bearing and a coarser *external*: 'Whereas complaints have been made that some undergraduate members of the University are in the habit of smoking at *public entertainments* and otherwise creating annoyance, they are hereby cautioned against the repetition of such ungentlemanlike conduct.'"

Trying to check smoking was a losing battle, since dons and undergraduates alike both smoked. It was the same regarding drinking. Woodgate and Willmott Dixon indicated that hard drinking amongst both dons and undergraduates was accepted as nothing exceptional at this period. Both mention being drunk themselves on a number of occasions and also various dons who were famed for their potations. This was in the time-honoured university tradition, as was the training for the rowing eight. Woodgate recorded that "Training was old fashioned and barbarous; raw steaks and a run round the 'parks' before morning chapel."

It was while training for the university eight that Woodgate was involved in what might have been an unfortunate affair on the wedding day of Prince Edward and Princess Alexandra in 1863. Through no fault of his own he found himself engaged in a fracas with a slightly drunken porter which could have ended in serious trouble. His reaction to the entire event, however, is a very clear indication of the Victorian gentleman's high-handed attitude with servants at this time.

After a day's strenuous training it was the habit of the crew to meet for "gruel" in one or another's rooms. On that occasion it was the turn of an undergraduate named Jacobson of Christchurch to provide the

In full flight from the Proctor at Oxford. (*Radio Times Hulton Picture Library*)

refreshment. The rest of the crew had already arrived in turn and Woodgate was the last one to reach the college.

"I knocked and gave Jacobson's name: An under porter of the college, probably more or less elated by hearty drinking on such an important occasion, ejaculated as he held the half-open wicket gate: 'By God, we won't have no more Jacobson's tonight' and jammed the gate across my half entered body. . . . [It] caught me across the chest. . . . A tussle ensued . . . he trying to drive me back, I to free myself . . . and to enter. At last I grabbed him by an extra thick shock of hair . . . I jabbed his skull against the sharp rectangular staple of the door, until it cut through wool and all, and he dropped bleeding; then I walked in proudly over the fallen carcase . . . unmolested further."

The next morning, inevitably, he received a message from the Dean of Brasenose, Dr Cradock, asking him to call. The Dean had received a letter from the Dean of Christchurch claiming that he had fought his way into the college and half killed a porter. Woodgate gave his explanation of the events and the Dean suggested he should write a letter of explanation and apology. This was not good enough for Woodgate. He indicated that he regarded the matter as a social not an academic issue. He claimed that he had been assaulted and was entitled to an apology from the appropriate college authorities, otherwise he proposed to prosecute. The Dean listened to this argument and somewhat surprisingly approved.

Thereafter, in Woodgate's own words, "I tidied myself up, brushed a beaver, put on a frock coat; bought a new pair of gloves, borrowed a tidy umbrella, and sailed in mufti down St Aldates to call on the Dean, sending up my card. I was ushered in. There stood the handsome and reverend-looking Dean; warming his nether man over his study fire . . . . 'Then you are the gentleman who committed this outrage in my college last night?' I replied. 'I have come to talk over this matter with you, sir.'

"'How is it that you are not in cap and gown?' said the Dean.

"'Because the matter is a purely social issue between gentlemen as regards a servant's misconduct: there's nothing academic at stake.'

The Dean said no more on the subject of attire; and asked me to explain how it was that I had cut open his porter's head and fought my way into college."

Woodgate, incipient barrister that he was, required no second bidding. He began by explaining that he had arrived at the gate at the invitation of his friend Jacobson. He continued:

"There was no intimation nor notice that customary civilities between B.N.C and Ch.Ch. had been suspended. Hitherto there had been every *entente cordiale* between the two colleges. I desired that *entente* to continue; and for that reason instead of adopting off-hand a hostile course, prosecuting this porter for jamming me in the wicket (and bruising my collar bone black and blue), and perhaps depriving Ch.Ch. of his services, while he did six months on the tread-mill, I felt that it would only be courteous to postulate that the authorities of Christ Church in in no way approved of their menial's misconduct, and of his violation of inter-collegiate hospitalities, and that they were ready as gentlemen to a gentleman, to tender *amende honorable*; in which case I would, in consideration of my many friends in that college, forbear to prosecute!

"The Dean abandoned his censorious attitude and was suavely polite; accepted my version, and expressed his regret for my injuries, and his hopes that they would not affect my oarsmanship. I bowed with all the grace I could muster, and thanked him for his politeness – the interview was over."

The attitude of the mid-Victorian gentlemen to "menials" is very clearly illustrated by this reasonably unembroidered account of what amounted to a fight between a college servant and an undergraduate. It is significant that the Dean as "a gentleman" accepted the word of another "gentleman" without question. Woodgate's impudence was fairly considerable and his suggestion that the porter might have received six months on the treadmill was stretching it somewhat, but by keeping the matter on a social level he effectively silenced any grounds for criticism of his own conduct that the Dean might have had.

The sequel from the porter's viewpoint was not so satisfactory. Woodgate added: "I fancy that the unfortunate under-porter got the sack for his share in the row. At all events, some years later, when I was growling at a waiter (at the Mitre or Randolph, I forget which) for dilatoriness in service, he pleaded that I should not be too hard on him, for he still bore the scars where I had cut his head open. I looked up – sure enough, it was my shock headed friend of that wedding night. I gave him an extra half-crown to show no ill-will."

As this incident and its aftermath suggest, Woodgate was quite a formidable character, generally ready to rise wholeheartedly to a challenge of any kind. This was a typical Georgian trait stemming basically from the wilder, less disciplined attitudes of the times, usually only to be encountered in Victorian days amongst undergraduates. It would, however, be entirely wrong to imagine that the Victorians were not capable of the sort of physical feats that the Georgians indulged in after dinner for a wager. Woodgate, once again, may be quoted as proof that this was certainly not the case:

"It was that same year (1863) that for a silly bet of a sovereign, I . . . ruined a set of nearly new evening dress . . . . Jack Morley of B.N.C bet me a sovereign that I would not walk straight away from where we were (Pearce's Hotel, 10 Bury Street) to Oxford, and I took him. I changed my dress coat for a serge jacket; but made no other alteration in my rig, and was off in a few minutes. I regret I did not take the exact time; but it was a very few minutes past 9 p.m. I began badly, going over Hammersmith Bridge, instead of sticking to the Bath road. I had to recross the river at Kew. I did not do fair heel and toe all the way. I jogged much of the distance; at a sort of cart-horse trot some six or less miles an hour. I reached the door of the Red Lion Hotel, Henley at 6 a.m. .... I got into Oxford just as the bells of a church near Magdalene ... were finishing the call for 11 a.m. service .... My waistcoat and trousers were badly spotted with perspiration that had dropped all night from my face. My kid, elastic sided evening boots [the fashion of the day] had split ... and I had torn my pocket handkerchief into strips to bind them up. After I had tubbed and breakfasted, some B.N.C friends, up reading for vacation, must needs chaff me about alleged fatigue; so, for wanton bravado, I went down to the river, got my sculling boat, and sculled to Nuneham Black Bridge and back. I slept well that night."

All the wildness at the universities in Victorian days was not necessarily attributable to the undergraduates. There was the Vice-Principal of Brasenose in the 1850s, mentioned by Woodgate, who drank too much and eventually in 1859 was forced to resign with incipient D. Ts. Willmott Dixon capped this with the story of the sporting Fellow of St John's, Cambridge, named Mark Tapley, who used regularly to return from Newmarket at a late hour and scandalise the dons by blowing a coaching horn in a decidedly merry condition. For years, apparently, he had been courting the landlady of an inn frequented by sportsmen on the outskirts of Newmarket and eventually he married her, after which his midnight blasts on the "yard of tin" ceased to waken the college.

Willmott Dixon recalled the scene when the Oxford Volunteers visited Cambridge in the 1860s:

"The overwhelming hospitality shown to the visitors at each of the 'Varsities was productive of disastrous results. Railway traffic was entirely disorganised for hours, owing to the mad freaks of inebriated undergraduates and the damage to the rolling stock was frightful. I remember well the scene along the road to the station when the Oxford Volunteers were leaving Cambridge. Rifles, bayonets, belts, cartouche boxes, shakos strewed the ground as if a panic stricken army had fled that way with fierce pursuers at its heels. Lines of linked riflemen from both 'Varsities lurched erratically along, filling the air with deafening drinking choruses. The railway officials were driven frantic, with Pandemonium let loose at the station."

According to Dixon similar sights were witnessed at Oxford on the Cambridge Volunteers return visit and the same thing happened when the Athletics Clubs first met. In the end it was decided that the best plan was to meet in London on neutral ground. Another scene which might have happened in either university was recounted by Woodgate.

His "set," the best of the College, known as "Phoenix," had been celebrating. This entailed supper, after the usual indifferent 6 p.m. dinner in hall, with oysters, dressed crab, grilled bones and poached eggs, washed down with wine and followed by steaming punch bowls of whisky, rum, gin and brandy. Woodgate's friend Farquhar "had no head for wine" and feeling "indisposed" had retired to his rooms. Woodgate continued:

"I went, later, with others to see how he was going on, and to help him to bed if required. The room was in darkness. Farquhar snoring on his sofa. I pioneered first into the room, feeling my way with my hands. In due time I lit upon his recumbent figure, and essayed to diagnose him by touch. My hands presently lit upon his patent leather dress boots. I stroked them scientifically and remarked: 'Extremities are cold: beggar's dead! Better leave him' and cleared off . . . ."

In view of his interest in acting and sport Woodgate was rather more than what might be termed "simply a rowing man." Augustus Hare, at Balliol in the mid-1850s was also not easily defined. Two other Oxford students of the same period at Exeter College were Pre-Raphaelites Edward Burne Jones and William Morris, who do not seem to have made outstanding names for themselves. The most Burne Jones could say for Morris was that he "never seemed to be particularly busy . . . had plenty of leisure for fishing . . . a great instinct for knowing what would amuse him and what not to read." In Cambridge at much the same time it would also have been difficult to define Francis Burnand, who founded the A.D.C (Amateur Dramatic Club) as simply keen on acting and stage production. Unlike the public schools, the Universities still fostered individuality.

Although still small by comparison with present day standards the universities were also, like the public schools, expanding considerably. During the 1860s the education of girls began to develop strongly. In 1869 a College for Women was opened at Hitchin, eventually to become Girton College, Cambridge. In 1871 a woman's college was opened at Cambridge itself. In the same year Lady Margaret Hall, Oxford was also founded, shortly to be followed by Somerville College, also for women. Oxford and Cambridge were developing on lines undreamed of in the early Victorian period.

In 1874 after a classical education at Trinity College, Dublin, a brilliant unstable young Irishman named Oscar O'Flahertie Wilde arrived at Magdalen College, Oxford. By 1878 he had won the Newdigate Prize for Literature and obtained a first-class honours degree. Intellectually brilliant he had set himself at the head of the "art for art's sake" school of thought newly introduced by J. M. Whistler. Wearing velvet suits and knickerbockers and languishing before lilies, the "too-too" cult of "Aesthetes" became a natural target for *Punch* and the satirists. Expressing scorn for athletics he was duly ducked in

Sporting Cambridge undergraduates in their rooms. (*Mary Evans*)

the Cherwell and his rooms were wrecked, but for a short while his languid pose attracted followers. Yet within a decade his influence had passed and by the 1890s and his final downfall Oxford might never have known of his existence. Here also was the strength of the universities as an institution, in that they have a continuity which remains unshakeable by passing phases.

Writing of the wrecking of rooms, a thing unheard of in the 1860s, Willmott Dixon expressed his disgust, "Though there were occasional outbursts of rowdyism, there was no deliberate 'ragging' in my day. That odious form of ebullient blackguardism – the last expression of 'bounder's' hooliganism – we were happily spared. I have seen men's rooms wrecked after a 'drunk' . . . but organised malignant 'ragging' is a very different thing . . . ."

As well as Trinity College, Dublin, in Ireland, there were, of course, other universities in the north, Durham University (founded in 1832), Edinburgh, Aberdeen, St Andrews and Glasgow universities in Scotland. Those who went to such universities were usually younger than in the older universities in the south, but all provided good educations, even if those who passed brilliantly there often went on to Oxford or

Cambridge for the benefit of the extra status obtained. For an academic career this was almost an essential.

If the tremendous growth of the railways during the 1850s and 1860s had any noticeable effect on the universities, it was only to make them easier of access. The young men could more readily visit London, or return to their homes at the beginning and end of term. With the advent of the women's colleges and the introduction of the bicycle as a means of locomotion in the 1870s and 1880s the universities began to approach more closely their recognisable modern image.

By the 1890s the aesthetes had come and gone and the young undergraduates were discussing such matters as the Webbs, the plays of Bernard Shaw, the poetry of Kipling, the position in South Africa and the Jameson Raid, not forgetting the internal combustion engine. The Queen Empress was an accepted fact and a background figure who seemed assured of immortality. There was the prospect of strawberries and cream in a punt on the river, of cricket, of croquet and lawn tennis in long glorious summer days. It was a halcyon period for the young man or woman at university.

There were still great and eccentric figures amongst the dons, such as Benjamin Jowett, Master of Balliol and Vice Chancellor of Oxford, whose death in 1893 ended an era. The old antipathy between dons and undergraduates, however, was largely a thing of the past. There was a much more friendly attitude throughout the universities. A freer and less repressive tone was prevalent throughout society.

The enormous expansion of the past century had provided an assured and complacent feeling of permanency by the end of the 1890s. Visits to the continent, to climb the Alps in the footsteps of Whymper, or taste the cream of the French or German wines, yachting at Cowes, or more mundane recreations such as golf, tennis, or cricket in the summer vacation, followed by grouse shooting on the Twelfth, then partridges in East Anglia in September and hunting in the winter months — these were the certainties of life. There was a place for everything and everything and everybody had their place. Such was the life of the wealthy young gentleman at the turn of the century, as enjoyed by many young undergraduates. There might be those who had vaguely heard of some obscure revolutionary called Karl Marx, but most were more concerned with the latest de Dion or Benz automobiles, or the remarkable experiments in flying and the new theories of flight which seemed so near success. It is sad that few of these young men lived to write their memoirs since almost to a man they died in the Great War to end all Wars of 1914–18.

# CHAPTER FOUR

# *Taste and Manners*

The first three chapters have concentrated on the upbringing of the young Victorian from his nursery to leaving university. It seems reasonable next to concentrate on his background, on his home life, his tastes in art and architecture, in furniture and clothing, in relaxation with his family, as well as his dining and wining habits. Inevitably, as in any age, there were vast differences between individuals in such matters, as well as between various parts of the country, but with their strong desire to emulate the class above them and thus ultimately the Royal Family, the Victorians achieved a recognisable uniformity typical of the age.

Perhaps the most obvious reminder of Victorian taste still with us today is to be found in their architecture, solid, gothic and unmistakeable. According to Robert Kerr, in *The Gentleman's House*, this should consist of something in the region of twenty four rooms with the usual offices, such as they were, distributed round the building in suitably selected areas. Written in 1864 his book remains a fair guide to Victorian ideas on housebuilding and on what was considered requisite for a gentleman's house. What Kerr proposed was admittedly his ideal and the suggestions he put forward were not really intended as more than a guide but on certain matters he was very definite in his views, as when he enlarged on the subject of bathrooms:

"No house of any pretensions would be devoid of a general Bath-room; and in a large house there must be several of these. The sort of apartment usually required is simply one that shall be large enough to contain a reclining bath and a fireplace, with perhaps a shower bath,

Cardiff Castle was one of the trophies of gothic taste, built by William Burgess in the 1880s. (*Radio Times Hulton Picture Library*)

either separate, or over the other and sufficient space for dressing. The light may be either by window or skylight . . . .

"If the house has but one Bath-room it will be best placed in a retired position amongst the Bedrooms and not too far off the principal staircase.

"If there be hot water apparatus of any sort in the house the Bath-room ought to be placed with special reference to a supply . . . . Cold water of course must be supplied, and a waste-pipe laid to the drain."

Despite Kerr's insistence on several bathrooms there is little doubt that many Victorian houses, even by the end of the century, were ill equipped on this score. Many of the extremely large parsonages built in Victorian days had no bathrooms at all. Whether there was a bathroom or not the Victorian water supplies and plumbing were generally extremely inefficient. Lead pipes without lagging frequently burst in winter time. Inefficient water heating methods and lengthy stretches of pipe often resulted in so-called hot water being nearly cold by the time it reached the bathroom. In general anyway the Victorians relied throughout the century on servants bringing them hot water each morning rather than on plumbing. They regarded a cold bath as normal and a hot bath as sheer luxury, even possibly somewhat effeminate.

The great majority of Victorians were not particularly hygiene conscious as early as 1864, or indeed in most cases even by the end of the century. When the issue was a social one, however, there was always a very clear dividing line. It is obvious from Kerr's book that sharing a lavatory with servants was quite inconceivable. On the subject of lavatories he wrote:

"In the smallest house there will be one for the servants, separate from that for the family. As the next advance ... one for the Bedchambers upstairs, the ordinary one being on the Ground Floor . . .. In the country an additional one is often provided in the garden for Gentlemen . . .." He added that another was often added to the billiard room and that when there was a nursery wing it was a wise precaution to supply one there too.

No less authority than Florence Nightingale, however, in her *Notes on Nursing* published in 1860 had already pointed to a common flaw in house design of the period, which Kerr appears to have overlooked. She warned:

"Another great evil in house construction," she warned, "is carrying drains underneath the house. Such drains are never safe . . .. How few there are who can intelligently trace disease, in their households to such causes? Is it not a fact that when scarlet fever, measles or small-pox

BILLIARDS.

appear among the children, the very first thought which occurs is 'where the child can have 'caught' the disease? And the parents immediately run over in their minds all the families with whom they may have been. They never think of looking at home for the source of the mischief.''

Some idea of Kerr's conception of the ideal house may be gauged from his chapter headings, which included the following: diningroom, morningroom, breakfast/luncheon room, drawingroom, boudoir, library, billiardroom, study, gentlemen's room, or business room, saloon, family suite, conservatory, or winter garden, smokingroom, principal bedroom suite, principal guest's suite, other special bed-chambers. Amongst the "miscellaneous" he listed: tutor's or governess's room, children's rooms, nurseries, schoolroom. Amongst the "supple-mentaries" he included lavatory, plunge bath, bath, water closets, kitchen offices, scullery, pantry, dry larder, salting room, smoking house and bacon larder, dairy and dry saltery. Amongst the upper servants' offices were butler's pantry and appurtenances, serving room, housekeeper's room, still room, china closet, house steward's office, gun room, housemaid's closet, cleaning rooms and servants' hall. Finally he listed wash-house and laundry, drying room and hot closet, linen room, brewhouse, cellars, coal, wine, beer, etc.

It is obvious after reading such a list how much the Victorians depended for their comfort on the ready availability of domestic

*AMBITION.*

Lady. "BUT I THOUGHT THAT YOU AND THE OTHER SERVANTS WERE PERFECTLY SATISFIED!"

Flunkey. "WELL, MEM, I AIN'T IN NO WAYS DISCONTENTED WITH MY WAGES, NOR WITH THE VITTELS, NOR NOTHINK OF THAT—BUT THE FACT IS, MY FRIENDS SAY THAT A YOUNG MAN OF MY APPEARANCE OUGHT TO BETTER HISSELF, AND GET INTO A SITUATION WHERE THERE'S *TWO* MEN BEHIND THE CARRIDGE!" *(Poor Fellow !)*

servants. The enormous amount of work required simply to keep a house of this size reasonably clean must have been immense. The short answer, of course, was that Victorian standards of cleanliness inevitably were not as high as they liked to think they were. Neither candles or gas light showed up dirt as readily as the glare of electricity and this was not introduced until the 1880s and was not in general use before the end of the century.

Dealing with the lamps and candles represented a large part of a servant's life for the greater part of the century. William Tayler, Oxford born yeoman farmer's son, forced by the breakdown of rural society to take up domestic service, kept a diary of his work in the year 1837. He was footman to a wealthy widow in Great Cumberland Street in London, with three maidservants, and only his mistress and her daughter to look after. He sketched a typical day's work in his diary on 1st January 1837 as follows:

"Got up at 7.30, cleaned the . . . knives and lamps, got the parlour breakfast, lit my pantry fire, cleared breakfast and washed it away, dressed myself, went to church, came back, got parlour lunch, had own dinner, sit by fire and read Penny Magazine — and opened door when any visitors came. At 4 o'clock had my tea, took the lamps and candles up into the drawing room, shut the shutters, took glass, knives, plate, etc. into the dining room, layed the cloth for dinner, took dinner up at six o'clock, waited at dinner, brought the things down again at seven, washed them up, brought down the desert, got ready the tea, took it up at eight o'clock, brought it down at half past, washed up, had my supper at nine, took down the lamps and candles at half past ten, went to bed at eleven. All these things I have to do every day."

Although perhaps not entirely typical William Tayler obviously knew how to make the best of a fairly easy job and indicated that a domestic servant was considered above a mere "tradesman." In general, domestic servants were able to lead fairly comfortable lives during the Victorian age despite the shortage of "labour-saving devices." In any gentleman's household, however reduced in circumstances he might be, there would be at least three maidservants and in a house of any pretensions a good many more. It is only necessary to read Kerr's description of the Housekeeper's Room to appreciate that the social distinctions of the Victorian age extended to all levels.

"This is primarily the Business-room and Parlour of the housekeeper. The fittings, besides the ordinary furniture of a plain Sitting-Room, will consist of spacious presses, from 18 to 24 inches deep, filled with drawers and shelving, for the accommodation of preserves, pickles, fancy groceries of all kinds, cakes, china, glass, linen and so forth . . .. The upper servants take breakfast and tea and perhaps pass the evening with the housekeeper in this room . . .. The same persons dine here also if there be no steward's room . . .."

The elaborate rituals attached to smoking even in late Victorian times in a bachelor's rooms are well illustrated here. (*Mary Evans*)

The power of the "upper servants" in the Victorian era should never be underestimated, but it was not until 1902 that J. M. Barrie in his play *The Admirable Crichton* dared to suggest that the leader of a shipwrecked aristocratic family could turn out to be their butler. Although each household theoretically revolved around the requirements of the Victorian gentleman, it was generally the wife who really controlled the household and she in turn was often subtly influenced by her housekeeper or butler. There is not much doubt that despite the vaunted superiority of the Victorian male he did not necessarily exercise supreme authority in his own house, as so often suggested. A good example of this was the straits to which the mid-Victorian gentleman was driven if he wished to smoke. Kerr noted under the heading "Smoking Room":

"The pitiable resources to which some gentlemen are driven, even in their own houses, in order to be able to enjoy the pestiferous luxury of a cigar, have given rise to the occasional introduction of an apartment specially dedicated to the use of Tobacco. The Billiard-room is sometimes allowed to be more or less under the dominion of the smoker, if contrived accordingly; but this would in other cases be impossible; and there are even instances where, out of sheer encouragement of the practice, a retreat is provided altogether apart . . .."

Until well into the 1860s and even later, Victorian ladies strenuously objected to the smell of tobacco smoke around the house, largely because it was considered unladylike for them to smoke and was socially unacceptable to do so. It was tacitly understood that only females of easy virtue smoked and tobacco thus had sinful connotations. A cynical observer noted that they raised no objections to kissing their father's snuff covered cheek, but already by mid-century snuff was largely giving way to tobacco as the prevalent vice of the day. By 1860 smoking was fully accepted in every gentleman's club and smoking carriages were provided on most of the railways.

If he wished to smoke in his own house, however, the mid-Victorian gentleman was forced to indulge in an elaborate ritual. First he had to remove his coat and put on a special quilted, frogged silk "smoking jacket" with a tasselled cap to match, so that no smell should adhere to his clothes or hair. Thereafter, armed with a candle, he withdrew to his smoking room, the gun room, or billiard room, in an isolated part of the house, where he was joined by his friends to take part in a masculine smoking orgy. Presumably his quilted jacket was intended to keep him warm, but was no doubt assisted by a brandy and soda.

In *The Habits of Good Society*, an anonymous author wrote in about 1855:

"I have no wish to see English girls light their own cigarettes . . . but . . . as smoking is now so much a habit of Englishmen, it would be wise if it were made possible . . . in the society of ladies.

"As it is there are rules enough to limit this indulgence. One must never smoke, or even ask to smoke, in the presence of the fair . . .. One must never smoke in the streets, that is, in daylight. The deadly crime may be committed, like burglary, after dark . . .. One may smoke in a railway-carriage, in spite of the bye-laws, if one has first obtained the consent of everyone present, but if there be a lady there, though she give her consent, smoke not . . .. One must never smoke, without consent, in the presence of a clergyman, and one must never offer a cigar to any ecclesiastic over the rank of curate.

"But if you smoke, or if you are in the company of smokers, and are to wear your clothes in the company of ladies afterwards, you must change them to smoke in. A host who asks you to smoke, will generally offer you an old coat for the purpose . . . When you are going to smoke a cigar yourself, you should offer one at the same time to anybody present if not a clergyman or a very old man . . .. You should always smoke a cigar given to you, whether good or bad, and never make any remarks on its quality."

Obviously the writer thought the situation was absurd at the time and by the 19th November 1861 a letter to *The Times* emphasized the extent to which these customs were ignored and how widespread smoking had become in the interval:

"There can be no doubt that smoking is a habit, or vice, if you

The solid interior of the Reform Club epitomised Victorian taste and grandeur.

please, which has of late years much increased among the upper classes of this country . . .. There is not a club in London which does not now possess a commodious smoking-room. But last week the *Illustrated London News* published a striking sketch of His Royal Highness the Heir Apparent cantering cheerily across Newmarket Heath with a cigar in his mouth; His Royal Highness the Commander-in-Chief may be seen any morning smoking his way down Constitution Hill to his duties at the War Office, our Cabinet Ministers are known to smoke in their offices, our Judges to refresh themselves with a smoke as soon as they can escape from their foul and ill-ventilated courts; the smoking-rooms of the Houses of Parliament attest to the prevalence of the habit among the members of our legislature: I have myself seen the Poet Laureate enjoying his clay pipe; and I have no doubt, sir, that many of the ablest literary contributions which pass under your chastening pen are strongly impregnated with the flavour of tobacco."

It was in the late 1860s that William Frith the popular mid-Victorian painter described an evening he had with Maria Louise Ramee, better known by her pen name *Ouida* as the best selling authoress of such flamboyant novels as *Under Two Flags* (1867). He recorded:

"Dinner and the company were delightful. One charm of it to me (being I regret to say an inveterate smoker), was the introduction of cigarettes during the course of the dinner, beginning, I think, after the

The Drury Lane theatre was a good example of Victorian magnificence in public buildings.

fish. I had heard of the fashion in foreign countries, but it surprised me as occurring in England."

Even by the end of the century this was not a fashion likely to be encountered frequently in England, although smoking had become generally accepted. The Victorian gentleman of the 1890s no longer had to retire to his own domain to smoke after dinner, for by this time ladies were also beginning to smoke, at least in the privacy of their own homes. It was still not customary for ladies to be seen smoking in public, although perfectly acceptable for gentlemen.

Of course, Frith was an artist and artists, actors and writers were expected to be Bohemian in their tastes. Although they might be gentlemen by birth, upbringing and education and even be knighted for their services to art, as for instance Sir Edwin Landseer, or Sir Edward Burne-Jones, the famous artists, or Sir Francis Burnand, Editor of *Punch* from 1880 to the 1900s, they were generally regarded as a breed apart. Whereas it was regarded as gentlemanly, or ladylike, to be an amateur artist, actor, or writer, and indeed many upper class Victorians of both sexes were extremely talented in one or more of these fields, to be a professional was another matter altogether.

Taine in the 1860s thought the English did not regard an artist as a gentleman because he worked with his hands, but he had missed the real point. In a society where conformity with an accepted pattern of behaviour was regarded as essential, non-conformity was viewed with suspicion and the popular conception of an artist's, actor's or writer's life was one of general dissipation. Hence the Victorians tended to view all artists, actors and writers with a mixture of awe and fascination, or else blank incomprehension often tinged with envy and suspicion as something quite outside their understanding. These same attitudes, unfortunately, often extended from the man to his work. Too often the Victorians were Philistines, ignorant, uncomprehending and uncaring.

Thus the Victorians readily appreciated art that was within their comprehension and preferred their pictures "to tell a story" without complications. Popular mid-Victorian art is characterised by William Frith's paintings such as "Derby Day" (1858) or "The Railway Station" (1862). The first of these was a large canvas depicting Epsom Downs on Derby Day with a multitude of interconnected scenes and characters. When first shown it created a sensation. The latter also was a large and crowded canvas showing the numerous incidents of travel and departure at a London railway station with a train about to leave. This too was immensely popular. By the end of the century, however, Frith's popularity had waned and public taste had grown rather more sophisticated.

An equally popular contemporary of Frith's was Landseer, whose famous animal pictures, such as his "Stag at Bay" or the well known "Dignity and Impudence" featuring a Bloodhound and a Scottie, appealed enormously to Victorian taste, perhaps especially as little artistic appreciation was required to enjoy them. Although Landeer's animals tended at times to be too humanised he remained popular throughout the reign of Victoria. That both Frith and Landseer were talented artists and able draughtsmen is by the way.

It was the Pre-Raphaelite school characterised by Holman Hunt, Millais and Rossetti, who appealed to later Victorian taste. Their artistic ideal was an extreme concentration on attention to detail and Holman Hunt with his deeply religious allegorical themes was the one who held most firmly to it. Millais is perhaps best known today for his much publicised picture "Bubbles" extensively used as an advertisement for soap. He was extremely successful, being created a baronet in 1885 and President of the Royal Academy in 1895, but his art had long deteriorated from sentiment to sentimentality, the besetting sin of many Victorian artists.

There were good, even great, artists in the Victorian era, but to some extent almost all were affected by the age in which they lived and moreover their art was seldom seen at its best in private houses. The Victorians unfortunately could hardly ever be content with just one picture on their walls and the tendency too often was to hang several ill-assorted pictures side by side, mixing good, bad and worse in an indiscriminate clutter. Equally unfortunate was the desire for enormous works of art, either merely to cover the vast wall spaces of the large Victorian rooms, or based on the mistaken belief that the greater the size of the picture the greater the work of art. Exhibitionism of this nature, the trait of the self-made industrialist, a stock butt of Victorian humour, was all too common.

The sad truth is that most Victorian taste in art was bad. So also was much of their taste in architecture, furniture and furnishings. Yet many Victorian knick-knacks or minor art forms are now eagerly collected. Stevengraphs, the woven pictures produced after the collapse of the English ribbon industry in 1860 following the removal of duty on imported ribbons, have a distinct charm of their own. Much pottery of the period is decidedly not unattractive. A typical glass case of exotic stuffed birds, a tiger skin, or a mounted animal head, can all be effective ornaments in their place. The Victorians simply could not leave well alone. Their rooms were heavily overfurnished with all these, also with beaded anti-macassars, embroidered mottoes, silver framed

A typical Victorian sitting room showing the superfluity of ornament and fussy designs of the times. (*Mary Evans*)

photographs, carved ivory ornaments, china souvenirs and much more, on small side tables, on the mantelpiece, on shelves, bookcases, tables and even on the piano. The result was a visual calamity.

The same refusal to leave well alone affected the design of furniture. The simple clean line, or unfussy utilitarian concept became anathema to the mid-Victorian craftsmen. A simple piece of furniture such as a sideboard was gradually added to until it emerged in the late Victorian period as a flute-legged, claw-footed, gothic erection with frescoed back supporting additional cupboards and mirrors which covered an entire wall. Such solid mahogany furniture was suitably designated a "handsome piece." Perhaps unconsciously the Victorians were seeking to reflect their pride in their progress, in the stability of their way of life and of the Empire, by the solidity of the furniture with which they surrounded themselves. Perhaps they needed the reassurance of its solidity, the scrollwork and frescoes, the claw feet and fluted legs and shining expanses of mahogany. It was all of a piece with the architecture and surroundings.

C. L. Eastlake in his *Hints on Household Taste* written in 1878 had some trenchant comments on Victorian taste, as follows:

"The public are frequently misled by terms of approbation now commonly used by shopmen in a sense widely differing from their original significance. Thus the word 'handsome' has come to mean something generally rather showy, often ponderous and almost always encumbered with ornament: the word 'elegant' is applied to any object which is curved in form (no matter in what direction, or with what effect). If it succeeds in conveying to the spectator a false idea of its purpose and possesses the added advantage of being so fragile that we cannot handle it without danger it is not only 'elegant' but 'graceful.' If an article is simple and of good design, answering its proper purpose without ostentatious display of ornament, pretending to be neither more nor less than it is, they only call it 'neat' in the shops."

The reason so many Victorian gentlemen and their wives were seduced by the honeyed phrases of shopkeepers was contained inadvertently in Arthur Freeling's *Gentleman's Pocket Book of Etiquette* written in 1840. In this he summed up his advice to would-be gentlemen as follows:

"Always seek the society of those above yourself . . . The man who is content to seek associates in his own grade (unless his station be very exalted) will always be in danger of retrograding. What is good company? becomes an important question. If it is composed of persons of birth, rank, fashion and respectability . . .. If you cannot, from your station, obtain entrance to the best company, aim as near to it as your opportunities will permit."

Manuals of Etiquette inevitably followed one another in steady succession throughout such a notably self-conscious and socially insecure century. Manners on smoking, manners on leaving calling cards, manners at the dinner table, all these were the subject of continuous study and streams of literature. O. B. Bunce, writing under the pseudonym "Censor" in his *Don't, A Manual Of Mistakes and Improprieties More Or Less Prevalent in Conduct and Speech*, published around 1890, advised:

"Don't tuck your napkin under your chin, or spread it upon your breast. Bibs and tuckers are for the nursery. Don't spread your napkin over your lap; let it fall over your knee.

"Don't eat from the end of your spoon, but from the side.

"Don't gurgle, or draw in your breath, or make other noises when eating soup. Don't ask for a second service of soup.

"Don't bite your bread. Break it off. Don't break your bread into your soup.

"Don't eat vegetables with a spoon. Eat them with a fork. The rule is not to eat anything with a spoon that can be eaten with a fork. Even ices are now often eaten with a fork.

"Don't leave your knife and fork on your plate when you send it for a second supply."

Despite such books of etiquette the Victorians enjoyed their meals. The upper classes both ate and drank well and took their time about doing so. Taine commented on the amount the English ate. He noted that according to economists an average Englishman ate four sheep a year to an average Frenchman's sheep and a half. He added mildly that since the English considered the French abstemious it followed that they naturally considered the English voracious. Nor were the English by any means restricted in their diet to meat

In his *Recollections* Woodgate recalled, "In those times (1860s) oyster suppers were fashionable about Christmas time. Dinner invitations for 6 p.m. dinner would perhaps contain a significant 'Oysters' which meant 10 p.m. supper and early dinner, which gave time for second appetite. When supper time came, whist and music or charades adjourned. Every man having deposited his lady at the table, adjourned to a sideboard, turned up his sleeves and opened oysters (servants did not do the opening). Pimms was the great emporium which supplied the country with this commodity. Most gentlemen could do two to five dozen at a sitting. About 1861 I recall my father's lamenting to us youngsters. 'We must set some limit on oyster suppers. They have become a matter of *eating money*! Do you know! oysters are now all but a penny apiece.' "

If a country gentleman in the Midlands at this time could obtain oysters at less than a penny each it is understandable that in London they would be considerably cheaper. Even the lower middle classes in London could afford to produce a considerable dinner by modern standards, although perhaps not always well cooked or well served.

Alexis Soyer, a distinguished chef and author of several books on cookery writing as from the viewpoint of a lower middle class wife gives an amusing impression of the sort of indifferent dinner which might have been served in such circles in the 1850s:

"Dinner was served pretty punctually, only half an hour after time. On my entrance in the room my first glance at the table showed me that there was a want of *savoir faire* in its management; the plate, very abundant and splendid, was of so yellow a cast that it looked as if it were plated, and the cut glass was exceedingly dim. My first surprise was that there were no napkins, the next the soup plates were quite cold . . . : after being served with fish and waiting until it was cold for the sauce to eat with it, I was rather sceptical how the rest of the dinner would progress. After the first, the second course made its appearance, which was heavy and too abundant; the plain things were well done, but there was only one servant in the room for the whole party of fourteen, and from the strict formality of the table it would have been sacrilege to have handed your plate for any vegetables or anything else you might require. There were four salt cellars, certainly very massive silver ones, at each corner of the table, and a beautiful cruet frame in the centre; the hot dishes of this course, like the previous one, became cold and tasteless before being eaten, and during the time the servant was serving the champagne all the plates were empty; in fact it was a good dinner spoilt . . ..

"About half an hour after the cloth was removed, and just as the conversation was being thawed from the freezing it had received at the dinner table, Mrs D. and ladies withdrew and for an hour and a half we had to bear the insipid conversation of the drawing-room, the hissing of the urn at the tea-table bearing a prominent part. Several messages were sent from time to time to the dining room to say that the coffee was ready; and when at last the gentlemen came, two had had quite wine enough which caused them to receive sundry angry looks from their wives . . . "

The method of service at this execrable dinner was the old style known as á la Française, by which each course was laid on the table at once, the different dishes being taken off to serve them. Apart from laying considerable strain on the cook this was necessarily very slow and often resulted in the food getting cold. In the 1860s the method of serving meals à la Russe was introduced. By this method fruit, flowers and wine were on the table with one course at a time, served, already cut up, in front of the host. This was much faster and more important even in Victorian days was easier for the cook. By the 1870s it had become much more popular.

Writing to her sister in America in 1873 Lady Jebb, recently married to a Cambridge don, recounted in some detail a dinner party she had given:

"Cambridge, 5th April 1873: I gave a dinner party on Thursday and left the preparation of most of the dinner to Mrs Bird (the cook) simply giving my orders and everything was perfect. I got a girl in to help . . . . First [Mrs Bird] made the rolls herself. (One is laid at each plate, you know, instead of bread. She makes excellent rolls.) Then she made a white soup, she fried twelve fillets of sole, and made the lobster sauce to go with the fish. Next we had two entrees ordered from the College . . . the first . . . 'timballes de fois gras' and then, when this was eaten and the plates changed, the second entree, 'sweetbreads stewed with mushrooms and truffles,' was passed. With these Mrs Bird had nothing to do, which gave her a breathing time to dish the main dinner. She roasted the leg of mutton, boiled the turkey, made its sauce of oysters, and cooked all the vegetables – potatoes, cauliflower, and celery which go with this course. When we were through with this, she sent up the roast duck with its sauce . . . I hired two waiters to help Martin (the butler) and everything passed off delightfully. We had a plum pudding from the College and after that a Charlotte Rousse, then cheese . . . and then the table was cleared for dessert. All the wine glasses, decanters, etc., were taken off, the crumbs brushed away, and then new decanters put on and dessert plates. The waiters handed round one dish after another, of the dessert, after which we ladies arose and left the room to the gentlemen . . . . Entertaining here is a great pleasure and no trouble to the hostess."

Lady Jebb, of course was fortunate in having the assistance of the College kitchens to call on in need. However entertainment of this sort

Such scenes at political dinners were not unknown in the early part of the Victorian period, although latterly unlikely at public dinners. (At private dinners when the ladies had left drunkenness was not uncommon.)

was quite common in any well-off Victorian gentleman's household. Dinner parties of from eighteen to twenty people were nothing out of the ordinary. The menu provided for such a dinner party in The Young Housewife's Daily Assistant published in 1874, very clearly underlines the sort of variety normally expected on such occasions:

### July and August

Coventry Soup, spring soup.
Water souchet of flounders, stewed eels.
Curried lobster, salmon pudding.
Fried salmon with Tartar sauce.
Boiled trout with sweet herbs.
Whitebait, both plain and devilled.
Thin brown bread and butter, cut lemons.

Fried sweetbreads with mushrooms.
Lamb cutlets with fresh tomatoes.
Fricandeau of veal with spinach.
Saddle of mutton (currant jelly).
French beans, potatoes.
Roast capon, ham.
Quail, pate de fois gras
Mayonnaise of lobster.
Conservative pudding, iced.
Summer fruit salad.
Raspberry cream, pineapple jelly.
Savoury macaroni"

At a formal dinner there was a strict etiquette regarding partners which changed little throughout the latter half of the 19th century. This is well outlined in Lady Colin Campbell's *Etiquette of Good Society*, which though published in 1911 would have been as correct on the subject of "Going in to Dinner" as anything written forty years earlier:

"The host communicates to each gentleman the name of the lady he is to take into dinner. If they are strangers to each other, the host introduces his friend to the lady. When the 'guests are met and the feast is set,' the butler announces the latter to his master, who then offers his arm to the lady appointed to be escorted by him. This should either be the oldest lady, the lady of highest rank, or the greatest stranger; but in smart society precedence is no longer allowed for brides. The other guests follow arm-in-arm and the hostess closes the procession, escorted by the gentleman who has been appointed to the honourable post, and who has been elected for one of the three reasons above mentioned, as being the oldest, or of highest rank &c."

Despite the dazzling dinners and formality, the glitter and the gluttony, which continued to make up part of the social scene, there was a growing servant problem towards the end of the 19th century. As early as 1837 the footman William Tayler had dutifully chronicled in his diary every Sunday that as a matter of course he went to church, but he gave the show away in one entry which ran "Today I really went to church." As the century wore on servants, especially in London, increasingly expected at least part of their Sunday free and the average gentleman's household had to be satisfied with cold meat for dinner in the evening. In the circumstances it is not surprising that by the 1890s it had become the accepted custom in many London households to dine out on Sunday.

This was not a custom that could have arisen in the 1870s simply because then there were no restaurants suitable for ladies. By the 1880s a few large restaurants had begun to appear and by the 1890s there was a considerable choice. In his book *Dinners and Diners* published in 1901 Lt. Colonel Newnham-Davis mentioned people who "ring the changes for their Sunday dinner from the Savoy to the Carleton, from Princes' to the Berkeley." Not least among the popular restaurants were those at the railway stations. Colonel Newnham-Davis described the appearance of the Marylebone Great Central Hotel:

"The banqueting hall is a magnificent room, a sight in itself. The walls are of Norwegian marble, a marble of light greens and yellows and pinks; its ceiling is of cream and gold; the twelve marble columns that support the roof are white in colour, thickly veined with pink and grey; and over the grill which is at one end, is a long frieze depicting a number of beautiful ladies who are apparently meant for the Seasons . . ..

"We went through the lounge, which is all *faience* and marble, and Oriental rugs, and great palms and easy chairs, and came at last to the coffee room. And a very magnificent room it is, second only in gorgeousness to the banqueting hall."

One of the features on which most of these restaurants prided themselves was on their broadly based cellars and choice of wines. Although every gentleman's household had its own cellars, the average gentleman tended to rely on his wine merchant, or on experience gained at his club, or on visits abroad, for his choice of wines. It is true that the first vintage wines had been laid down as early as the 1770s, but it was not until after Waterloo in 1815 that the practice of laying down vintage wines and ports became steadily more widespread. By then the right shape and size of bottle had been perfected and practical rules learned concerning laying wines down successfully. Clarets and burgundies, sherries and madeira, and above all port, were to be found by the 1830s and 40s in almost every gentleman's cellar, although not always as well cared for as they might have been.

In the 1870s the insect pest *phylloxera vastatrix* which attacked the roots of the vines began its deadly work and by the 1880s the European vinyards had been devastated. There were still stocks enough of champagne, the most popular Victorian wine, or suitable substitutes, but for a decade brandy, the most popular after dinner drink was almost unobtainable. It was then that Scots salesmen of the dynamic calibre of Alexander Walker, James Buchanan and Tommy Dewar began successful large scale selling of Scotch whisky. Brand names such as Johnnie Walker, Buchanan's Black and White, Dewar's, Teacher's, Haig, Sanderson's Vat 69, Mackie's White Horse and Hill Thomson's Queen Anne became familiar in the south. Scotch became the national after dinner drink in place of brandy.

In the view of at least one Victorian this was not the only change in dining habits which was required. In his *Hints on Household Taste* (1878) C. L. Eastlake commented, "Our evening dress needs radical reform. How it happens that black cloth has come to be associated with occasions of public and private festivity in common with occasions of public and private mourning is a riddle which we must leave to posterity to solve. But it is certain in the existing state of society, Englishmen wear the same dress at an evening party and at a funeral. Nor is this all, for many a host who entertains his friends at dinner has a butler behind his chair who is dressed precisely like himself. To add to this confusion, the clergyman who rises to say grace, might, until recently, have been mistaken for either."

Certainly when compared with their Georgian forefathers the Victorians were a drab lot. The edict of Beau Brummel lived after him that black and white was the only suitable evening wear for gentlemen. Yet day wear was also dull and uninspiring. Typical dress for a gentleman of the 1860s might consist of a "promenade costume" consisting of a double breasted top coat of barathea with deep cuffs and wide sleeves. If brown it would be lined with black, otherwise with crimson silk. His trousers might be check patterned of medium width with a close fit at the foot, generally strapped underneath for riding. A patterned brocade, satin or silk waistcoat was one of the few remnants of Georgian fashion. A beaver hat (top hat) was essential and the portly male might wear stays.

Dress in the country in the 1870s and 1880s might consist of a Norfolk jacket and knickerbockers, with gaiters and boots. In the latter decades of the century tweeds, Inverness capes, deerstalkers and more comfortable easier dress became general. For formal wear, however, frock coats, top hats and stiff collars remained in fashion until the end of the century. Eastlake's strictures on evening wear had little or no effect.

As regards clergymen, however, there was a considerable change in garb as Woodgate noted in his *Reminiscences*. In the 1840s and 1850s

The Norfolk jacket attained new heights of popularity towards the end of the century.

he recorded, "The normal cleric claimed to be a 'gentleman' and to dress as such, as regards cut and fashion of clothing; while as regards colour, he adhered to the University statute of 'sub-fusc' hues. His nether garments were not forced to be black as now; iron grey, pepper and salt, Oxford mixture and so on would suffice for day time. His coat was swallow-tailed a la Regency; his hat a beaver, full height; his overcoat broadcloth, buttoning to the chin if required. The still surviving breeches and gaiters, affected in this day episcopally, decanally and archdiaconally are but the record of a protest by the superior order of clergy in the early nineteenth century against the slovenly innovations of dressing gowns for the legs called trousers, to which the rest of the clergy had begun to succumb, and to swim in the wake of fashion."

In any fashions there are liable to be pitfalls for the unwary or uninitiated as that comparatively harmless young clergyman the Rev. Francis Kilvert found out unexpectedly in 1873. He had visited the seaside and decided to have a bathe from a bathing machine on the edge of the sea as was the custom. He noted in his diary:

"Thursday 24th July. This morning Uncle Will, Dora and I drove to

Brighton was an elegant seaside resort early in the period. Here the German Spa in Queen's Park, Brighton.

Seaton with Polly and the dogcart. It was a lovely morning. At Seaton, while Dora was sitting on the beach, I had a bathe. A boy brought me to the machine door two towels, as I thought, but when I came out of the water and began to use them I found that one of them was a pair of very short red and white striped drawers to cover my nakedness. Unaccustomed to such things and customs I had in my ignorance bathed naked and set at nought the conventionalties of the place and scandalised the beach. However some small boys who were looking on at the rude man appeared to be much interested in the spectacle and the young ladies who were strolling near seemed to have no objection."

In the early part of the 19th century seaside resorts proliferated and with the spread of the railways in the 1850s and 1860s the holiday at the seaside became almost a national institution. Indeed with the possible exceptions of Bournemouth and Scarborough the majority of seaside resorts ceased to cater for the gentleman's family and turned increasingly to what were termed in Victorian parlance "confined establishments" or what might now be called "lower income brackets." According to the *Visitor's Guide to Bournemouth* of 1842 it was founded by a local landowner, Sir George W. Tapps-Gervis, who "became satisfied that Bournemouth was endowed by nature with those special features and circumstances which eminently fitted it to become an approved resort . . . . Thus on spots where, before, the foot of man rarely pressed . . . a number of detached villas . . . sprang into existence, apparting accommodation of varying extent . . . to the convenience of either large or small families."

103

Shanklin, from East, J.O.W.

Seaside resorts: Ramsgate and Shanklin. Note the horse-drawn bathing machines.

The Beach, Ramsgate

From mid-century onwards the Scottish Highlands became increasingly popular following the example set by Queen Victoria.

With the "vulgarisation" of so many seaside resorts and following the example of "the dear Queen," many English gentlemen took to visiting the Highlands in the latter half of the century. Renting a shooting box for the "Glorious Twelfth," or for the stalking or the fishing, became a regular custom. Queen Victoria and the railways opened up Scotland and particularly the Highlands in a way that had not appeared possible in the eighteenth century. The Balmoralisation of the Highlands was a purely Victorian phenomenon.

Increasingly during the entire Victorian period the English gentlemen accepted travel on the continent as a right, feeling that it was perfectly reasonable that they should travel where they willed without passports and speaking only their native language. Small expatriate communities were formed in most European capitals and the universal acceptance of English gold or paper money made travel easy. During the 1850s and 1860s the German spas, Baden Baden in particular, had considerable popularity. In the 1870s and 1880s France was possibly more popular, although Switzerland and Italy also had their devotees. In his *Manual of*

*Diet in Health and Disease* (1876), Thomas King Chambers, M.D., had some words of advice for the unwary:

"In almost all country places out of England it is impossible to avoid the greasy dishes which are apparently preferred by all except our own countrymen; and a frequent consequence is rancid indigestion, with nauseous taste in the mouth, and flatulence or diarrhoea. A few drops of vinegar or lemon juice and a little cayenne pepper in the plate are the readiest correctives.

"Another article of cuisine that offends the bowels of unused Britons is garlic. Not uncommonly in southern climes an egg with the shell on is the only procurable animal food without garlic in it. Flatulence and looseness are the frequent results. Bouilli, with its accompaniments of mustard sauce and water melon, is the safest resource, and not an unpleasant one, after a little education."

Not altogether surprisingly the English on holiday were one of the stock English jokes. Like the English on holiday, however, the English sense of humour developed on more sophisticated lines as the century progressed. In the 1860s Taine likened the English sense of humour to the English bitter beer, which he claimed was a wholesome drink and, if persevered with, it was possible to acquire a taste for it. He considered the French humour more spontaneous and subtle and quoted a letter in *Punch*:

> Letter from a Secretary of the Treasury to a Member of Parliament: Library, The house of Commons. Dear Sir, Lord P – has passed me your letter in which you draw his attention to the fact that the session is nearly over, that you have lent his Lordship's policy a support as judicious as it has been constant, and that your services merit a reward in the form of a place.
>
> In reply to your letter I must ask your permission to point out that your first proposition is the only one on which Her Majesty's government has the honour and pleasure of finding itself in agreement with you, and that, personally, I have the honour to be, Sir,
>
> Your very faithful and humble servant . . . . .

It is only necessary to take a few bound volumes of *Punch* at random over the years of the 19th century to see the steady development of the English sense of humour as the years pass. The ponderous jokes of the early part of the century with their lengthy explanations appear heavy and laboured beside the much more amusing and effective wit of the end of the century. Despite his ultimate complete obliteration from the Victorian scene after his downfall, Oscar Wilde left his mark on the humour of his period. Many of his aphorisms were sophisticated nonsense, but witty just the same, as for instance:

The first duty in life is to be as artificial as possible. What the second duty is no one has as yet discovered.

No crime is vulgar, but all vulgarity is crime. Vulgarity is the conduct of others.

The only way to atone for being occasionally overdressed is by being alway absolutely overeducated.

There is something tragic about the enormous number of young men there are in England at the present moment who start life with perfect profiles and end by adopting some useful profession.

Compared with an example of early Victorian humour quoted by Rommilly in his diaries "Why is the Queen like a besieged castle? Because she is always enceinte", Wilde's wit is an enormous bound forwards. Yet such comparisons with the punning early form of humour are, of course grossly unfair since tastes had changed so radically for so many different reasons. It is as fair to compare Wordsworth to Kipling which is rather a gigantic hop sideways. Yet Kipling was essentially the poet and writer of the Empire, of India and of the Common man, the soldier and the sweat. He may not have been considered quite suitable for the drawing room, but there were few Englishmen by the late 1890s who could not quote a few lines at least of such epics as "Gunga Din."

Wilde and the Aesthetes he led were themselves the target of much humour in *Punch* and elsewhere. Gilbert and Sullivan, whose light operas delighted the late Victorians held them up to ridicule in song. The Victorians by the end of the century had accepted the music hall and light opera as part of their life. George and Weedon Grossmith in *The Diary of a Nobody*, J. M. Barrie and Bernard Shaw on the stage, and Sir Francis Burnand in *Punch* were but a few who in the 1890s poked fun at the earnestness of the age. The Victorians had at last learned to laugh at themselves and had cast aside their stays. By the end of the century there was much more ease and freedom of expression than the start of Victoria's reign had seemed to promise, but both tastes and manners had radically changed.

# CHAPTER FIVE

# Morality and Sex

One of the particularly noticeable features of the Victorian age was the steadily increasing literacy of all classes combined with the rapidly increasing output of literature of every kind. From temperance leaflets to biblical tracts, from political pamphlets to penny journals, from ballads and poetry to popular novelettes and more serious literature, from local newspapers to national magazines, the sheer quantity of print produced as well as the variety was infinitely greater than in the previous century. Yet the one book which was to be found in every household and which remained the most frequently read throughout the nineteenth century was the Bible. It was on the Bible that Victorian morality was based. It was round the Bible that some of the fiercest controversies of the age were waged.

At the same time the influence of popular works such as those of Sir Walter Scott in perpetuating the taste for gothic art and architecture and encouraging a renaissance of interest in mediaeval taste and ideals of chivalry cannot be overlooked. A book by a now forgotten author, Kenelm Digby, entitled *The Broadstone of Honour*, first published in 1822, but frequently reprinted, was particularly notable in this respect. By lengthy quotations from Cicero and early French and English examples of knightly chivalry, he strove to advance his ideal conception of gentlemanly behaviour and honour. One extract from the strange nooks and crannies of his gothic prose was also the coping stone of much early Victorian thought:

"Let then every class of man be satisfied with the status of life to which they have been appointed. Every station has its advantages and with regard to happiness its equal position."

And there was the hymn:

> The rich man in his castle,
> The poor man at his gate
> God made them high and lowly,
> And ordered their estate.

*Hymns Ancient and Modern.*

It was in part such literature, dilating on the advantages of birth and the ideals of knightly chivalry, in part his indignation at the omission of the Queen's Champion hurling down the gauntlet at Queen Victoria's coronation in 1838, which caused the 26 year old Earl of Eglinton to announce his intention of holding a full scale tournament of knights in armour in 1839. To his surprise he was inundated with applications to enter, but the fates were unkind to him. What might at least have been a colourful spectacle was washed out by the heaviest rainfall in memory and the affair became a laughing stock as well as leaving his estate in debt for the rest of his life.

Despite such occasional aberrations and the deplorable results of gothic taste in architecture, the Victorians, whether through the Bible, through their literature, or through example, or perhaps through a combination of all three, had a very real admiration for what they termed nobility of character. True nobility of mind was their highest aim in many cases. That such nobility of mind might be difficult to live with, and might even prove uncomfortable in the extreme to those in close contact with it, was by the way.

It was this nobility of mind, allied to Christian manliness, which Arnold strove above all to inculcate at Rugby in the 1830s and 1840s. This was shown to be the height of the hero's ambition in *Tom Brown's Schooldays*, by Thomas Hughes, to give only one example from popular literature of the time.

"'I want to leave behind me,' said Tom, speaking slow, and looking much moved, 'the name of a fellow who never bullied a little boy, or turned his back on a big one.'"

This, of course, was based on Hughes' own experiences under Arnold at Rugby. At University the products of the Arnold system were termed somewhat cynically "muscular Christians." In *Tom Brown at Oxford*, published in 1861, but based on his experiences in the early 1840s, Thomas Hughes wrote:

"... the least of the muscular Christians has hold of the old chivalrous and Christian belief, that a man's body is given him to be trained and brought into subjection and then used for the protection of the weak, the advancement of all righteous causes and the subduing of the earth, which God had given to the children of men."

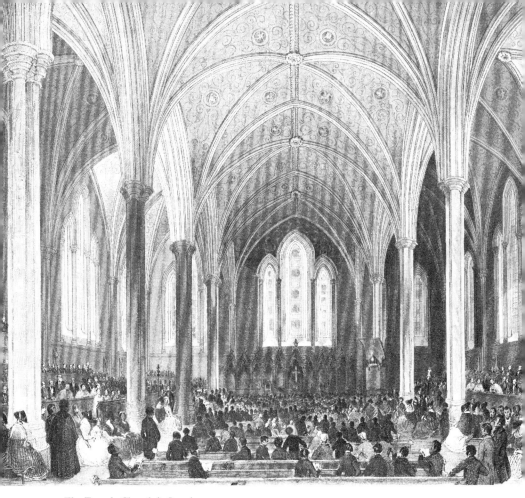

The Temple Church in London.

It is obvious that at times there was an extremely narrow line between what passed for true nobility of mind and obsessive priggishness, or pure bigotry. It must not be forgotten, however, that the Evangelism of the early Victorian period was a dismal gloomy religion and a ripe breeding ground for bigotry. It was well described by Sir Walter Besant in *Fifty Years Ago*, a review which appeared in the "Graphic Jubilee Number" of 1887, in which he wrote:

"He who can remember the ordinary Church Service in the early Fifties knows what they were in the Thirties .... The musical part of the service was, to begin with, taken slow – incredibly slow; no one now would believe, who is not old enough to remember, how slow it was .... Two hymns were sung; they were always of the kind which expressed either the despair of the sinner, or the doubtful joy of the believer. I say doubtful because he was constantly being warned not to be too confident .... There were many kinds of preachers, just as at present ... but they all seemed to preach the same doctrine of

110

hopelessness, the same Gospel of Despair .... Wretched, miserable creed!"

He went on to note the changes which had taken place in the Church in the intervening fifty years, not entirely favourably:

"What we now call the 'life' of the church, with its meetings, fraternities, guilds, societies and organisations, then simply did not exist. The clergyman had an easy time; he visited little, he had an Evening Service once a week, he did not pretend to keep saints' days and minor festivals and fasts — none of his congregation expected him to keep them; as for his being a teetotaller for the sake of the weaker brethren, that would have seemed to everybody pure foolishness; yet a good man, for the most part, who lived a quiet and exemplary life, and a good scholar — scholars, are, indeed, sadly to seek among the modern clergy — a sound theologian, a judge of good port, and a gentleman. But processions, banners, surpliced shows, robes, and the like, he would have regarded as unworthy of the consideration of one who was a Churchman, a Protestant, and a scholar."

Parallel with the dissemination of "muscular Christianity" in the 1830s and 1840s was the development of what came to be known as the "Oxford Movement," started by Keble, Pusey and Newman in Oxford in an attempt to break away from the narrow-minded, severe Protestantism which Besant had found so uninspiring. Although Keble and Pusey remained Protestants, Newman fulfilled the worst forebodings of many Evangelicals by "going over" to Roman Catholicism in

THE CLERICAL BEARD MOVEMENT.

111

1845 and taking many of his followers with him. Those who did not join Newman turned increasingly to "Ritualism" or High Church practices, to the considerable indignation of many who objected to "surpliced shows" as the pages of *Punch* and other satirical publications showed.

In the first half of the century dissension was all within the church. Religious and scientific beliefs had not yet seriously clashed for at this stage Science was still in its infancy, even if there had been considerable developments in many fields. Summing the matter up, Thomas Babington Macaulay fervently praised the advances made by Science in the following eloquent terms without a dissenting voice being raised:

"It has lengthened life; it has mitigated pain: it has extinguished diseases; it has increased the fertility of the soil; it has given new security to the mariner; it has furnished new arms for the warrior; it has spanned great rivers and estuaries with bridges of form unknown to our fathers; it has guided the thunderbolt innocuously from heaven to earth; it has lighted up the night with the splendour of day; it has extended the range of human vision; it has facilitated intercourse, correspondence, all friendly offices, all despatch of business; it has enabled man to descend to the depths of the sea, to soar into the air, to penetrate securely into the noxious recesses of the earth, to traverse the land in cars which whirl along without horses, to cross the ocean in ships, which run ten knots against the wind. These are but a part of its fruits, and of its first-fruits, for it is a philosophy which never rests, which has never attained, which is never perfect. Its law is progress."

For much of the first half of the nineteenth century William Buckland (1784–1856), Dean of Westminster and erstwhile Reader of Mineralogy at Oxford, was regarded as the leading geologist in the country. His practical knowledge was considered so immense that it was seriously related of him that on one occasion when lost between London and Oxford he merely examined a handful of soil and said confidently, "Ah, as I thought, Ealing." His eloquence attracted sizeable audiences to his lectures, which were largely devoted to equating his geological discoveries with his theological belief in a Universal Deluge.

In the 1830s Charles Lyell (1797–1875), who had qualified as barrister but had been attracted to geology by Buckland's lectures, published his *Principles of Geology* which discreetly, but firmly, ignored any reference to theological viewpoints. The earth, he argued, was millions of years old, not just a few thousands as had previously been maintained. Buckland, predictably, opposed this strongly along with other authoritative men of the day, but many were converted to this theory. In the 1840s came fame and in 1848 Lyell was knighted.

Amongst Lyell's supporters and friends was Thomas Huxley (1825- 1895), a younger man, who had achieved the post of professor of palaeontology at the Royal School of Mines and was in considerable demand as author of popular scientific papers intelligible to the layman. A powerful debater of impressive intellect, Huxley thoroughly enjoyed controversy. It was at the urging of both Lyell and Huxley that Charles Darwin eventually in 1859 published his *Origin of Species*.

Darwin (1809–1882) had deliberately attempted to avoid provocation by relating his theory of natural selection only to animals, although including a mild hope that as a result "light will be thrown on the origin of man and his history." The so-called Fundamentalists, who held to the Bible as the basis of all belief, immediately attacked this new and revolutionary theory fiercely. Huxley, his most vociferous supporter, deliberately encouraged the controversy that ensued largely because he delighted in this sort of furore.

It is significant that Darwin, who had studied Theology at Cambridge with a view to becoming a clergyman admitted in his *Life & Letters,* "I did not then in the least doubt the strict and literal truth of every word in the Bible. I soon persuaded myself that our Creed must be fully accepted."

This was an attitude common to most gentlemen, even to the firebrand Huxley, in the first half of the nineteenth century. Hence it is easy to understand the violent reactions of many clergymen and theologically minded scientists at what appeared to be an attack on the foundations of their beliefs. There was thus a good deal of support for Bishop Samuel Wilberforce in 1860 at a meeting of the British Association at Oxford when he attacked Darwin's theory in a witty half hour speech. He concluded by enquiring whether Huxley, who was present, claimed descent from a monkey through his grandfather or grandmother. At these words, Huxley, who coined the word "agnostic" to define his beliefs, or lack of them, somewhat inconsistently in the circumstances, whispered to his neighbour, "The Lord hath delivered him into mine hands." He then stood up to reply and the conclusion of his reasoned defence of Darwin's theory was devasting:

"A man has no reason to be ashamed of having an ape for his grandfather. If there were an ancestor whom I should feel shame in recalling, it would rather be a *man* – a man of restless and versatile intellect – who, not content with success in his own sphere of activity, plunges into scientific questions, with which he has no real acquaintance, only to obscure them by aimless rhetoric, and distract the attention of his hearers from the real point at issue by eloquent digressions and skilled appeals to religious prejudice."

Although the controversy over Darwin's theory continued fiercely for some time with scientific agnostics ranged against the Fundamentalists, it was as nothing to the furore which ensued when Dr Colenso, the Bishop of Natal, found himself troubled with doubts about the Book of Genesis in 1863. In the preface to Part I of his essay on the subject entitled *The Pentateuch*, he wrote:

One of the many cartoons ridiculing Darwin for his theory of evolution. (*Mary Evans*)

"While translating the Story of the Flood, I have had a simple minded, but intelligent native . . . ask, 'Is all that true? Do you really believe that all this happened? My own knowledge of some branches of science, of Geology in particular, has been much increased since I left England and I now know on geological grounds . . . that a Universal Deluge . . . could not possibly have taken place in the way described in the Book of Genesis . . . . The story . . . is utterly incredible."

The strange thing to us today is not that the Bishop should have had doubts about the story of the Flood, but that he should have felt it necessary to go into details of the height of Mount Ararat, "17,000 feet . . . 3,000 feet above the region of perpetual snow," and to point out that if they had lived there for seven months as the story claimed "the . . . living creatures in the Ark must have been frozen to death."

Even more extraordinary to us now is the fact that, far from being hailed as a champion of the obvious, Dr. Colenso was attacked from all sides. A particularly virulent attack came from J. B. Young in 1865 in a treatise entitled *Modern Scepticism*. A former Professor of Mathematics at Belfast University, Young fulminated, "If Bishop Colenso be really in a condition of mind which renders him fully accountable for what he writes (and there is reason to suspect otherwise), then we say that a more reprehensible instance of scientific *guess-work*, deliberately promulgated as established scientific truth, has rarely been witnessed."

After dealing with Bishop Colenso in tortuous sarcastic detail, Young also attacked Lyell, Darwin and Huxley in much the same manner and ended:

"Revelation neither invokes human science to confirm its truths, nor does it challenge human science to disturb them. It does not stoop even to notice science at all; and in thus not deigning to regard it silently

114

Edward Bouverie, a typical mid-Victorian high-church cleric. (*Radio Times Hulton Picture Library*)

declines its feeble support – and as silently defies its puny opposition."

Even Young with his tortuous reasoning and laboured sarcasm found it hard to substantiate some of the Old Testament in the light of accepted scientific knowledge, but there is no need to go into any further detail on his arguments. The mere fact that, whether Fundamentalist or scientific agnostic, the average Victorian gentleman could argue heatedly over such matters indicates the unthinking acceptance of much of their belief and the shallowness and pettiness of much of their thoughts. Their minds really were in chains and their eyes in blinkers in the first half of the century. The revision of the Bible in 1870 was a much greater step towards the twentieth century than might appear on the face of it.

The appointment of Edward White Benson as Archbiship of Canterbury in 1883, following on that of the invalid and vacillating aged Tait, brought new life to the church and justified Besant's comments in 1887. With fresh vision the new Archbishop refused to allow matters of petty detail to assume undue importance and his primacy was one of almost unprecedented activity. His aim was to make the Church a greater force in English life and up to his death in 1896 he worked unflaggingly to this end. The old narrow Evangelism gave way to a no less sincere but much broader faith.

In his approach to marriage, however, Edward Benson (1829–1896) epitomised many early and mid-Victorian gentlemen's extremely ambivalent attitudes to women. On the one hand they set their women on a romantic pedestal as feminine, helpless creatures to be chivalrously protected and on the other they treated them quite simply as lesser beings. As wives, mothers and daughters they could not be permitted to occupy themselves in any way which was not considered socially acceptable; thus much of their time was occupied in utterly stultifying and useless occupations such as pointless embroidery, or in the dull social round of daily visits. They were not required, or expected, to have any education, or any thoughts beyond the management of a household and fashion. Until the Married Women's Property Act of 1870 all their joint property belonged in the eyes of the law entirely to the husband, for they were not legally considered fit to have control over any money or property in their own right. They were, of course, not allowed to vote. The husband, in his own eyes and often in theirs also, was the dominating factor in their lives.

Even by early or mid-Victorian standards Edward Benson was a little unusual. In 1852, as a young man of 23, he decided to marry Mary, the eleven year old daughter of his widowed cousin Mrs Mary Sidgwick. He noted in his diary:

"Mrs Sidgwick's little daughter, Mary, is this year eleven years old . . . As I have always been very fond of her and she of me with the love of a little sister . . . it is not strange that I who from the circumstances of my family am not likely to marry for many years to come . . . and who am fond indeed (if not too fond) of little endearments . . . should have thought first of the possiblity that some day dear little Minnie might become my wife."

He also noted that after reading Tennyson's "The Princess" with her and talking to her "the palms of my hands grew very hot." He then approached his cousin, Mary's mother, who was naturally somewhat startled and tactfully suggested that there were many more mature examples of her daughter to be found and that it was too early to make up his mind. However the following year he persuaded her to let him "speak" to the now twelve year old Mary. As he recorded in his diary, she repeated the words of Tennyson's poem "The Princess," "Love, children, happiness," and added, "Two of these are mine now." When she was just eighteen and he was newly appointed the first headmaster of Wellington, they were married.

The result was really just what might have been expected. He was a dominating and exacting figure, a natural schoolmaster who firmly believed that he could mould others as he wished. She was a happy, rather romantic, child with a quick mind, but in no sense an academic, who could never attain the same heights of religious and emotional feeling as her gifted husband. He was also an ardent physical lover and she, he complained, was cold and unloving. Although they both tried to make the best of it, their married life in the early years at least was very hard for both of them, but particularly for her. It was almost invariably the wife who suffered most in such circumstances. She noted in her diary:

"An utter child, I danced and sang into matrimony with a loving, but exacting, a believing and therefore an expectant spirit, twelve years older much stronger, much more passionate, whom I did not really love . . . . But let me try to realise how hard it was for Edward. He restrained his passionate nature for seven years and then got this unloving, weak, unstable child. I know how disappointing this must have been to him, how evidently disappointed he was . . . ."

In the manner of many other Victorian wives Mary Benson learned to accommodate herself to her husband and eventually to manage him tactfully, although never reaching the stage of loving him. His brilliant career as Archbishop of Canterbury was not to her taste, but she succeeded in rearing three sons and a daughter and managing his household for him. It is not really surprising, however, 'that after his death in 1896 she felt a sense of freedom.

"For the first time," she wrote, "I am answerable to nobody, No one has right to question my actions and I can do as I like. What a tremendous choice."

The pattern of Mary Benson's married life was common in Victorian England. It was accepted and even expected that it should be thus. In 1846 Mrs Ellis published a book entitled *Domestic Habits of the Women of England*, which sold extremely well and was in effect a marriage guidance manual. In this she wrote:

"In her intercourse with man, it is impossible but that woman should feel her own inferiority, and it is right that it should be so . . . she does not meet him on equal terms. Her part is to make sacrifices in order that his enjoyment may be enhanced. She does this with a willing spirit, but she does it so often without grateful acknowledgement. Nor is man to be blamed for this . . . ."

Although she included much sound advice and criticised the emptiness of many fashionable women's lives who cultivated an attitude of helplessness and ignorance, Mrs Ellis drew the line at mentioning anything to with the sexual side of marriage on the grounds that this was "a theme too delicate for the handling of an ordinary pen and a venturing beyond that veil, which the sacredness of such a connection is calculated to draw over all that is extreme in the happiness or misery of human life."

Had Mrs Ellis wished to break the accepted Victorian ban on sexual matters in print, her book would in all probability never have been published. Charles Mudie, who started his famous lending library in 1842, was already sufficiently successful by 1846 to ensure that no author dared to transgress his strict rulings on such issues. If he refused to accept a book the sales were automatically minimal and his ban on an author as good as ensured that no publisher would be prepared to accept him.

It is noteworthy that none of the early Victorian novelists, or writers of any books other than medical text books, ever specifically mention sexual relationships. Dickens and Thackeray are particularly good examples. Despite Dickens' lively descriptions of London life, including dens of vice, as in Oliver Twist, he never uses the word prostitute, or indicates what must clearly have been the occupation of some of the women he describes, although in every other respect his prose amounts to a vivid reportage of the scenes and individuals. As a result of this self-imposed censorship the average woman in Victorian fiction is an insipid and improbable being. It was only in poetry that the Victorians allowed themselves greater licence, although this could well have been because poetic allusions were often missed, or misinterpreted.

The remarkable extent of the Victorian reticence on sexual matters frequently resulted in the almost total ignorance of many young wives about the elementary facts of life. Their knowledge of sex and the workings of their own bodies was sometimes so incomplete before marriage that it came as a surprise to them to learn that they were pregnant. The discussion of such matters as birth, or birth control, between male and female, other than doctor and patient, was something that simply could not arise in early Victorian England. The foolish, fashionable women referred to by Mrs Ellis often failed completely to explain to their daughters what they should have known about sexual intercourse or pregnancy. Pregnancy was something to be concealed beneath voluminous petticoats and the usual euphemism "in a delicate condition." In at least one case the sum total of information a mother gave her daughter on her wedding eve consisted of the not very illuminating advice, "After you are married you will find a great deal that is unpleasant, but pay no attention. I never did."

It is not altogether surprising perhaps that a double standard of morality was prevalent throughout Victoria's reign, with one standard for the men and another for the women. A man might keep a mistress as long as he did not flaunt her openly. Divorce was a stigma from which no woman, however innocent she might be, could recover socially. However unfaithful her husband might be, she would resolutely turn a blind eye. A classic example was that of the Duchess of Beaufort when the butler reported the arrival of a packing case containing a picture for the Duke and enquired what he was to do with it. Accompanied by a number of guests the Duchess went to see the picture, which turned out to be a painting of a pretty girl whom everyone knew to be his latest mistress. The Duchess duly admired it and informed the butler firmly, "His Grace would like it hung in his own room, I expect."

Such reserve was not expected of the Victorian male and when a

Rotten Row in Hyde Park towards the end of the century.

little later the Duke's mistress deserted him for another, he tearfully informed his sons and daughter-in-law of the details. Then seeking consolation in religion he ordered that the entire household, family and servants, should attend church on the following Sunday to receive the Sacrament.

Taine was very puzzled by the Victorian double standards of morality. He found the utmost difficulty in getting Englishmen to talk about their sexual adventures and complained bitterly about their reticence. Nor could he understand an Englishman who enjoyed his Sunday in France in the French manner suddenly reverting to stiffness and refusing even to allow billiard-playing on his return to England. This desire to conform with accepted standards he put down as hypocrisy, but in fact it was merely a dread of flouting convention and thus being considered "no gentleman."

That a gentleman could and did have his mistresses, or visit prostitutes, was fully accepted by almost everyone with the proviso that it was "done discreetly." As ever the Victorians preferred not to face the facts of life, but took refuge in turning a blind eye, or employing a euphemism. In this instance the term "pretty horse-breakers" was the common one used for the hordes of kept woman who daily rode in Rotten Row in the afternoon. George Augustus Sala, one of the principal journalists of his day described the scene at four in the afternoon in the season:

"Watch the sylphides as they fly or float past in their ravishing riding-habits and intoxicating delightful hats, some with the orthodox cylindrical beaver with the flowing veil; others with roguish little wide-awakes, or pertly cocked cavaliers' hats with green plumes. And as the joyous cavalcade streams past … from time to time the naughty wind will flutter the skirt of a habit and display a tiny, coquettish, brilliant little boot, with a military heel, and tightly strapped over it the Amazonian riding trouser."

No mention of "pretty horse-breakers" would be complete without mention of the most famous of them all, the one and only Skittles. Catherine Walters born in 1839, the daughter of a Liverpool publican, she arrived in London at around the age of seventeen and eventually became acknowledged leader of her profession by the time she was twenty. In 1862 Sir William Hardman was writing to his friend Holroyd in Melbourne as follows:

"A gossip anent 'Anonyma.' And who is 'Anonyma'? Thereby hangs a tale. 'Anonyma' is 'Skittles,' or according to the name on her cards, Miss Walters, of equestrienne and pony-driving celebrity. 'Anonyma' was the name given to her by *The Times*. 'Skittles' was bestowed upon her by equally discreditable sponsors …. A whore, sir, much sought after by fast young swells. Well, my friend, she has bolted to that hot bed of abomination, the City of the West, New York to wit. Her luxuriously decorated house in the hands of the auctioneer, her horses and carriages are sold; fair patricians, eager with curiosity to know how such a one lived, and if possible, to learn the secret of her attraction to the young men of their acquaintance, throng the deserted halls of 'Skittles,' and admire *le cabinet* with its seat padded with swansdown …. Skittles has bolted with a married man of good family. His name is Aubrey de Vere Beauclerk …."

In fact 'Skittles' was supposed to have derived her name originally from having as a girl had the job of setting up the skittles in a bowling alley. By 1861 she had attained the status of a near national figure. In that year she was painted by Sir Edwin Landseer and the equestrienne portrait ostensibly of a Miss Gilbert was one of the main attractions at the Royal Academy. In the same year she was featured in a lengthy letter to *The Times* under the title *Anonyma* ostensibly enquiring who the young lady was whose presence attracted crowds in Rotten Row each day. Greatest achievement of all, however, was her conquest of the Marquis of Hartington, heir to the Duke of Devonshire, who settled an annuity of £2,000 on her. Then in 1862 she departed with de Vere Beauclerk for New York, to spend the next decade in Paris, where again she had the fashionable world at her feet, returning only to hunt with the Quorn each winter.

One of her "amours" in Paris was Wilfred Scawen Blunt, the poet and Victorian eccentric who remained her friend after his marriage in

"That Girl seems to know you, George" – the mistress was a frequent character in Victorian humour. (*Mary Evans*)

120

121

1869. On her return to London in 1872 she took as her lover the Hon. Gerald Suamarez and they remained attached until her death in 1920. Another of her friends throughout her latter years was Edward, Prince of Wales. One of her visitors during these latter years was Gladstone. Although she had a reputation for hard swearing, especially in the hunting field and stories about her were legion she clearly had a fascination all her own. Her interests were wide, encompassing modern art, music and serious reading and her comments were cogent and witty. It is not surprising that the fashionable ladies of London flocked to her house when it was put up for sale in 1862. Many of them must have come to the conclusion that a life of sin had it compensations.

Nor is it surprising that in one of the first studies of the subject entitled weightily *Prostitution: considered in its Moral, Social and Sanitary Aspects in London and other Large Cities and Garrison Towns with Proposals for the Control and Prevention of its Attendant Evils*, Dr William Acton should come to some almost precisely similar conclusions:

"If we compare the prostitute of thirty five with her sister, who perhaps is the married mother of a family, or has been a toiling slave for years in the over-heated laboratories of fashion we shall seldom find that the consitutional ravages often thought to be necessary consequences of prostitution exceed those attributable to the cares of a family and the heart wearing struggles of virtuous labour."

In 1862 Henry Mayhew in the fourth volume of his massive survey of conditions in London entitled *London Labour and the London Poor* estimated the total number of prostitutes at over 80,000 in a population of some 2,000,000. He gave an interesting account of an interview with one of the top class of prostitute, whom he labelled "Seclusives, or Those Who Live In Private Houses and Apartments":

"'I am not tired of what I am doing,' a woman once answered me, 'I rather like it. I have all I want, and my friend loves me to excess. I am the daughter of a tradesman at Yarmouth. I learned to play the piano a little, and I have naturally a good voice. Yes, I find these accomplishments of great use to me; they are perhaps, as you say, the only ones that could be of use to a girl like myself. I am three and twenty. I was seduced four years ago. I tell you candidly I was as much to blame as my seducer; I wished to escape from the drudgery of my father's shop. I have told you they partially educated me; I could cypher as little as well, and I knew something of the globes; so I thought I was qualified for something better than minding the shop occasionally, or sewing, or helping my mother in the kitchen and other domestic matters. I was very fond of dress, and I could not at home gratify my love of display. My parents were stupid, easy-going old people, and extremely uninteresting to me. All these causes combined, induced me to encourage the addresses of a young gentleman of property in the neighbourhood, and without much demur I yielded to his desires. We then went to London, and I have since that time lived with four different men. We got tired of one another in six months, and I was as eager to leave him as he was to get rid of me. So we mutually accommodated one another by separating. Well, my father and mother don't exactly know where I am or what I am doing, although if they had any penetration they might very well guess. Oh, yes! they know I am alive, for I keep them pleasantly aware of my existence by occasionally sending them money. What do I think will become of me? What an absurd question. I could marry tomorrow if I like.'"

It was small wonder that gentlemen's wives tried to ignore this other world of less virtuous women which attracted their menfolk when they were so frequently indisposed in "a delicate condition." The streets of the West End, the Burlington Arcade and Haymarket in particular, were thickly populated by prostitutes who plied their trade there in the evenings and also in broad daylight. Frequent letters to the papers indicated the indignation of country parsons and others whose wives or daughters had suffered the indignity of being approached by gentlemen who had mistaken them for prostitutes.

Yet it was an evil inevitably favoured by the very conditions on which the prosperity of the country depended. The factory owners whose girl workers slaved for a pittance could not be surprised if they turned to prostitution to eke out a living. The craft work of the Victorian age might be in appalling taste, but it was well turned out, perhaps the last work to be well produced, by means of sweated labour. Model factory owners such as Owen rather earlier in the century, thought little of a ten hour day for children. Girl milliners produced wonderful dresses for ladies of fashion with perfect stitching all done by hand in sweat shops under appalling conditions and for a mere pittance of a wage. Small wonder they, too, turned to prostitution.

The year 1861 was notable for more than Skittles' triumphs in London. Albert Edward, Prince of Wales, after a boring couple of years successively spent at Oxford and Cambridge carefully supervised by equerries and professors, was sent on a ten week training camp with the army at the Curragh near Dublin. Here he acquired his first mistress, an actress named Nellie Clark, who was smuggled nightly into his living quarters. She was to be the first of a long, long procession, for as well as being a gourmand the Prince had a very loving nature. Unfortunately news of this particular adventure only reached the ears of the Court after travelling round the London Clubs and on his way to discipline his erring son Prince Albert died of typhoid at Windsor. Victoria, quite unreasonably, blamed her son for the death of her "dear Albert."

In 1864 Prince Edward married Princess Alexandra and within the next seven years she bore him six children. Thereafter it is clear she wished to call a halt and the Prince discovered that seduction was an

A "fancy house" near St James's Street in 1864, as it appeared in the *Illustrated Police News*. (*Radio Times Hulton Picture Library*)

easy matter for the heir apparent. There were many married ladies who were only too willing to oblige a handsome and willing Prince, and since their husbands were usually bored with them they raised no objections. The Mordaunt Case in 1870 was somewhat unfortunate. Sir Charles Mordaunt brought a divorce case against his wife, who was by then locked up in a lunatic asylum and the Prince was called as a witness. His letters, when read out in court, proved entirely innocent, but Victoria summed the situation up correctly:

". . . the fact of the Prince of Wales's intimate acquaintance with a young married woman being publicly proclaimed will show an amount of imprudence which cannot but damage him in the eyes of the middle and lower classes, which is to be lamented in these days when the higher classes, in their frivolous, selfish and self-seeking lives, do more to increase the spirit of democracy than anything else."

Then the following year, while visiting Londesborough Lodge, near Scarborough, for a country week-end party in October, the Prince contracted typhoid as a result of inefficient drainage contaminating the drinking water. His life was despaired of and not only the Queen, but the entire nation, suddenly realised they would miss their profligate Prince if he were to die. When the crisis was past there was general rejoicing, Thereafter, although there were occasional scandals and although the Prince continued to indulge his taste for food and other men's wives, he enjoyed a good deal of popular affection.

"Laura Clarendon and three fashionably-dressed females of notoriety discovered in a house of questionable character near Blythewood Square, Glasgow. Fined £7." (*Mary Evans*)

Another major scandal was imminent in 1876 when the Prince challenged Lord Randolph Churchill to a duel. Lord Randolph named his second and sent a note back pointing out that as Prince Albert had been the prime instigator in forbidding duelling in 1843 Prince Edward must be aware that it was out of the question. All this arose because the Marquis of Blandford, Randolph's elder brother, was in danger of being cited as co-respondent by Lord Aylesford, whose wife he had seduced. Randoph had unforgiveably approached the Princess of Wales and threatened to publish the Prince's letters to Lady Aylesford, unless he urged his friend Lord Aylesford to withdraw his threatened action. In the end "not wishing to create a public scandal and mischief" Lord Aylesford did call off his action. It was, however, a long time before the Prince forgave Lord Randolph.

There can be little doubt that the easing of moral restrictions from the 1870s onwards was in no small measure due to Edward's example, but it is unfair to put all the blame on him. From the death of "Albert the Good" in 1861, Victorian gentlemen appear to have gradually reverted with a certain feeling of relief to the easier moral standards of the Georges. With the Queen shutting herself away in Balmoral and the young Prince setting the example this is not perhaps surprising. Queen Victoria noted this herself:

"The animal side of our nature is to me — too dreadful and now — one of the new fashions of our very elegant society, is to go in perfectly light-coloured dresses — quite tight — without a particle of Shawl or Scarf (as I was always accustomed to wear and to see others wear) — and to dance within a fortnight of the confinement, even waltzing at 7 months !!!! Where is delicacy of feeling going to!"

In the long week end house parties there were ample opportunities for flirtations and for sexual experiment. A wife who had borne her husband four of five children was generally considered fair game by husbands who were bored with their own wives. What might have been lost on the marital roundabouts was thus usually regained on the social swings.

There were, of course, many stories of scandals and near scandals, or of occasions when guests had to leave in a hurry without explanations or apologies. A notable occasion of near scandal was when the Earl of Cardigan entered a lady's bedroom confident that her husband was likely to be in the billiards room for some time. He had barely closed the door and was tiptoeing towards the bed when the husband entered.

"Hush," said Cardigan with great presence of mind. "She's asleep. Don't wake her. I was passing and thought I smelt fire, but all's well."

Whether he had his suspicions or not, there was little the other could do except thank the Earl for his good intentions, but it was not always so easy. There was the case of Lord Charles Beresford, who tiptoed into a bedroom in the dark and leaped onto the enormous double bed with a cry of "Cock-a-doodle-doo," only to find, when a candle had been lit, that he was lying between a bishop and his wife. This contretemps exceeded his ingenuity to explain and he left very early the next morning.

At least all this was healthy enough. Unfortunately the repressions of the Victorian era did not always breed healthy sex. Prostitution catering for perversions of all sorts, including particularly the introduction of child prostitutes, guaranteed "disease free," was common in the 1880s. In the Minutes of Evidence of a Report of the Lords Committee in 1881 a police superintendent described a visit to a house in Windmill street:

"I went in with a chief inspector, and in each of the rooms in that house I found an elderly gentleman in bed with two of these children. They knew perfectly well I could not touch them in the house; and they laughed and joked me, and I could not get any direct answer whatever. I questioned them, in the presence of the brothel keeper, as to what they were paid and so on. They were to receive six shillings each from the gentlemen, two of them; and the gentlemen had paid six shillings each for the room. It was four shillings if there was only one girl, but six shilling if there were two girls in the room."

Male prostitution, flagellation, transvestism and similar perversions were all catered for in the late Victorian period. A somewhat unusual example of the effects of repression was that of A. J. Munby, born in 1828 and on the face of it a perfectly normal barrister, minor poet and literary figure, interested in social work and with a past in the Ecclesiastical Commission. This outwardly respectable Victorian gentleman was sexually fixated on strong, muscular and dirty working women in menial jobs. On the pretext of social investigations he took photographs of women labourers in all sorts of heavy, dirty jobs, such as Midlands mining wenches in trousers. He ended by marrying a maid of all work in 1873 at the age of 45 and for the next 37 years, until his death in 1910, kept the fact secret from his family and all but two or three of his closest friends. His diaries reveal the extraordinary dual life he led with his wife outwardly employed as his maid. They also provide a glimpse of the amazingly muddled state of his thinking at times, particularly in relation to other perversions:

"Wednesday 13th April 1863: ... I had chanced to see an advertisement of a masked ball tonight at some pleasure gardens in Camberwell; admission *one shilling*. Who would be attracted by such a ball? It was a fine night and I resolved to make it the excuse for a walk, and go and see. I set off at midnight . . . . I went on; found the gardens and went in; to a large wooden shed . . . . Only about fifty or sixty people were present; most of them in fancy dresses of a tawdry kind. They seemed to be people of the class I expected to see; young artizans and workgirls.

"Several of the girls were drest in men's clothing, as sailors and so on; one as a volunteer in uniform, I took for a man until somebody called her Jenny. Moreover not a few of the youths were elaborately disguised *as women* of various kinds; and some so well that only their voices showed they were not girls — and pretty girls. This is a new thing to me, and is simply disgusting. Nevertheless it was clearly 'only a lark,' and the youths affected a quiet and feminine behaviour. Of the women, I should conjecture that very few were professional harlots, but that many were more or less immoral, though . . . they all had a trade to live by. I looked on for about half an hour; during which time I saw no indecency whatever . . . ."

A rather commoner expression of unhealthy sex during the Victorian period was the steady growth in pornography. One of the earliest pedlars of pornography was a certain John Camden Hotten, who died in 1873. His library of erotica was bought up by his friend and biographer William Ashbee, another notable figure in the pornographic literature of the period, who published an immensely pedantic and boring three volume work, disguised very thinly as a scholarly bibliography.

Although both Hotten and Ashbee had some pretensions to respectability, the same was not true of William Dugdale the other notable Victorian pornographic publisher. He died in prison in 1868 and was described by Ashbee as "one of the most prolific publishers of filthy books." These were the first of many sleazy followers and at least in the case of Ashbee are noteworthy principally for their pedantry rather than the boredom of their content which remains common to all.

The desire to be known as an authority on any subject was a typically Victorian failing and in this respect Ashbee was no different from many others. Another example in a different sphere was Sir Ralph Payne Gallwey, author of three books on the crossbow, all boring and all copied from previous works. He was also responsible for a small and tedious pamphlet on *High Pheasants in Theory and Practice* and he went on to publish Colonel Peter Hawker's *Shooting Diaries*, not hesitating to alter them drastically where he felt they lacked interest. He finally produced a book on wildfowling which contained the remarkable advice to a gentleman pursuing that sport to remember after dinner on his "wildfowling yacht" to avoid "smoking a cigar in the magazine."

To take such liberties with diaries, or literary material, in order to "make a name" as an authority, was a typically Victorian practice. The smaller immoralities were conveniently ignored. It was thus that many gentlemen regarded cheating at cards or seducing another man's wife. So long as they were not caught such minor immoralities did not count. In at least two famous cases, the de Ros scandal at the start of the Victorian age and the Tranby Croft affair towards the end, when the principal characters involved had been publicly exposed as cheating at cards, they both continued to deny the offences. Lord de Ros remained quite literally unable to see what the fuss was all about. The Victorian gentleman's morality was remarkably elastic.

# CHAPTER SIX

# *Trials and Tribulations*

It is easy to think of the Victorian age as being one of untroubled peaceful serenity for those who were fortunate enough to belong to the upper classes. In practice, however, although Britain was not involved in any prolonged wars, such as those of the previous or subsequent centuries, there were almost continual minor Colonial wars, or skirmishes on frontiers and periodic threats of unrest or civil strife amounting to revolution at home. The rick burnings and riots in the name of the sinister "Captain Swing" of the 1830s, the Chartist riots of the 1830s and 40s and latterly the Irish troubles, as well as periods of serious political dissension were disturbing enough. With the example of Europe in the late 1840s at hand there was understandably a fear of revolution in the minds of many.

In her diary for Sunday 6th February 1887, Mary, Lady Monkswell, a representative example of her class, wrote revealingly:

"On the way to Church this morning I was much comforted by Bob (her husband, Lord Monkswell) expressing the most supreme contempt for a fear which I have meditated upon a good deal lately – it is this: – That with all the appalling changes pressing upon us politically on every side, a threatened European war, Ireland upside down, the paralysis of Parliamentary government, & the exceeding badness of the Prince of Wales, it would be wise to prepare a refuge for ourselves when the deluge comes. Suppose the rates and taxes are doubled & our investments don't pay at all, what we must do is to get ourselves some little country place & farm in which we can supply ourselves with the necessities of life, because we should be cleared out of *here* in double

Interior of Lord Raglan's headquarters in the Crimea.

quick time. My idea was to face boldly this state of affairs & I am glad to say that when I unfolded my fears to Bob he was exceedingly scornful and called me an *old Tory*."

Due to the steadily increasing speed of communications throughout the Victorian era, from the introduction of the railways to the development of the telegraph and telephone, as well as to the vastly greater number of newspapers, the average Victorian gentleman was much better informed of events both in the outside world and at home than his Georgian counterpart. Affairs which had previously not concerned country gentlemen to any degree suddenly seemed of much greater interest and importance when they were the subject of a leading article read in his newspaper at the breakfast table. The world was suddenly much smaller and the names of outlandish places such as Timbuctoo, Khartoum, Waziristan and Spion Kop became familiar in most households. War correspondents at the Crimea, such as Sir William Russell of *The Times* although an entirely new phenomenon, were eagerly read as they sent back "despatches from the front." Winston Churchill at the turn of the century was already only one of a number of such notable figures.

The Victorian newspapers were as aware as any papers today of the importance of providing their readers with sensational news. Their uninhibited reporting of murders, murder trials and divorce cases, or indeed of any item calculated to excite their readers' interest, was strikingly at variance at times with the cant and humbug so often

A Christmas Dinner on the heights before Sebastopol during the Crimean War.

displayed in other walks of life. The Victorian journalist, of course, in the first half of the century was not regarded as a gentleman. It was only in the latter part of the century that journalism began to be an acceptable profession.

The effect of such reporting on the course of a trial could often be to bias the public for or against the defendant or accused. It would be a mistake to imagine that in Victorian days justice was always fair, or unbiased. The judges, like the bulk of their fellow men of the age, when brought face to face with something they did not wish to see, were quite capable of looking the other way. A particularly striking example of this was to be found in the trial of Boulton and Park with Fiske and Hurt.

These rather extraordinary proceedings involved the American Consul in Edinburgh, John S. Fiske and Lord Arthur Pelham Clinton, third son of the Duke of Newcastle, although the principals in the case were Ernest Boulton, son of a London stockbroker and Frederick Park, son of one of the Masters of the Superior Courts. These last two were good looking, effeminate youths with soprano voices and a taste for amateur theatricals, in which they invariably took the leading feminine parts. Unfortunately for all concerned they carried their enthusiasm for their roles into real life and went around in female dress.

On the evening of 28th April, 1870, the police at long last took action. William Chamberlain, a detective, who had been watching Boulton and Park disporting themselves as women around London since the previous year, followed them from a house in Regent Square, between 7 and 8 p.m., to the Strand Theatre, where they met two men and entered a private box. They then went to the bar and, according to his evidence, "Park went to the ladies' retiring room." They were than arrested together with their companions, one of whom escaped. On the way to the police station they tried to bribe the sergeant who escorted them in a cab, but to no avail. They were duly charged.

The original charge was merely that of appearing in public in women's clothes, a misdemeanour. Following the report of a police surgeon, who examined the accused without a warrant from a magistrate, a graver charge was preferred, but eventually, finding the evidence insufficient to substantiate this, they were indicted together with six associates, including Lord Arthur and Mr Fiske, with conspiracy to commit a felony. From the first the case attracted enormous interest and the courtroom was besieged when they came up for trial. *The Times* of 30th April 1870 reported as follows:

> At Bow Street (on 29th April, 1870) Ernest Boulton, 22, residing at 23 Shirland Road, (Paddington), Frederick William Park, 23, of 13, Bruton Street, Berkeley Square, law student, both of whom were in female costume and Hugh Alexander Mundell, 23, of 158, Buckingham Palace Road, were brought before Mr Thomas charged with frequenting the Strand Theatre with intent to commit felony. The prisoners Boulton and Park were defended by Mr Abrams. When placed in the dock Boulton wore a cherry coloured silk evening dress trimmed with white lace; his arms were bare and he had on bracelets. He wore a wig and plated chignon. Park's costume consisted of a dark green satin dress, low necked, trimmed with black lace, of which material he also had a shawl round his shoulders. His hair was flaxen and in curls. He had on a pair of white kid gloves.

The sensational reportage of the trial under such headings as "Men in Women's Clothes" excited tremendous attention both at a subsequent hearing and at the ensuing trial. It transpired that with two other defendants, Gibbins and Thomas, they had lodgings in Wakefield Street, owned by a landlady named Martha Stacey. Inspector Shenton, in charge of the case, identified clothes and other articles found here as follows:

"There were sixteen dresses, satin, rep and glace; green cord silk . . . a dozen petticoats, ten cloaks and jackets, half a dozen bodices, several bonnets and hats, twenty chignons, and a host of miscellaneous articles – stays, drawers, stockings, boots, curling irons, gloves, boxes of violet powder . . . etc. The estimated value was about £170."

When it came to the trial, revelation followed revelation. A

Masquerades or Fancy Dress Balls were frequent "low-life" amusements.

succession of witnesses testified that they had known the accused as women, or as women dressed as men, or as men, or as men dressed as women. One honestly confused witness, who had flirted with "Lady Arthur Clinton," then dressed as a man, but looking like a woman, admitted that after standing Lord Arthur Clinton and Boulton a Champagne lunch, "I kissed him, she, or it, believing at the time it was a woman."

Letters were produced from John S. Fiske, American consul in Edinburgh, to Boulton, of which the following is an example:

Office, Edinburgh. April 20:

My Darling Ernie — I had a letter from Louis (Hurt) which was charming in every respect except the information it bore that he is to be kept a week or so longer in the North. He tells me you are living in drag [the Victorian slang for women's dress]: What a wonderful child it is! I have three minds to come to London and see your magnificence with my own eyes. Would you welcome me? Probably it is better I stay at home and dream of you. But the thought of you — Lais and Antinous in one — is ravishing. Let me ask your advice. A young lady, whose family are friends of mine, is coming here. She is a charmingly dressed, beautiful fool with £30,000 a year. I have reason to believe that if I go in for her I can marry her. You know I never should care for her; but is the bait tempting enough for me to make this further sacrifice to respectability? Of course, after we were married, I could do pretty much as I pleased. People don't mind what one does on £30,000 a year ... .What shall I do? You see I keep on

133

writing to you and expect some day an answer to some of my letters. In any case with all the love in my heart, I am yours, John S. Fiske.

There were over 2,000 such letters from Fiske to Boulton, Hurt to Boulton, Hurt to Fiske, Hurt to Lord Arthur and Park to Lord Arthur. From these alone their relationship to each other, it might be thought, left nothing to the imagination. It is hard to see how anyone reading such letters could have any illusions as to the interests and inclinations of the parties concerned.

The Boulton/Lord Arthur Clinton letters are explicit:

> 4th December 1868: My dear Arthur, I am just off to Chelmsford with Fanny. We stay until Monday. Not sent me any money, wretch! Stella Clinton.

The Park- Clinton letters are equally clear in tenor:

> Duke St. November 21.
> My dearest Arthur — How very kind of you to think of me on my birthday! I had no idea you would do so. It was very good of you to write and I am really grateful for it. I require no remembrance of my sister's husband, as the many kindnesses he has bestowed on me will make me remember him for many a year and the birthday present he is so kind as to promise me will only be one addition to the heap of little favours I already treasure up. So many thanks. ... Believe me, your affectionate sister-in-law, Fanny Winifred Park.

The unexpected death of Lord Arthur Clinton prior to the trial due in part to stress probably aided the defence, but the case for the defendants was undoubtedly saved by their chief witness, Mrs Boulton, wife of the stockbroker and mother of Ernest. According to her, Ernest, or Stella, had always dressed up as a girl from the age of six onwards and had always been immensely interested in private theatricals. He was in the habit of dressing up as a housemaid, in which guise he had taken in his own relations. She knew Lord Arthur as a friend of her son's who had frequently acted with him. She and her husband had visited them at Lord Arthur's rooms. They had performed together as male and female leads in Chelmsford, Brentwood and Scarborough amongst other places. She also knew Mr Park and Mr Hurt well. She knew her son's nickname was Stella and as a delicate boy she kept him well supplied with money. She was not aware he had been going about London in women's dress.

Mr Park, father of Fanny, was a Master in the Court of Common

Pleas. He also was aware of his son's theatrical proclivities and allowed him a liberal £2,500 a year. He knew Boulton who had visited their home. Significantly he was not further examined. The law, like any other close fraternity, stands by its own.

After eloquent defence pleas the Attorney General made a rather weak summing up for the Crown, winding up:

"... It is my duty to submit to you that, considering the conduct and demeanour of these persons, the manner in which they were associated, the terms upon which they lived, and the way in which they wrote to each other — for to the letters I attach great importance — it is for you to say whether all these appearances are to be referred to innocent friendship and idle frolic or to a guilty and immoral confederacy."

The Lord Chief Justice summed up strongly in favour of the defendants, expressing disapproval with the form in which the prosecution had presented its case: "... Where the proof intended to be submitted to a jury is proof of the actual commission of crime it is not the proper course to charge the parties with conspiring to commit it, for that course manifestly operates unfairly and unjustly and oppressively against the parties concerned"

He admitted that the proven fact of going into the ladies rooms at the theatre was an offence deserving corporal punishment and stamped the defendants with the deepest disgrace, but he pointed out that they had a genuine theatrical reason for buying ladies' dresses and no doubt they had got into the habit of wearing them, but there was no proof of incitement to immorality. The evidence of witnesses had been contradicted by others. The letters quoted might well be construed in fun and as a method of habitually addressing each other in theatrical terms, but nothing improper had been proved. In his view Hurt and Fiske should never have been charged and it was up to the jury to decide whether anything was proved by their letters, which it was suggested implied no more than personal admiration and affection without any evil being construed. In the face of this summing up it is not surprising that the jury took only fifty three minutes to return a verdict of "Not Guilty."

Few clearer examples exist of the Victorian English gentleman's remarkable ability to look squarely at something he did not wish to see and prove publicly that it was in fact something quite different. *The Times* of 16th May, 1870, in a leader welcomed the proof that the British were thus morally vindicated:

It is not without a certain sense of relief that we record this morning the failure of a prosecution which nothing but a strong conviction of public duty would have justified the Government in instituting. THE QUEEN v BOULTON AND OTHERS is a case in which a verdict for the Crown would have been felt at home and received abroad as a reflection on our national morals, yet which, for that very reason, could not be hushed up after popular rumour had once invested it with so grave a complexion. Viewing it as it now appears by the light thrown on it in the Court of Queen's Bench, we may wonder that it was not disposed of before the magistrates in April last, instead of being exalted to the dignity of a State Trial. ... Now that justice has been satisfied and the whole story thoroughly sifted, the verdict of the jury should be accepted as clearing the defendants of the odious guilt imputed to them.

The reverse of the coin in a case concerning heterosexual morals, demonstrating the danger of uncontrolled Press reporting as well as the Victorian gentleman's determination to punish severely any who apparently contravened the strict social code of the day is seen in the trial of Colonel Valentine Baker in 1875. The Colonel, who had been publicly mentioned by the Duke of Cambridge as one of the most brilliant officers in the army, was travelling in a train from Aldershot to London. At Liphook a Miss Dickinson, aged 22, one of whose brothers was an army officer and another a barrister, entered the Colonel's compartment. It was a hot June day and the rest was revealed in court where Miss Dickinson acused the Colonel of attempted rape.

If ever a man was prejudged, it was the unfortunate Colonel, for during the slack days of July the papers made the most of it. The trial itself, when it eventually arose, was on none other than 1st August Bank Holiday Monday at Croydon. The court room was besieged and the witnesses could scarcely be heard at times. The Colonel's counsel clearly expected the case to be adjourned to a more suitable venue, for the jury, which was composed of Brighton shopkeepers and similar tradesmen could scarcely be termed the Colonel's peers or in the circumstances be expected to give him a fair trial. Unfortunately the judge, Mr Justice Brett, was famed for his severity in sexual offences and refused to countenance an adjournment.

It boiled down in essentials as to whether Miss Dickinson or the Colonel was lying. Both admitted to an innocent enough opening conversation about the heat and the weather. Thereafter Miss Dickinson accused the Colonel of grappling with her and kissing her with glaring eyes. She then reached for the communication cord, which failed to function, and she was forced to open the door and step out onto the running board, when the engine driver looking back saw her and stopped the train. The Colonel denied the charge completely and claimed that he had merely tried to coax her back into the carriage when she had suddenly opened the door and stepped onto the running board.

RAILWAY MORALS.

Guard. "NOW, MISS! ARE YOU GOING BY THIS TRAIN?"

Miss Rebecca. "YES! BUT I MUST HAVE A CARRIAGE WHERE THERE ARE NO YOUNG MEN LIKELY TO BE RUDE TO ONE."

It was the sort of unsupported evidence which no court would accept today with the knowledge of the hysterical self-delusions of suggestible young females which can lead to genuine belief that they have been raped. There was no evidence worth the name on which a dog should have been hanged, but the Colonel had been condemned by the Press for some weeks beforehand. He was found guilty and sentenced to a year's penal servitude. Even though he went on to become a general in the Turkish army, serving with great distinction and honour, it was a sadly wasted career. It is significant that his wife and friends stood by him and eventually popular opinion veered round in his favour, although unfortunately all too late.

One of the results was that wise men thereafter took care not to travel alone in trains with unaccompanied females in the same carriage. In his *Reminiscences* W. B. Woodgate recalled one such occasion when he took avoiding action somewhat unnecessarily as it turned out:

"At a Hants railway station, in the seventies, an angel-looking *ingenue* climbed into the smoking compartment wherein I sat alone.

" 'Smoking carriage, madam!' I growled.

" 'Oh, yes; I know,' she replied, smiling amiably.

"In terror I hailed the guard, and bade him shift my kit to another coach; he demurred – as the train was due to start. I insisted; and out came my gun, bags, birds and the like, I murmuring:

" 'Sooner have a mad dog than a single woman in the carriage.'

"Retribution befell in a subsequent year, at Lord's. A young Oxonian whom I knew hailed me and introduced his sister. It turned out that she was the aforesaid angel *ingenue.* He had noted my face as the train drew up that day, and bade his young sister get in (relying on my escort and protection for her to town), while he superintended her baggage. When he reached the carriage to introduce me, he heard of my flight and unflattering preference for a mad dog."

Another hazard of Victorian life which Woodgate mentioned at some length was that any attempt to take a policeman's number for misconduct was courting an almost certain charge of being "drunk and disorderly." On one occasion he himself reported a policeman who was using bad language in public and the Police Commissioner, Sir Edmond Henderson, sent an Inspector to interview him. The Inspector indicated that when the complaint had been brought to the policeman's notice he had argued that it was "very ungentlemanly" of any member of the public not to make their complaint at the time of the offence. According to Woodgate, the Inspector appeared to agree with the policeman. On the other hand, Woodgate, himself a barrister, quoted a police magistrate as saying that taking a policeman's number was "like a red rag to a bull" and a most dangerous proceeding for any layman.

Certainly in the latter decades of the century Woodgate was not alone in having a low opinion of the police. He indicated that bribery was commonplace. He described how the notorious night club "Kate Hamilton's" was regularly raided by police who were well paid to make sure they noticed nothing untoward. As late as the 1890s he instanced a baccarat club close to Chancery Lane, which paid a regular £15 a week to the police to ensure that it remained unraided.

Montagu Williams in his *Leaves from a Life* cited several cases of corruption amongst the police, but in general this was unusual, although they, too, might often enough be prepared to acknowledge the double standards of morality of the Victorian gentleman by accepting small bribes to overlook minor offences, or even sometimes to avoid scandal. In 1889, for instance, Lord Arthur Somerset, "Podge" to his friends, who included the Prince of Wales, was caught in a homosexual brothel during a police raid, but was allowed to slip out of the country. This was no minor matter, for by the Amendment Act of 1885 almost any sexual impropriety between males in private or in public had been made a serious criminal offence. A leading lawyer had described the Act, not inaccurately, as the "black-mailer's charter" and it had drastically altered matters between the Boulton-and-Park trial and that of Oscar Wilde.

Although the Victorian age saw many notorious trials, it was perhaps that of Oscar Wilde in 1895, twenty five years after the case of Boulton and Park, which demonstrated that at last the nation was prepared to face up to reality. It was a long drawn out drama, started by Wilde's

A typical scene at an early Victorian gaming hall.

own folly in bringing an action for libel against Lord Queensberry. When crossexamined inexorably by Mr Edward Carson, Wilde answered flippantly, apparently careless of the effect. He drew roars of laughter in court, but the evidence against him piled up steadily. As a result at the end of the three day trial he not only lost his action for damages, but the Home Offce then instituted a prosecution against him for indecent offences. When the jury disagreed at the first trial on this count the Home Secretary, Mr Asquith, ordered a second trial. At his third court appearance Wilde was found guilty and sentenced to two years with hard labour, the maximum for the crime.

In this case the forces of law and order and Victorian morality were fully aligned against the transgressor. As the leader of the "Aesthetes," the intellectual movement of the 1870s by this time nearly forgotten, he was a natural target for attack and he had laid himself wide open by his own behaviour. The Victorians might be prepared to allow a great deal to pass unseen, or unacknowledged, but they were not prepared to have their social conventions openly flouted, or to allow the code of normal gentlemanly conduct to be openly disregarded without seeking full revenge. Nor in such matters was there any hope of pardon. By 1900 Wilde had died, an outcast in exile in France, expelled from society by the Victorian gentlemen of the day.

Three notable trials concerning gambling, on cards and horse racing, during the Victorian era, cast an interesting sidelight on Victorian gentlemen's attitudes to such matters. The earlist case was the famous one of Lord Henry de Ros. In 1836 he had been detected repeatedly cheating at cards in his club, Graham's, by marking them with his thumb nail. He had been warned by his friends and promised to cease the practice, but had still continued it. In 1837 he was then foolish enough to bring an action for libel against John Cumming and predictably lost not only the action but his public reputation as a man of honour. Even after that he continued to protest his innocence until his friends were forced to marvel at his hypocrisy. Greville in his *Memoirs* went as far as to suggest that he seemed completely unaware of having committed any offence. Be that as it may, by the following year he was dead, shunned by his friends and society.

In 1844 there was a notable scandal when the Derby was won by a colt supposedly a three year old named Running Rein, but actually a four year old substitute. The subsequent disreputable revelations came to light in the Exchequer Court when Lord George Bentinck, the moving spirit of the Jockey Club, urged the owner of the second horse to denounce the substitution and claim the race and the owner of the substitute Running Rein, a Mr Wood, took the case to court to vindicate his position. The arch villain of the piece was a scoundrel named improbably Goodman, who had been involved in so many turf malpractices and swindles that his name alone was sufficient proof of roguery. He had transferred the horse to Wood and the latter withdrew his action before the trial was over when it became clear how much trickery had been involved. He claimed, not perhaps untruthfully, that he had been made to look a fool.

The judge in his summing up stated with considerable reason:

"Since the opening of this case a most atrocious fraud has been proved to have been practised; and I have seen with great regret, gentlemen associating themselves with persons much below them in station. If gentlemen would associate with gentlemen, we should have no such practices, but if gentlemen will condescend to race with blackguards, they must expect to be cheated."

The third famous scandal was much nearer the end of the Victorian age, the notorious Tranby Croft affair of 1891. This had a certain similarity to the case of Lord de Ros, but since it involved the Prince of Wales it had far wider repercussions. It all started in 1890 when the Prince went to stay for the St Leger race meeting with a Mr Arthur Wilson at his house Tranby Croft near Hull. After dinner a game of baccarat was suggested and the Prince's own gambling counters were used. The son of the house, Mr A. S. Wilson, thought he observed his neighbour at the game, Lt Colonel Sir William Gordon-Cumming, cheating by increasing or decreasing his stake under cover of his hand according to whether he received high or low cards.

After the game the young man informed several of his friends and relations and the following evening they tacitly agred to watch the Colonel's play, when they all decided that he was indeed cheating as had been suggested. Their observations were finally referred to the Prince for adjudication. He summoned Sir William and offered him the alternatives of signing a document binding him not to play cards for

140

money again and all concerned to secrecy, or leaving everyone free to make the matter public. Protesting his innocence, Sir William duly signed the document, but, almost inevitably, the story leaked out the following year.

Somewhat belatedly deciding to defend himself Sir William brought an action for defamation against Mr A. S. Wilson and the four others of the party who had originally claimed to observe him cheating. In June 1891 the case came to court and the Prince was cited as a witness. By any reckoning it was a fairly sordid story. One of his friends had cheated at cards, another had given his word not to divulge the facts and had done so. In his own defence Sir William maintained that he had only signed the document in order to keep the affair quiet for the sake of the Prince's reputation, even at the sacrifice of his own. Unfortunately when the Prince was asked if he thought his friend had cheated he had to admit that on the facts he had no other option. The five who had claimed to see him cheat in the first instance all affirmed their story and predictably Sir William Gordon-Cumming lost his case.

The scandal was immense, not only at home but abroad. Sir William was forced to resign from his clubs and withdraw to the confines of his country estate in Scotland. At least one of his contemporaries was to admit that as a matter of course they almost all cheated in a similar way, but Sir William had committed the cardinal sin of being caught in the act. This to the Victorian morality was the ultimate offence. Compounding his error he had involved royalty. The press had a field day and it might almost have seemed as if the Prince himself had been involved in cheating. One German paper went so far as to print a cartoon of the Prince of Wales's feathers with "Ich Deal" beneath them. Although the scandal at last died down Sir William never recovered his place in society. The Victorians did not forgive easily.

The same, of course, could be said of the Irish, even if all too often they were uncertain of what they were fighting about in the first place. Throughout the latter half of the Victorian age the troublesome Irish situation was a source of endless tribulation. In his autobiography Montagu Williams recalled an event which was common enough then as now:

"in the afternoon of the 13th December 1867, the Clerkenwell explosion took place. Two men – Burke and Casey by name – were confined in the House of Detention on a charge of treason-felony and a plot was formed among the Fenians of London and Manchester to liberate them. A barrel of gunpowder was placed against the prison wall and exploded. The effects were deplorable. Many houses in Corporation Lane were shattered, four persons were killed on the spot and about forty others were maimed or otherwise wounded, in some cases fatally. A large proportion of the victims were women and children and all were of the poorer classes."

Such political disturbances were a part of Victorian life, as were murders, burglaries and garottings, the equivalent of today's muggings. The gaslit streets of latter day Victorian London were no safer than nowadays. A common arrangement in a gentleman's household was for the butler to sleep downstairs with a loaded gun ready to repel housebreakers. Even though they might have to escape with their loot in a horse drawn cab rather than a motor car the principles were very similar to those of today. There were, however, certain types of typically Victorian pest. One, in particular, was the begging letter writer. In Henry Mayhew's *London Labour and the London Poor* under the heading *Those That Will Not Work* he included a section on the Decayed Gentleman. Of the period around 1862 he wrote:

> It is not uncommon to find among these degraded mendicants one who has really been a gentleman, as far as birth and education go, but whose excesses and extravagances have reduced him to mendacity. Such cases are the most hopeless. Unmindful of decent pride, and that true gentility that rises superior to circumstances, and finds no soil upon the money earned by labour, the lying drunken sodden wretch considers work "beneath him"; upon the shifting quicksands of his own vices, rears an edifice of vagabond vanity, and persuades himself that, by forfeiting his manhood, he vindicates his right to the character of gentleman.
>
> The letters written by this class of beggar generally run as follows:
>
> Three Mermaids Inn, Pond Lane, April — 18 —
>
> Sir, or Madam,
>
> Although I have not the honour to be personally acquainted with you, I have had the advantage of an introduction to a member of your family, Major Sherbrook when with his regiment at Malta; and my present disadvantageous circumstances embolden me to write to you, for the claims of affliction upon the heart of the compassionate are among the holiest of those kindred ties that bind man to his fellow-being.
>
> My father was a large landed proprietor at Peddlethorpe, - —shire. I, his only son, had every advantage that birth and fortune could give me claim to. From an informality in the wording of my father's will the dishonesty of an attorney, and the rapacity of some of my poor late father's relatives, the property was, at his death, thrown into Chancery, and for the last four years I have been reduced to — comparatively speaking — starvation.
>
> With the few relics of my former prosperity I have long since parted. My valued books, and, I am ashamed to own, my clothes

are gone. I am now in the last stages of destitution, and, I regret to say, in debt to the worthy landlord of the tavern from which I write this, to the amount of eight and sixpence. My object in coming to this part of the country was to see an old friend, whom I had hoped would have assisted me. We were in the same form together at Rugby – Mr Joseph Thurwood of Copesthorpe. Alas! I find he died three months ago.

I most respectfully beg of you to grant me some trifling assistance. As in the days of my prosperity I trust my heart was never deaf to the voice of entreaty, nor my purse closed to the wants of the necessitous; so, dear sir, or madam, I hope that my request will not be considered by you as impertinent or intrusive.

I have the honour to enclose you some testimonials as to my character and former station in society; and trusting that the Almighty Being may never visit you with that affliction which it has been his all-wise purpose to heap on me, I am

> Your most humble and Obliged servant,
> Frederick Maurice Stanhope.
> Formerly of Stanhope House ――shire.

It is clear from one of Beetons's *Complete Letter-Writer* examples that these sort of letters were not the only ones which from time to time plagued the Victorian gentleman. A classic reply is provided by Beeton in answer to the "Person who wants to borrow money without any claim but assurance." This particularly pleasing example of the art of letter writing in Victorian days runs as follows:

Sir,
                                                    Address . . . .
                                                    Date . . . .

While I was out of town I find you did me the honour of inquiring two or three times for me; and among my letters I found one from you desiring the loan of £10. You must certainly have mistaken me or yourself very much to think we were enough known to each other for such a transaction. Should I answer the demand of every new acquaintance, I should want power to oblige my old friends, and even to serve myself. Surely a gentleman of your merit cannot be so little beloved as to be forced to seek new acquaintances, and to have no better friend than one of yesterday. Be this as it may, it does not at all suit my convenience to comply with your request, and there I must beg you to excuse,

> Yours obediently ( . . . . . . . . )

(Name and Address)

As may be judged from these letters the question of financial stability loomed large in the eyes of the Victorian gentleman. Yet Taine noted in the 1860s that every gentleman he met in England seemed to live to the full extent of his income, seldom saving much each year. Thus a large scale fraud or the unexpected bankruptcy of a financial house could have disastrous effects on many Victorian gentlemen, who could literally be transformed in a moment from being comparatively well-to-do to near penury.

The death of a Victorian gentleman could often thus spell disaster for his family, who might be left with the necessity of earning their own living while totally unequipped to do so. The widow might be forced to move into cramped lodgings and the daughters to seek work, which almost inevitably meant becoming a governess, or lady's companion. The sons might emigrate and make their own way in the world, or perhaps continue to support their mother and sisters in much reduced circumstances. It is thus understandable that the death of the "pater-familias" could be regarded as the most serious tribulation which a family could suffer.

"Arrest" from W.P. Frith's "The Road To Ruin". Ruin was something which most Victorian gentlemen feared. (*Radio Times Hulton Picture Library*)

144

A view of Marine Parade in Brighton in early Victorian days: (*By Courtesy of the Chief Librarian, East Sussex County Libraries*)

The Victorians, however, had a considerable preoccupation with Death. Black-edged notepaper, blinds pulled down in a house of mourning, black bands on coats, black swathed top hat, and complete mourning clothes were the outward trappings. Black horses magnificently matched for mourning carriages and hearse were a part of every undertakers stock in trade. Letters of condolence, themselves black-edged, sent in black edged envelopes were sent in formal stereotyped terms. Professional mutes, carrying the coffin to the graveside, leading a solemn and lengthy procession of relatives equipped with black-edged handkerchiefs were part of the solemn scene at every funeral. The Victorians undoubtedly had a strong feeling for death and the outward trappings, which remained as a legacy of Evangelistic beliefs to the end of the century.

The appearance of a funeral cortege was one of the few things that could bring temporary peace to the normal Victorian London streets, for it would be a mistake to imagine that they were quiet. The organ grinder with his inevitable monkey was regarded as one of the permanent afflictions of anyone sick in bed. The cries of hawkers, the sound of horses' hooves, the jingling of harness and the grinding of iron-shod wheels over cobblestones combined with the reproving voices of their drivers produced an eternal cacophony.

For the greater part of the century it should also be remembered that the streets of London were extremely dirty and smelt very strongly of horse. The ragged crossing sweeper, who expected some small acknowledgement of his or her services, would sweep a way through the muck for the gentleman who wished to cross the road, but even so ladies dresses almost inevitably trailed in the filth. The heavy, choking, pea-soup London fogs which invariably accompanied the winter months

145

were another tribulation the Victorians suffered. As the century progressed and the volume of smoke London produced increased, so these choking fogs grew worse, providing perfect cover for garotters and their like.

If London could be noisy there is no doubt that the menace of the "Cheap Tripper" had ruined the enjoyment of the seaside for the average gentleman and his family by the 1880s. A sarcastic entry in *Punch* for 15th September 1877 appeared under the title 'How to spend a Happy Day (at Ramsgate, Folkestone and Elsewhere):

*Eight o'clock* – Wake early, with the shout of "shr—r—imps in your ears."

*Nine o'clock* – Be regaled with the music (?) of a German band endeavouring to get through the overture of *Zampa* with a clarinet, cornet and a trombone all more or less beginners.

*Ten* – Breakfast, weak tea, stale eggs and sea-salt bacon.

*Eleven* – Off to the sands for a bathe. Machine full of sand, sea dirty and towels wet.

*Twelve* – All the fun of the fair. Donkey-drivers, "comic" songs, and general vulgarity.

*One* – Lunch. Sawdust sandwich and lodging-house sherry.

*Two* – Rain. The only books in the house, *Bradshaw* and the second volume of *Only a Daisy*, by the authoress of *A Crushed Heart*.

*Three* – More rain, with a dash of thunder and lightning.

*Four* – Fine weather. Walk on the pier in company with 'Arry, 'Enery, 'Ugh and 'Umphrey.

*Five* – Arrival of the steamboat. 'Arry, 'Enery, 'Ugh and 'Umphrey particularly facetious.

*Six* – Dinner. Feeble soup, cold fish, and underdone mutton.

*Seven* – Amusements of the evening. Town band dreadfully noisy and awfully out of tune. The *elite* of Clapham and Lower Tooting promenading on the Esplanade. 'Arry, 'Enery, 'Ugh and 'Umphrey smoking and laughing in close proximity.

*Eight* – The pleasantest hour of the whole day – devoted to taking the train for the Metropolis and returning to London.

One of the more tedious tribulations of the Victorian age was the "practical joker." Frith in his *Memoirs* described how Toole, the actor, on one occasion to enliven a railway journey stuffed his glove with cotton wool and waited until the guard came round to check their tickets. He recounted with glee how when the guard took the ticket and the hand with it, although "a robust person," he staggered back in a near faint.

Sothern, another actor of the period around the 1860s and 1870s,

146

famous for his part as Lord Dundreary, a witless peer, was also an inveterate practical joker. Frith recounted how on one occasion he sent an anonymous passionate note as from an old admirer to a good looking young woman sitting in a box with an elderly companion. He then watched the lady try to thrust the note into her pocket while being cross questioned by her companion. He was delighted with the success of his "joke" when the gentleman finally seized the note, read it with evident rage and jealousy and rushed his companion out of the box.

In the 1880s Lord Charles Beresford with a number of friends dressed in navvy's clothes solemnly dug up the roadway in Piccadilly. They then put down warning signs and left the road closed to traffic. It was three days before the authorities appreciated that they were not returning and set about having the hole filled in again. As this was then a largely residential rather than shopping centre less people than might have been expected were inconvenienced, but consideration for other people's feelings seldom troubled the practical jokers of the period.

It is unlikely that the Burlington Arcade was affected, then one of the favourite haunts of the higher class prostitutes. A writer in the *Saturday Review* of 1871 noted that photographs of notorious demi-mondaines were often displayed there and described the tribulations of an innocent clergyman wandering into the Arcade by accident:

"You meet a respectable country parson, all eyes and boots, creaking out of step between his wife and daughter . . . of a sudden general start and shudder. A print in a shop half way down has turned the hearty rector into a scandal-struck figure of stone."

As early as the 1850s there were few streets in an area bounded by Oxford Street, Great Portland Street, and Fitzroy Square, where prostitutes were not likely to be outrageous in behaviour, especially after dark. Their favourite form of solicitation was to address a gentleman as "Charlie" and enquire, "Are you good natured, dear?" In some areas they went a good deal further than this. In Norton Street, according to a writer in 1857 the prostitutes "were in the habit of appearing naked at the windows, and lounging on the sills to attract the attention of the passer-by. At other times, the same wretched creatures would rush into the streets with only one undergarment on; and it was a common occurrence for them to run out and drag men in as they were passing."

It is not really so surprising that syphilis, gonorrhea and other venereal diseases were sufficiently common to be the subject of advertisements in the papers lauding patent cures. The Victorian gentleman's double standard of morals was bound to catch up with him occasionally and one of the tribulations suffered undoubtedly was venereal disease. General Paralysis of the Insane, G.P.I., as a result of advanced syphilis was not an uncommon cause of death in the Victorian age, amongst all classes of society.

It is true that gentlemen did not always escape the consequences of their actions and even on occasions suffered without due cause. Divorce proceedings were, of course, invariably fatal to a woman's social position, although generally not so to a man. There were, however, exceptions. Sir Charles Dilke, who started his political career as a leading republican but recanted to become one of Gladstone's ministers and considered by many as his likely successor was a case in point. The somewhat unbalanced wife of a fellow Liberal Member of Parliament, Donald Crawford, falsely named Dilke to her husband as being her lover. Thereupon he cited Dilke, who was forced to withdraw from public life for a period. He returned subsequently, but his career had suffered a setback from which it never recovered.

Perhaps the greatest tribulation which the Victorians suffered from was maintaining the elaborate facade of double morality which was such a necessary part of their life. Taine commented on the young man who was rowing in the Thames with his mistress when he saw a lady friend. He at once rowed for the shore, highly embarrassed, even though he had not been seen. Similarly a clergyman encountered by a gentleman and his wife on holiday resolutely refused to introduce the lady who accompanied him to them. He finally explained confidentially to the gentleman that she was merely a governess who had accompanied him for a week's holiday. Yet another clergyman was reported as being most perturbed to learn that his mistress was not confirmed. Once this had been duly corrected he returned to her with all his previous ardour.

Such dual standards must have been extremely wearing on the people concerned. Thus A. J. Munby spent almost all his life concealing his undoubtedly eccentric, but not particularly reprehensible, tastes for dirty serving wenches from the world. He concealed his marriage from his family, but felt free to make it known to his wife's family. They were not gentlefolk so they did not matter. Such strange double standards of morality indicate a confusion of mind and thought which were ingrained by the social behaviour of the times. There were glorious exceptions who flung convention to the winds, such as Burton, the great explorer. There were others like him, who preferred to call a whore a whore, but by the standards of the day, of course, they were simply "not gentlemen."

# CHAPTER SEVEN

# Travel and Transport

The Victorian age was the last to be dominated by the horse. It is true that it is more generally thought of as the age of steam, but this applied principally to the use of steam for locomotives on the railways, to propel ships at sea, or to power industrial machinery. On the roads other vested interests, at first the horse haulage and coach service proprietors in the 1830s, then the railway companies in the 1860s, blocked the development of steam driven transport. Throughout the century, on the roads and in the towns, the horse remained the principal form of transport.

Quite what an astounding experience rail travel was in the early days for those who had never even seen a steam engine before is extremely well illustrated in a charming account by Fanny Kemble, the actress, who travelled on the footplate with George Stephenson on the Liverpool-to-Manchester railway in August 1830. She wrote:

" . . . We were introduced to the little engine which was to drag us along the rails. She (for they make these curious little firehorses all mares) consisted of a boiler, a stove, a small platform – a bench, and behind the bench a barrel, containing enough water to prevent her being thirsty for fifteen miles – the whole not bigger than a common fire-engine. She goes upon wheels, which are her feet, and are moved by bright steel legs called pistons; these are propelled by steam, and in proportion as more steam is applied to the upper extremities (the hip joints, I suppose) of these pistons, the faster they move the wheels; and when it is desired to diminish the speed, the steam, which unless suffered to escape would burst the boiler, evaporates through a safety

A view of the Old Stein, Brighton. It remained one of the elegant seaside resorts. (*By courtesy of the Chief Librarian, East Sussex County Libraries*)

valve into the air. The reins, bit and bridle of this wonderful beast is a small steel handle, which applies or withdraws the steam from the legs, or pistons, so that a child might manage it. The coals, which are its oats, were under the bench, and there was a small glass tube affixed to the boiler, with water in it, which indicates by its fulness or emptiness, when the creature wants water, which is immediately conveyed to it from its reservoirs. There is a chimmney to the stove; but, as they burn coke, there is none of the dreadful black smoke which accompanies the progress of a steam vessel. This snorting little animal, which I felt rather inclined to pat, was then harnessed to our carriage, and Mr Stephenson having taken me on the bench of the engine with him, we started at about ten miles an hour . . .

"You can't imagine how strange it seemed to be journeying thus, without any visible cause of progress other than the magical machine, with the flying white breath and rhythmical unvarying pace, between those rocky walls, which are already clothed with moss and ferns and grasses . . . the engine having received its supply of water . . . set off at its utmost speed, thirty-five miles an hour; swifter than a bird flies (for they tried the experiment with a snipe). You cannot conceive what that sensation of cutting the air was; the motion is as smooth as possible too. I could either have read or written . . . . When I closed my eyes, this sensation of flying was quite delightful, and strange beyond description; yet, strange as it was, I had a perfect sense of security and not the

The Brighton viaduct across the Preston Road. A good example of Victorian railway architecture. (*By courtesy of the Chief Librarian, East Sussex County Libraries*)

slightest fear . . . [as] this brave little she-dragon of ours flew on . . . ."

George Osbaldeston, who died in 1866, an unrepentant and unregenerate Georgian buck, the "Squire of All England," reduced to living on an allowance from his wife after gambling vast sums away on the turf, gives a different account of early train journeys in his autobiography:

"Travellers by railway in these days [1862] cannot know what it was to go by train in the early days. I went many years ago with a friend from Birmingham to Liverpool; railroads were not so general then as they are now, and people were not accustomed to them; they were new, and those who did not often go by train were always fearful of accidents. On our journey we had to pass through a tunnel before we got to the station. The carriages were not lighted and there were a good many women in the one we occupied. The whistle was but little known then, and as I had seldom travelled by rail I had never heard it before this journey. Just as we entered the tunnel the whistle was blown; the sound created such consternation as I have rarely seen; the women were most dreadfully alarmed and began screaming awfully. The guard had locked the door and the gentlemen in the carriage had the greatest difficulty in preventing them from jumping out of the window. They were pacified at last and their cries ceased. Just before we entered the station the driver blew his whistle again, and it was so like the screams of the females that I thought they were frightened again, and said to

The Victorian era started with the coaching scene.

my companion, 'What are those silly creatures screeching about now?' I felt quite ashamed of my ignorance when he laughed and told me it was only the signal that we had reached our destination."

Throughout the 1830s the stage coach services achieved as near perfection as was possible, but the steady expansion of the railways spelled the end for them. By the 1840s it was obvious they could not compete and they gradually went out of business. During the 1840s the railways proliferated all over the country as "railway-mania" seized the investing public until finally in 1849 the crash of George Hudson "the railway king" brought ruin to thousands.

In his book *The Coaching Age*, written in 1885, Stanley Harris, noted:

"It is well, perhaps, that the great supporters of our roads in years long since past cannot see them in their present altered and dilapidated state, looking almost like country lanes; about one half only of what was once a fine broad road being now metalled and kept in repair, while the remaining portion is more or less covered with weeds and grass, as is also the case with a considerable part of the footpaths. Main roads as they used to be and as they are now are vastly different."

The old thirty yard wide turnpike roads with insufficient income from tolls to pay for their upkeep, simply could not continue after the final breakdown of the coaching system in the 1840s. Gradually the grass encroached on them and the neighbouring landlords enclosed the grass grown verges, until the roads in many cases became a shadow of their former size. Their only traffic was the occasional gig, or farm wagon. This did not mean to say there were not necessarily hazards to be encountered in travelling on them, as Colonel Peter Hawker recorded in his *Diaries* on 6th April 1850:

"Had a narrow escape from a serious accident. Being engaged to be

152

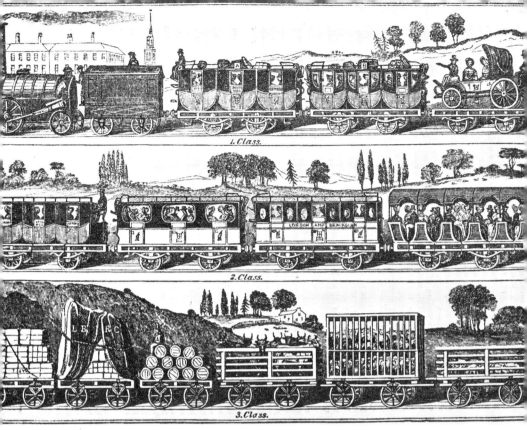

The London and Birmingham
Railway carriages (*Radio
Times Hulton Picture Library*)

Private coaches did not
disappear until late in the
period. (*By courtesy of the
Chief Librarian, East Sussex
County Libraries*)

with Mr Earle before twelve today, I put my favourite mare into my gig and drove off for Andover soon after eleven o'clock. As the mare was as quiet as a lamb I required no servant. When about two and a quarter miles from Andover, the poor mare was suddenly seized with megrims, or mad staggers, and in all my life I never saw any animal in such an awfully horrid state. She suddenly stopped and shook her head, and then lay down; she then sprung furiously up again, and violently ran back so as to throw herself and the gig into a quickset hedge on top of a rising bank. With a still more violent struggle she precipitated herself down into the road, falling on her back and twisting the gig to what a sailor would call 'keel uppermost;' by further struggles she then got on her side and there lay, kicking and plunging in a desolate turnpike road, where, for half an hour, I had not a soul come near me. At last a waggon and cart came by, and the men belonging to them, helped me to extricate the mare. She then ran bout like a mad bull and fell down and got up repeatedly; at last she made one finishing fall and I made sure she was dying, when I proceeded to Andover with the man in the cart, and hastened off to a veterinary surgeon to bleed her as a last resource. On completing my business I went back and found that the mare had been saved by bleeding and was actually led off to Longparish [his home]."

Although Richard Trevithick, an enterprising Cornish steam engineer, had invented a successful steam carriage to run on the roads in the first decade of the century he was unable to obtain backers. Yet by the 1830s there was a regular steam coach service travelling at about ten m.p.h., weighing some three to four tons unladen, between Cheltenham and Oxford. Although a Select Committee of the House of Commons appointed to enquire into these steam carriages was entirely in favour of them the country squires and coach service operators, who complained that their horses were frightened of them, were able to block them. In 1861 a Locomotives on the Highway Act enforced a minimum of three as crew, a man to go in front with a red flag, a maximum speed limit of 4 m.p.h. and no permission to blow off steam. These stiff restrictions, which were confirmed in an Act of 1875, were inspired by the railway companies who saw steam transport on the roads as possible competition. Thus the development of the automobile in England was handicapped from the start, despite which there were some nine steam carriages invented during the years 1860 to 1878.

Strangely enough there was a little known resurrection of the mail coach services on short routes during the late 1880s, when the post office considered the railway fees for transport unduly excessive. On certain routes they found thay could perform their own transport more cheaply, by horse and coach. London, Oxford, Brighton, Hitchin, Colchester, Tunbridge Wells, Guildford and Chatham were amongst the short-haul journeys, which continued well into the twentieth century.

A steam-car designed by Mr Rickett. (*Radio Times Hulton Picture Library*)

From the earliest days there was tremendous competition between the various railway companies, just as there had been between the various stage coach proprietors. The battle between broad and narrow gauge, ended with the triumph of the narrow gauge adopted by Stephenson and the final abolition of the broad gauge with its greater comfort for passengers in 1891. The cumulative effect of the consolidation of the various railway companies, following numerous amalgamations, the standardisation of the gauges and the advanced rolling stock, as well as the modern locomotives of the later years of the century induced competitive racing between the various routes, notably in the east and west coast routes to Scotland. This reached its height in the 1890s and in 1895 the route between London and Aberdeen was constantly being covered in record times by west — and east-coast trains. The final record achieved was that of an overall 63.3 m.p.h. which still stands as the record for the route.

It was small wonder that the mail also attained unprecedented speeds of delivery in the Victorian penny post. It was accepted as so reliable that letters were written to the papers when any delay was noted, as witness the following letter to *The Times* of 8th May 1881:

> Sir - I believe the inhabitants of London are under the impression that letters posted for delivery within the metropolitan district commonly reach their destination within, at the outside, three hours of the time of postage. I myself, however,

have constantly suffered from irregularities in the delivery of letters, and I have now got two instances of neglect which I should really like to have cleared up.

I posted a letter in the Gray's Inn post office on Saturday at half past 1 o'clock, addressed to a person living close to Westminster Abbey, which was not delivered till next 9 o'clock the same evening; and I posted another letter in the same post office, addressed to the same place, on Monday morning (6 May) before 9 o'clock, which was not delivered till past 4 o'clock in the afternoon. Now, sir, why is this? If there is any good reason why letters should be delivered in less than eight hours after their postage, let the state of the case be understood; but the belief that one can communicate with another person in two or three hours whereas in reality the time required is eight or nine, may be productive of the most disastrous consequences.

I am, Sir, your obedient servant . . .

Although internal communications in Britain had steadily improved from 1840 onwards with the spread of the railways, which coincided with the introduction of the telegraph system and the penny post, the brain child of Rowland Hill, it was a much slower process overseas. As late as the 1860s for instance the journey to India round the Cape of

A late nineteenth-century steam vessel. The comfortable steam-ship became the common form of international transport. (*Radio Times Hulton Picture Library*)

A scene in Port Said near the turn of the century.

Good Hope was still a lengthy business, although the introduction of regular steamships in the 1830s had begun to speed matters. The opening up of the overland route via Suez improved matters in the 1840s, but it was not really until the completion of the Suez Canal in 1869 that the passage to India became less of a nightmare and more speedy delivery of both mail and passengers was reasonably assured.

One result was that the British in India were no longer so isolated. As the journey took so much less time and was so much more reliable it became feasible to return to Britain for leave more frequently and it was no longer necessary to spend periods of ten years or more overseas without a break. The unpublished diaries of Stephen Gilham, who spent a large part of his life with the East India Company, provide a graphic account of the early days of the overland route via Suez. After sixteen years in India he was forced to return home due to ill health. The journey out by sail had taken five months and they had sighted the coast of Brazil, where they had a brush with pirates. Now he found matters greatly changed.

"I joined one of the East India Company's steam frigates in Bombay Harbour on the 1st December 1840; she had her steam up ready for a start with the Indian overland mail of Aden and Suez and at 8 p.m. put to sea. Arrived at Aden on the morning of the 12th. Coaled and left the same evening for Suez and reached there on the 19th under steam all the way, distance 2,500 miles."

His description of Aden typifies the Victorian gentleman's attitude to the haphazard acquisition of various strategic parts of the world,

Colmar Street in Suez, a frequent stopping place on journies to India and the Far East.

which continued throughout so much of the period. In his view by establishing peaceful conditions for trade the British intervention was entirely justified. His account of the area and the changes there at this time are clearly factual and not without interest:

"Aden is called the Gibraltar of the Red Sea, somewhat of a pretension, or misnomer, I thought, but it has since, I understand, acquired a better title to the comparison by the formidable fortifications which have been erected there. The inhabitants of the 'rock' are a mixture of all countries and creeds, from the Hindoo Banian, or shopkeeper, from the bazaars of India, to the Bedouin Arab of the neighbouring desert. The place had not long been taken possession of by the East India Company when I was there, but now it is a flourishing trading port and has drawn to it nearly all the exports of Mocha and other ports of the Red Sea. It is garrisoned by a Regiment of European infantry, a native regiment and a strong detachment of artillery. When we first took the place there was some desperate fighting and attempts at night surprises by the Arabs, but after they had come in collision three or four times with our disciplined forces their impetuous valour cooled down. They found that all their endeavours to recapture the town were useless and after some able negotiations between our Political Agent, Captain Haines, and their chieftains, all opposition to our peaceful occupation ceased. They found that the English had established a ready market for their provisions and garden produce; that what they brought for sale was punctually paid for and their persons as well as those of their women protected; our native merchants in their turn found good customers for their wares and in short that the coffee planters and other owners of different kinds of produce found an export market where they were not subjected to such heavy imposts as had been extorted from them by the Chief of Mocha which before Aden had risen to their notice had been the principal sea port in the Red Sea."

The Victorian gentlemen simply would not have understood the meaning of the phrase "Imperial exploitation," because in their view they were merely trying, quite genuinely, to set about improving trade and communications. That both British and native lives were lost in the process initially was part of the price to be paid and was accepted as such. Garrisoning such outposts in frequently appalling conditions was part of the "White Man's burden" and was borne philosophically by those concerned.

Gilham went on to describe the overland route:

"Suez at the extremity, or head, of the Red Sea is a miserable dirty Arab town depending entirely on the importance it derives from being the point of embarkation and disembarkation of the numerous passengers by the overland route; the steamer from want of sufficient depth of water lies three miles off the town. There is a branch of the Cairo Hotel here established by the late Mr Waghom, where the necessary preparations are made for the journey across the desert to Cairo. These are nowadays extremely simple. The modes of transport are three, viz, by iron carriages, something resembling omnibuses drawn by four horses each; on horseback and on donkeys. I chose a horse, for which and all expences of every description, including hotel expences both at Suez and Cairo and boat hire on the Nile with a servant who accompanied me to Alexandria I paid £18. A basket containing wine, beer and spirits, and provision of poultry already cooked with pickles, sauces, bread, in short all that a man could require (or a lady either) was included in the price I paid in abundance; there was more than a hungry man could consume, and all of the best description. Water is carried in huge leather bags or 'mussocks' (a buffalo skin sewn up) on camels. We were twenty six hours on the road, having left Suez at 9 a.m. on the 20th of December and arriving at Cairo at 11 o'clock the following morning. The distance between Suez and Cairo is seventy-two miles, the rate of travelling about three miles an hour. There are five stations on the route twelve miles distance from each other. We reached the central one at 4 p.m. where we halted to refresh the cattle for two hours . . .."

Here in typically Victorian manner, they ate a large, hot cooked dinner, which had been specially prepared for them by cooks who had come out from Cairo. The slow pace they maintained was due to the fact that they travelled in a caravan to avoid "the hordes of wandering Arab thieves, who are always on the look out for unprotected travellers." He also noted, "We had more than twenty camels laden with maii boxes and nothing could exceed the care and solicitude shown for their safety."

Lieutenant Waghorn, who had pioneered the overland route, had also set up a very fine hotel in Cairo, where Gilham went to stay on his arrival there, He recorded, "I . . . was made as comfortable as ever I was . . . in England or France . . . . The expensive establishment and fittings up of this enormous hotel must have cost the enterprising Waghorn a round sum; the servants are English men cooks, chamber-maids and waiters. They are well paid, receiving double the wages they would at home to induce them to stay in 'furrin parts' but I heard they were a discontented set and gave more trouble than the small army of native servants kept by the proprietors . . .."

Gilham's only hint of criticism concerning the discomforts of the journey which by any standards must have been considerable was contained in a comment concerning his need for a bath:

"After nineteen days aboard a steamer with its smoke and the dirty business of *coaling* to say nothing of one's clothes not being taken off for six and thirty hours after the dirt and perspiration of the desert, be sure that my first visit at Cairo was to a Turkish bath and barring the publicity, for I formed one of about thirty undergoing their ablutions in the same room, I found the whole programme of the proceedings very pleasant."

Before leaving Cairo for Alexandria Gilham recorded with typically British condescension his dinner with the Prussian Consul:

"On Christmas day, the last of my stay in Cairo, I dined with the Prussian Consul, a very gentlemanlike and pleasant man; as the majority of his guests happened to be English the dinner took place at the hotel where I was staying and we were regaled with English cheer — roast beef and a most respectable proportioned and well-seasoned plum pudding."

Gilham, however had the grace to record that Mohammad Ali, the Egyptian Pasha, was extremely forebearing in allowing any English to be present at all. Having noted that the Pasha provided an armed guard of fifty mounted men to protect the travellers on the overland route he added, "Considering that at the time I am writing about, 1840, Sir Charles Napier was battering down the walls of St Jean d'acre [sic] about the Pasha's troops ears this was a noble trait of magnanimity on the part of the white bearded old man. He made no difference in his treatment of peaceful travellers through his Country, let their nation be what it might; the magnificent silver candelabra representing a live palm tree and weighing 10,000 ounces and twelve feet in height given to him by the merchants of London as a token of their acknowledgement of his conduct in not interrupting the traffic by the overland route was a graceful tribute he richly deserved."

After all this it is sad to have to record that Gilham, having travelled safely to Alexandria and shipped on from there by coaster, was wrecked at the entrance to Malta harbour by a drunken skipper and lost all his belongings. He himself, however, was saved and eventually arrived in London, although not being insured he had no redress. The hazards of travel by land and sea were still quite considerable in mid-century, even if by the 1880s and 90s most of them had been effectively overcome. By the end of the century, indeed, travel by ship around the world was generally both comfortable and safe. British railways built by British engineers around the world had also made travel on land much less tiring or hazardous. The world was already shrinking.

One of the direct results of the enhanced ease of transport by sea, coupled with the railroads which opened up the interior of the United States of America, was a steady increase in the import of cheap wheat into Britain during the 1870s, which quickly grew to massive proportions. Under the old Corn Laws imports of wheat had been taxed on a sliding scale, so that in years of glut at home the import duty was high and the farmer protected, while in years of bad harvests the import tax was low so that the consumer benefited by obtaining his bread as cheaply as possible. When the landowners had abused their monopoly during and after the Napoleonic Wars by arbitrarily raising the price of wheat, thus causing the price of bread to rocket, there was widespread demand for repeal of the Corn Laws. Repeal came in 1846 with little effect at the time, beyond the claim that it allowed wheat into the country free of duty. For two decades this had little effect, until the trickle of wheat from the Mid-West States of America grew to a flood. By this time the cry of cheap bread had become a political sacred cow and there was no hope of reintroducing a protective tariff. The farming slump of the 1870s was thus inevitable.

Although a fairly sophisticated form of canning of meat had been developed by 1841, there was a considerable scandal in the 1850s when due to insufficient understanding of the processes involved, there were many instances of putrid canned meat. By the late 1860s, however canning had come into its own. It was in the year 1867 that a certain Fred Butler murdered a girl called Fanny Adams at Alton in Hampshire and chopped her into little pieces. It was almost inevitable, thereafter, that the Navy should term their canned meat "Sweet Fanny Adams" and equally understandable that for some considerable time thereafter it was not considered generally suitable for a gentleman's table.

The Victorian "ice-house" was the usual device, an underground cellar close to the back regions which was filled with ice for the purpose of keeping meat preserved during the summer months. Despite experiments with refrigeration in the 1860s it was not until the 1880s that the S.S. Strathleven first reached London with forty tons of

An early bicycle. (*Radio Times Hulton Picture Library*)

Australian beef refrigerated in good condition. Thereafter the import of refrigerated meat from abroad resulted in even the poor man's table being well served with roast beef, although not necessarily finding favour with the Victorian gentleman. The farming community suffered even further depression until towards the end of the century the topsy-turvy situation arose of farms being only worth the value of their shooting rights.

In the last three decades of the Victorian era, with a slump in agriculture and almost deserted roads, the countryside must have been a perfect place for the sportsman. It was certainly ideal from the point of view of the development of bicycling. "Velocipedes" consisted of nothing more than a rigid bar connecting two wheels on which the rider sat astride and propelled himself with his feet. They had been invented in the eighteenth century. But the bicycle was not really developed until the 1860s. In 1865 Pierre Lallemont in Paris constructed a bicycle with the front wheel driven by pedals. He obtained a patent for this in the United States of America in 1866 and it soon became popular in England. Known as a bicycle by those who liked it and the "boneshaker" by those who did not, it was soon improved.

By 1874 a front wheel of 54 inches was common and The Coventry Sewing Machine Company developed a machine with suspension wheels and wire spokes. The "penny farthing" was in being. By 1882 speeds of 20 m.p.h. were being achieved with steel tubed frames and hollow rimmed wheels with ball bearing axles. Tricycles and "sociables," in which the riders sat side by side, were developed and the roads with scarcely any traffic on them were ideal for this form of exercise. Admittedly the danger of being thrown over the handlebars of the penny farthing and the difficulties of mounting deterred many people, but the development of "pneumatic" tyres by J. Dunlop, a veterinary surgeon in Belfast, in 1888 improved comfort greatly.

The "Rover" of 1885, with chain drive to the rear wheel, was the

162

Early motorists. Cars remained a popular pre-occupation of gentlemen well beyond the Victorian era.

forerunner of the modern bicycle. The development of the drop frame, allowing ladies to ride without adopting "Bloomers" or "Sensible Costume" was the start of the craze for bicycling which swept through Britain. By 1895 the demand for bicycles was so great that speculation and over-capitalization began to affect the market. By the end of the century the bicycle was regarded as a convenient means of transport for everyone and was being used extensively throughout Britain. It was a truly classless machine ridden by ladies and gentlemen alike.

The early motor cars were far from classless. They were essentially a gentleman's transport, but only an eccentric gentleman would wish to have one. The English were too keen on horses to welcome these snorting, back-firing, smelly machines. On the other hand it is only fair to add that they were not developed in England as enthusiastically as on the continent because of the absurd laws, which had originally been encouraged by the railway companies to check any competition from steam wagons on the roads. The early motor cars were almost all produced on the continent. The names of the early pioneers of motor cars are distinctly un-British sounding, such as Benz, Daimler, Gottlieb,

Levasseur and De Dion. It was not really until the Edwardian era that British motoring began to find its feet.

Even so there were a few determined pioneers who were attracted by this new form of travel in the last decade of the century. A diary kept by one of these early automobile owners throws considerable light on the state of knowledge in this country on the subject of motor cars in 1895. Mr J. A. Koosen of Southsea saw an advertisement for a Lutzmann car, similar to a Benz, when in Germany and ordered one.

"I had then never seen a motor car and was under the impression that you take your seats, press the button and the machine does the rest. Well at last on November 21st, 1895, the thing arrived at Portsmouth Town Station. I had been told in a letter from the manufacturer that to start the engine you had to turn the flywheel towards you, which I did until darkness overtook me. The only result was a pair of worn out gloves."

Unfortunately for Mr Koosen he had not appreciated that the engine required fuel to make it go. It was some time before he finally discovered this detail. Mrs Koosen's diary, briefly, but graphically continues the story of the events which ensued:

"November 23. Took train to Lee and tried to make our motor work; wouldn't. Came home at five.

"November 24. Awfully cold; played with our motor – no result.

"November 25. After luncheon saw to our motor, but didn't get it out of shed.

"November 26. Drove to Lee and took Smith and Penning (engineers) Penning spent the day on his back without results.

"November 30. Motor went with benzoline for first time; awfully pleased.

"December 2. Waiting for new oil from Bowley and Son.

"December 9. Drove to Lee at 10; motor sparked at once and went well; After lunch started for home in motor car round by Fareham; had lovely drive; police spotted us; awful crowd followed us at Cosham; had to beat them off with umbrella.

"December 10. Police called at 1.30 took our names re driving through Fareham without red flag ahead.

"December 13. Went drive round common; tyre came off; sent her to Penning.

"December 16. Took train to Fareham . . . proceeded to Court House, filthy place. Hobbs spoke up well for motors. Silly old magistrate fined us one shilling and costs 15s. 7d."

If nothing more, these extracts indicate the tremendous handicaps afflicting early motorists in the Victorain age. It is difficult today to appreciate quite how remarkable the internal combustion engine appeared to the unmechanical minds of the average Victorian gentleman. It was a mystery to all but the most competent engineers and they were few and far between. In fact it is fair to say that the competent engineers were for the most part inventors themselves, for anyone capable of taking an engine apart was also capable of modifying and probably improving the design. Even if it was poised for some remarkable rapid advances the "horseless carriage" was still in a somewhat primitive stage of development at the end of the Victorian age.

In view of this, it required someone with Lord Byron's poetic vision to prophesy as he did, with remarkable, if premature, accuracy in 1822, "I suppose we shall soon travel by air-vessels; make air instead of sea voyages; and at length find our way to the moon, in spite of the want of atmosphere."

Ballooning, of course, had started experimentally in the 1780s and by the early nineteenth century had become a popular, if still novel, attraction. Charles Green, who made his first flight in 1821, was one of the greatest English balloonists of the early Victorian period. In 1836 in his Nassau balloon accompanied by two companions, he made a flight from Vauxhall Gardens and the following day landed near Weilbury in Germany, a distance of 480 miles, which was then a world record. One of his passengers, Monck Mason, recorded, "An unfathomable abyss of darkness seemed to encompass us on every side; and we looked forward into black obscurity ' . . . we could scarcely avoid the impression that we were cleaving our way through an interminable mass of black marble . . . ' "

Perhaps the most outstanding Englishman of the Victorian period as regards the advancement of flight was Sir George Cayley (1773–1857), who was hailed as "The Father of Aerial Navigation" and, indeed, richly deserved the title. A good example of the gifted amateur scientist of the early Victorian period, but one who truly applied sound scientific principles to his reasoning, he was responsible for clarifying ideas on mechanical flight and laying down the basic principles of heavier-than-air flight. "The whole problem," he stated, "is confined within these limits, viz. – to make a surface support a given weight by the application of power to the resistance of air."

One of Cayley's great admirers was the brilliant French inventor, Alphonse Penaud (1850–80), who dominated the decade of 1870-1880 in the aeronautical field. Amongst other inventions he designed a likely looking machine, but was unable to find a light enough engine to power it. Dogged by ill-health and deeply depressed, he committed suicide in 1880. The extent of his influence on ordinary Victorian thought is to be found in Lady Monkswell's diary for 1876, when his proposed machine was first designed. She recorded:

"30 August: Bob [Lord Monkswell, her husband] maintained incidentally that a man was going to try and fly across the Channel in some new machine and he [Malborough Prior, a friend] answered that he felt ashamed of his race for not having invented an effective flying machine before now; that the principle of it was perfectly understood and some day he hoped to have a hand in carrying it out!"

In the last quarter of the nineteenth century various experiments with balloons powered by engines, with man carrying kites, with hang gliders and with powered machines were attempted with varying degrees of success. One of the early pioneers, who might well have beaten the Wright brothers by a few years, was a Scotsman named Percy Sinclair Pilcher (1867–99). After leaving the Royal Navy at eighteen, Pilcher devoted the rest of his short life to attempting to fly. Following the example of Otto Lilienthal, from whom he purchased a glider, he successfully made several hang-glider flights. He had modified his designs and had also bench tested a 4 h.p. engine of his own design, when, like Lilienthal himself, he was killed in a flying accident, as were so many of these early pioneers.

In a lecture in Dublin in 1897 Pilcher gave his views on flying:

"The object of experimenting with soaring machines is to enable one to have practice on starting and alighting and controlling a machine in the air . . .. They are excellent schooling machines, and that is all they are meant to be, until power, in the shape of an engine working a screw propellor . . . is added, then one who is used to sailing down a hill with a simple soaring machine will be able to fly with comparative safety."

W. B. Woodgate who was present at Pilcher's last flight on Lord Braye's estate at Stanford Hill, near Market Harborough, in September 1899, described the scene graphically:

"Young Pilcher had two flying-machines on the ground; one of them fitted with some motor apparatus, the other was more in the style of a kite; each was his design.

"The weather was so wet and gusty that at first there was some doubt whether any flight could even be attempted; but so many friends as well as servants had faced the storm that the inventor pluckily decided not to disappoint his audience.

"My brother knew him, and took me up to his engineering arena in the park to introduce me. I rather fancy that we were the last persons to whom he spoke, short of instructions to his staff when he commenced his flight, a few minutes later. His apparatus – of the kite kind – when he took his stand in it, made him resemble in contour a sort of gigantic butterfly. A long cord was attached to the machine, and towed by horses harnessed to a cart, pulling him against the wind like a kite, and so producing a soaring action.

"The first start failed, and did not produce elevation; possibly the horses did not tow fast enough.

"On the second essay Pilcher sailed up and gradually soared higher than the tops of high elm-trees in the vicinity, so far as the eye could gauge.

"Then came the tragic *finale*. The canvas of the 'tail' had warped in the saturating rain; and put undue tension on the light bamboo framework which extended it. Something snapped, and one side of the tail furled and hung limp; balance was destroyed, and the machine and its rider revolved like a winged bird, and came down with a sickening crash on the still sun-baked turf – on which the morning's rain had made no saturating effect.

"The fall was fatal; the poor lad never recovered consciousness; both thigh bones fractured, and concussion of the brain. In less than forty eight hours he was no more . . .. "

The Victorian age ended with the world poised on the edge of powered heavier-than-air flight, but with the final successful step not quite achieved. The Victorians had successfully mastered steam power and used it to the full. The craftsmanship and comfort of their hand finished carriages, both railway and "horseless," was not often to be excelled in the ensuing century. Of course, this was a relic of the old days of horse carriages, which were not yet completely outdated. The Victorians might think of themselves as living in the age of steam, but they still naturally turned to the horse as the principal means of haulage in town and country. The towns and cities still stank of horse. The horse was still one of the most familiar spectacles on the roads. In essence the Victorians were still living in the age of the horse, while Byron's prophecy of visiting the moon was on the verge of fulfilment.

# CHAPTER EIGHT

# Sports and Pastimes

Sportsmen are notably conservative and slow to accept changes. Thus gentlemen's sports and pastimes during the first half of the nineteenth century differed little from those of their Georgian predecessors. Bare knuckle pugilism, the sport of the Prize Ring, attracted large crowds of ruffianly character as well as numbers of sporting gentlemen. Cock-fighting also attracted a widely varying cross-section of the community. Cruder sports, such as badger-drawing, dog-fighting and ratting were still commonplace. Hunting and shooting had altered hardly at all and the hard-riding sporting squire was still frequently to be found in country districts.

Perhaps the greatest Georgian survival of them all was George Osbaldeston, nicknamed affectionately and justifiably "The Squire of All England." Born in 1786, this small, hard-bitten Yorkshireman lived to the age of 80 in 1866. There truly does not seem to have been any sport at which he did not excel. He beat the reigning champion at the game of royal tennis. He was one of the best six amateur cricket players in England. He rowed for the Arrow Club, afterwards Leander. His love of coursing was famed. His fighting cocks were outstanding. He kennelled both fighting mastiffs and terriers for drawing badgers in his attics. He was a first-rate shot and one of the leading huntsmen of his day as well as an excellent amateur jockey.

In 1831 he won his famous thousand guinea wager at Newmarket by riding two hundred miles in under ten hours. He completed the ride in eight hours and forty-two minutes and then galloped into Newmarket for dinner, where he "kept it up till two o'clock next morning." He was described by an eyewitness at this time as "rather below the middle size with a large and muscular frame, the legs somewhat disproportioned to the body, and appearing when on horseback to belong rather to the animal than the man, so firm and sturdy was his seat; his weight was eleven stone."

Soon after his death, his friend and contemporary, Captain Horatio Ross, wrote of him, "As a general sportsman — as one who went in at everything in the 'ring,' he was the best man England has produced during the present century; and I could not say more in his praise. Besides, however, his high qualities of pluck, endurance and skill in all manly sports, he was a generous, kind-hearted, hospitable man. I lived much with him for a good many years and I can say that during all that time I never heard him speak harshly or in any unkind way about any human being; on the contrary he seemed always anxious to make excuses for those who were absent . . . . "

Inheriting vast estates as a minor, Osbaldeston once calculated that he had lost around £300,000 by gambling and by unsound investments. A good judge of a horse and a hound, he was unfortunately not a good judge of men and was easily misled by rogues. Thus far he conformed to a familiar pattern often seen in the previous century, but in several salient respects "The Squire of All England" differed from his Georgian predecessors.

In the year 1851 he succumbed to the spirit of the age by marrying a wealthy, respectable widow, who had already taken him in hand, and largely thanks to her management of his finances he did not die penniless as he otherwise might have done. At no time did he drink or womanise to excess, no doubt chiefly due to the fact that he was mostly too busy cock-fighting, coursing, drawing badgers, dog-fighting, shooting, racing, rowing, hunting, or otherwise indulging his very varied sporting proclivities and displaying his prowess at "manly sports." Finally, he only seems to have fought one duel and that was something of a farce.

The duel was fought in 1835, against none other than Lord George Bentinck, the arbiter of the Jockey Club, who had accused Osbaldeston with some justification of "damned robbery," in claiming a wager of £200 from him won on a horse which had deliberately been run so as to deceive the handicappers. Osbaldeston was in the wrong, though merely conforming to general practice at the time. He later claimed that the seconds failed to load the pistols with ball, though some accounts maintain that he put his bullet through Lord George's hat. He could certainly have killed his man with ease, but either way the affair scarcely redounds to his credit, even though the two were subsequently reconciled. It was a Victorian rather than a Georgian affair, all noise and protocol, although there was a fatal duel in 1843 which led to the Army Act being altered at the instigation of the Prince Consort and duelling being forbidden.

Osbaldeston was umpire at the prize fight in Northamptonshire in 1830 between Simon Byrne, the Irish champion, and Alexander Mackay, the Scots champion, when Byrne died as the result of a blow to his throat in the 42nd round. The fight was fair and well conducted, but Cribb, Cooper, Reynolds and Martin, the seconds, along with Mackay were committed for trial by the Rev. Mr Prettyman, J.P., who added that there were "persons more highly placed in society, who ought also to be in the dock." Osbaldeston entered in his diary "Cost me £200 or £300 to get out of it . . .. Prettyman the cause." Having been Master of the Pytchley, no doubt Osbaldeston knew Prettyman and, equally probably, the money was spent on shutting the mouths of those who might have testified to his presence. In the event his name was not mentioned at the subsequent trial at Buckingham Assizes and the jury returned a verdict of "Not Guilty" of the manslaughter of Byrne. This verdict was greeted with "boisterous acclamation" for public sympathy was all with a man who was unlucky enough to kill his opponent in a fair fight.

Although Osbaldeston retained his interest in the prize ring to the end of his life, even he complained in his autobiography of the criminal elements who also attended fights, often robbing other spectators with bare faced impudence. Pickpockets at any such meeting were an accepted hazard, but the prize-ring roughs far exceeded them, even being successful on occasion in stopping the fight if it was not going the way they wished. It was this sort of behaviour that brought prize fighting into disrepute.

An early-Victorian boxing match at Fives Court. Boxing gloves were generally used.

"Gentleman" John Jackson, who was bare fist champion from 1795 to 1800 and became the acknowledged arbiter of the sport, died in 1845, but by then the decline had already set in irrevocably. When the Amateur Athletic Club was founded in 1866 and the 8th Marquis of Queensberry with the help of John Chambers drew up the code of laws known as the Marquis of Queensberry's Rules it was the end of the prize ring. In 1868 the running of fight-trains became illegal and the old bare fist days were virtually ended. From that date onwards modern boxing became increasingly popular.

In 1835 the old primitive sports of bull- and bear-baiting were made illegal, but badger-drawing and dog-fighting remained popular back-alley sports, though patronised by all classes, including gentlemen, up to the end of the century. Cockfighting had already lost its general appeal, although immensely popular in certain areas of the country, when it was officially declared illegal in 1849. Illegal cock-fighting continued to the end of the Victorian age carried on in illicit cock-pits, even, according to Montagu Williams and W. B. Woodgate, close to Fleet Street. After mid-century these somewhat brutalised Georgian pastimes were generally only to be enjoyed in sporting public houses in the back streets of large towns. Despite the law they continued to flourish in such surroundings up to the end of the century.

With his discerning eye for the unusual, Henry Mayhew described a typical scene in just such a London sporting public house devoted to ratting, in 1851, as follows:

"The front of the long bar was crowded with men of every grade of

Bear-baiting was declared illegal in 1835, but illicit matches continued throughout the era. (*Mary Evans*)

Cock-fighting was made illegal in 1849. (*Mary Evans*)

society, all smoking, drinking and talking about dogs. Many had brought with them their 'fancy' animals, so that a kind of canine exhibition was going on: some carried under their arms small bull-dogs whose flat pink noses rubbed against my arm as I passed; others had Skye terriers curled up like balls of hair and sleeping like children as they were nursed by their owners. The only animals that seemed awake and under continual excitement were the little brown English terriers, who despite the neat black leathern collars by which they were held struggled to get loose, as if they smelt the rats in the room above . . .. "

In this specialist public house Mayhew went on to note the absence of the usual decorations to attract custom, apart from "clusters of black leather collars" on the walls and a silver dog collar, which was to be the prize in a forthcoming rat-match. On one chair in the hallway was an old fashioned bull-dog "with a head as round and smooth as a clenched boxing glove . . . its legs . . . as bowed as a tailor's." On the other side of the fireplace was a bull terrier. In the inner room there were sporting prints and stuffed dogs ranged against the dingy walls. In pride of place was a print of "the 'wonder' Tiny, 'five pounds and a half in weight' as he appeared killing two hundred rats." Mayhew continued:

"Among the stuffed heads was one of a white bull-dog with tremendous glass eyes sticking out, as if it had died of strangulation. The proprietor's son was kind enough to explain to me the qualities that had once belonged to this favourite. 'They've spoilt her in the stuffing, sir,' he said. 'That there *is* a dog,' he continued, pointing to one represented with a rat in its mouth, 'it was as good as any in

172

England, though it's so small. I've seen her kill a dozen rats almost as big as herself, though they killed *her* at the last; for sewer rats are dreadful for giving dogs canker, and she wore herself out with continually killing them, though we always rinsed her mouth out well with peppermint and water.' "

There seems to have been a considerable cross section of humanity present. Among others Mayhew mentioned costermongers in corduroy, soldiers with their uniforms unbuttoned, coachmen in livery and tradesmen "who had slipped on their evening frock coats and run out from the shop." He also noted "some French gentlemen, who had evidently witnessed nothing of the kind before" and were asking their interpreter for explanations as they tried "to drink their hot gin and water.

"About nine o'clock the proprietor took the chair in the parlour, at the same time giving the order to 'shut up the shutter in the room above and light up the pit.' This announcement seemed to rouse the spirits of the assembly, and even the dogs tied to the legs of the tables ran out to the length of their leathern thongs and their tails curled like eels, as if they understood the meaning of the words.

"The performance of the evening was somewhat hurried on by the entering of a young gentleman, whom the waiters called 'Cap'an'.

" 'Now, Jem, when is this match coming off?' the Captain asked impatiently; and despite the assurance that they were getting ready, he threatened to leave the place if they were kept waiting much longer. This young officer seemed to be a great fancier of dogs, for he made a round of the room, handling each animal in turn, feeling and squeezing its feet and scrutinising its eyes with such minuteness that the French gentlemen were forced to enquire who he was."

The arrival of the impatient young Captain and his friends appears to have livened up the evening, for the assembled party then moved up the broad wooden stairs of the inn, into what had once been the drawing room of the house. As they went they each paid a shilling entrance fee to the proprietor. Mayhew described the scene in the 'rat killing apartment' as follows:

"The pit, as it is called, consists of a small circus, some six feet in diameter, fitted with a high wooden rim that reaches to elbow height. Over it the branches of a gas lamp are arranged, which light up the white painted floor and every corner of the little arena. On one side of the room is a recess, which the proprietor calls his 'private box' and this apartment the Captain and his friends take possession of, whilst the audience clambered upon the tables and forms, or hung over the sides of the pit itself.

"All the little dogs which the visitors had brought up with them were now squalling and barking and struggling in their masters' arms; and when a rusty wire cage of rats was brought forward the proprietor was obliged to shout — 'Now you that have dogs, *do* make 'em shut up!' "

The "Captain," who appears to have been something of an exhibitionist, was first into the pit, demanding a dozen rats to test a dog he had been offered. Reaching into the cage he pulled the rats out by their tail despite a warning from one of the men not to let them bite him because "These 'ere are none of the cleanest." Then the dog was put in the ring, but despite the encouragement of its handler did not display much eagerness. Thereupon the "Captain" asked others with dogs whether "his little 'un would kill" and received a number of evasive answers such as "My dog's mouth's a little out of order," or "I've only tried him at very little 'uns." Then the preparations for the big match of the evening when fifty rats were to be killed began:

"The 'dead 'uns' were gathered up by their tails and flung into a corner. The floor was swept, and a big flat basket produced, like those in which chickens were brought to market and under whose iron top could be seen small mounds of closely packed rats. This match seemed to be between the proprietor and his son . . .. It was strange to observe the daring manner in which the lad introduced his hand into the rat cage as he fumbled about and stirred up with his fingers the living mass, picking up, as he had been requested, 'only the big 'uns.'

"When the fifty animals had been flung into the pit, they gathered themselves into a mound which reached one-third up the sides and which reminded one of the heap of hair-sweepings in a barber's shop after a heavy day's cuttings. These were all sewer and waterditch rats and the smell that rose from them was like that from a hot drain."

While they were waiting for the arrival of the dog the spectators seem to have amused themselves by blowing on the mound of rats. This caused them to scatter and during a contest the cry of "Blow on 'em" was kept up by the spectators whenever the rats grouped together and thus hindered the dog, when, as Mayhew phrased it, "the dog's second puffed at them as if extinguishing a fire." For a short while the "Captain" seems to have contented himself with tormenting the rats by flicking his pocket handkerchief at them, or offering them the lighted end of his cigar to sniff, thereby singeing their noses. Finally getting bored with waiting he once more threatened to leave and was only pacified by the arrival of the boy with a bull terrier "in a perfect fit of excitement."

". . . the second and the dog jumped into the pit. The moment the terrier was loose he became quiet in a most business like manner and rushed at the rats, burying his nose into the mound till he brought out one in his mouth. In a short time a dozen rats with wetted necks were lying bleeding on the floor, and the white paint of the pit became grained with blood. In a little time the terrier had a rat hanging to his nose, which, despite his tossing, still held on. He dashed up against the sides, leaving a patch of blood as if a strawberry had been smashed there.

" 'Hi, Butcher! hi, Butcher,' shouted the second, 'good dog, bur-r-r-h!' and he beat the sides of the pit like a drum, till the dog flew about with new life. 'Dead 'un! Drop it!' he cried when the terrier nosed a rat kicking on its side, as it slowly expired of a broken neck.

" 'Time,' said the proprietor, and the dog was caught up and held panting, his neck stretched out like a serpent's, staring intently at the rats that still kept crawling about. The poor little wretches in the brief interval, as if forgetting their danger, again commenced cleaning themselves, some nibbling the ends of their tails, others hopping about, going now to the legs of the lad in the pit and sniffing at his trousers, or strange to say advancing smelling to within a few paces of their enemy the dog."

On this occasion the dog lost the wager for the proprietor, who was not pleased with the result and indicated that he would "not give him house room." Meanwhile no doubt there was a good deal of settling up of side bets going on round the room, although surprisingly Mayhew makes no mention of this. He did however note that "A plentiful-shower of half-pence was thrown into the pit as a reward for the second." During the interval the landlord loudly exhorted his guests to "give up their minds to drinking" and the waiter added a cry of "Give your orders, gentlemen," while the boy with the rats also added to the clamour by asking "if any gentleman would like any rats."

Several more dogs were tried in turn, amongst them one very fat one, which was greeted with derisive cries of "Why don't you feed that dog?" and "Shouldn't give him more than five meals a day." Finally Mayhew recorded the end of the evening about twelve o'clock as follows:

"At last the landlord, finding that 'no gentleman would like a few rats,' and that his exhortations to 'give their minds up to drinking' produced no effect, spoke the epilogue of the rat tragedy: "Gentlemen, I give you a very handsome silver collar to be killed for next Tuesday. Open to all the world, only that they must be novice dogs, or at least such as is not ph*ee*nomenons. We shall have plenty of sport, gentlemen, and there will be loads of rat killing. I hope to see all my kind friends, not forgetting your dogs likewise . . .. Gentlemen, there is a good parlour downstairs, where we meets for harmony and entertainment.' "

Such diversions as rat-matches, badger-drawing and illicit cock-fighting undoubtedly continued to flourish in certain areas throughout the Victorian age. Increasingly, however, the tendency of the "public school" product was to turn towards the more "manly," or "gentle-manly," pursuits. Hunting, shooting and fishing were the field sports recognised by the Victorians as suitable for gentlemen. Such were the developments in each of these sports during the Victorian period, however, it is doubtful whether the sportsmen of the previous century would have approved of them.

By 1830 the introduction of the percussion cap had already largely

175

replaced the old flintlock in the shooting field, but we find no less authority than Colonel Peter Hawker, in his famous *Instructions to Young Sportsmen in all that pertains to Guns and Shooting* (seventh edition) stating, " . . . on further and more general trial, I find, so far from not having done justice to the percussion principle, I have, like all other modern shooters, been rather over-rating its merits than otherwise; for the more shots I fire, the more I am persuaded that the *flint-gun* shoots the *strongest into the bird* and by far the *easiest into the shoulder*."

It was not long before Hawker was forced to admit that the percussion cap was superior, but he was, of course, always against what was then termed "battue" shooting in organised parties of as many as a dozen guns. He preferred his sport alone over dogs, or at most with one or two companions. He would doubtless have approved of the following description of an ideal sporting dog in the *Sporting Magazine* of 1832:

"A Pointer or Setter to deserve the name should hunt high but steadily; quarter his ground with truth and judgement; turn to hand or whistle; drop to hand, bird and shot; back at all distances; be steady from a hare, yet follow a wounded one if necessary; and recover a dead or wounded bird well."

Then as now there were complaints that game was scarce and then as now the farming methods were blamed. In Hawker's *Diaries* there is the following entry for the year 1841:

"September 1st: The farmers it appears (in addition to mowing all the wheat stubbles and destroying for fuel all the turf banks where the birds could breed free from the rain and the scythe) have been using a solution of 1lb of blue vitriol in a gallon of hot water to fortify each sack of sowing wheat from becoming smutty and most people think that many

PARTRIDGE SHOOTING.

Keeper (who has never seen a breech-loader). "I DON'T THINK WERRY MUCH OF 'M; WHY HE'S BEEN AND BROKE HIS GUN THE WERRY FUST SHOT!"

birds have been poisoned by feeding on this corn . . . so few birds seen (and those few so wild) that I got only six partridges. Expected vile sport, but not quite so execrable as this."

An interesting sidelight on the effects of shooting with a muzzle loader is thrown in Hawker's *Instructions*:

"Many people cannot, or rather fancy that they cannot, shoot in gloves, and consequently their hands become as coarse as those of a gamekeeper, which, utterly as I abhor *dandyism*, I must yet observe is not quite in unison with the appearance of a perfect gentleman. I shall therefore recommend to them dark kid gloves, which will stand a month's shooting much better than might be supposed . . . . For gentlemen who require a delicate hand . . . I should advise them always to shoot in gloves, and the moment they return from the field to wash their hands in very warm water, using with it a more than usual quantity of soap; or their hands, by constant shooting, will, for a time, become . . . coarse and hard . . . . "

This minor hazard vanished in the second half of the century with the introduction of the breech loader, which revolutionized the sport of shooting. The ease of travel on the railways also resulted in the increasing popularity of grouse shooting in Scotland. Finally the total collapse of farming in the 1870s encouraged the leasing, or buying, of farms solely for the sporting rights and the development of game rearing on a scale that had never before been contemplated. The result of all these events in the last two decades of the century was that shooting over dogs became almost a rarity and driven game shooting became general, very nearly the reverse of the previous state of affairs. There was also a most deplorable tendency to glory in ever bigger

SPORT(?) FOWL SHOOTING.

An indication of public feeling against the later large bags of reared game. (From *Punch* magazine)

"record" bags. Although it was a halcyon sporting period it led inevitably to the nadir of sportsmanship.

In the year 1876 the exiled Maharajah of Lahore, Prince Duleep Singh, frequently host to the Prince of Wales at Elveden his sporting estate in East Anglia, shot 789 partridges in 1,000 shots. He subsequently shot 2,350 partridges in nine days. He also shot 440 grouse over three brace of dogs, while mounted on a pony, riding from one point to another and leaving the keepers to pick up the birds. In a single season at Elveden he shot 75,000 rabbits. All such organised slaughter, however pales before the effort of his friend Lord Walsingham who on 30th August 1888 shot 1,070 grouse, shooting with four guns and two loaders.

In the hunting field also the sport to be had in the early Victorian period differed greatly from that in the final decades of the century. The two great factors affecting Victorian sport were the spread of the railways and the introduction of barbed wire as a cheap means of fencing. It was thought at first that the deep cuttings bisecting the countryside and the sight of the puffing locomotives, so frightening to horses at first, would spell the end of hunting. Instead, however, the keen hunting man found that he could readily box his horses by rail to more distant meets, which he had never previously been able to attend. The sportsmen who lived perforce in towns were thus able to attend meets which before had been out of the question. Indeed the effect was to increase the number of supporters for many hunts, rather than cause any decrease in hunting.

As early as 1860 the Leicestershire farmers were circularised regarding the increasing use of wire in fencing, but this referred to the

THE WIRE FENCE.

The dangers of wire in the hedges before the days of barbed wire. A *Punch* cartoon.

old pit wires used for hauling the lifts up and down coal mines. In the Midlands, miles of these used wires were to be had cheaply and they were much used for fencing. Although no doubt something of a hazard, they were nothing like as unpleasant or as dangerous as barbed wire, which was first invented in the United States of America in 1875 and began to appear in Britain in considerable quantities in the 1880s. Since it was both cheap and efficient, its use became widespread, but due to the support that hunting enjoyed in the countryside it was generally possible to keep its use under some measure of control.

These two factors apart, the really great difference between fox-hunting in the early Victorian period and that in the later years of the century was in the speed of the hunt. Throughout the century there was a tendency to breed faster hounds. The publication of the Foxhound Kennel Studbook in 1866 with records going back in some instances over fifty years was an enormous aid to breeding for nose, speed and other attributes. By the end of the century it was common to find packs which could "burst" their fox in the first forty minutes of the run. The older type of slower hound had by then almost completely disappeared.

Another point of interest is that whereas in the 1830s there had been 138 packs of harriers recorded as against only 101 packs of foxhounds, by the end of the century, against all the odds, it was the packs of harriers that had dwindled in numbers. Fox-hunting was regarded as the gentleman's sport and towards the end of the century this snobbishness had been extended to the very packs of hounds hunted. To hunt in the 'Shires, was to have the pick of the fast hunting country and stamped a follower as one able to afford two blood horses and theoretically as a

Hunting was a source of much satirical comment from the time of Surtees onwards.

good rider and a good sportsman. To hunt with a "provincial" pack was almost the equivalent of social death in the eyes of the same young Victorian gentlemen who regarded driven shooting as the only kind possible socially since "only cads shoot over pointers."

It might be thought that fishing was one sport where such petty-minded snobbishness could not exist, but the rising Victorian gentlemen of the middle classes were generally able to find fine grades of difference, usually related to cost, in all matters which did not really interest them except as an exercise in social climbing. Thus fly-fishing for trout or salmon was more expensive than bait-fishing for pike or similar fish and the description "game" and "coarse" fishing developed as a social snobbery in some minds as much as a distinction between two forms of sport. It escaped the minds of those who wished to make such fine distinctions that it was decidedly ungentlemanly to do so.

The changes in the art of fishing and the development of fishing as a sport during the 19th century were considerable. In the early part of the century it was not uncommon to use a net for fishing and worms and bait were freely used. Until 1851 Pulman's *Vade Mecum of Fly Fishing for Trout* does not mention the art of dry fly fishing, although there had been two previous editions in 1841 and 1846. It may therefore be accepted that almost all fly fishing prior to 1850 had been wet fly fishing. In 1844, for instance, the Itchen was still a wet fly stream, although in the later decades of the century famed as a dry fly fisherman's paradise. Thus yet another division and petty snobbery arose in the latter half of the nineteenth century between wet and dry fly fishermen. With the opening up of the Highlands of Scotland, however, in the latter half of the century there were ample opportunities for fishermen of all tastes and inclinations.

This regrettable and unsporting tendency to back-biting and divisiveness inside field sports such as hunting, shooting and fishing also extended to the sports themselves. The unfortunate predilection for large bags of hand-reared pheasants resulted in many gamekeepers being encouraged to kill foxes, as well as anything with a hooked beak. The hunting and shooting interests within a county were often at odds as a result and inevitably the countrymen themselves took sides, although almost inevitably they favoured the hunt rather than shooting since the former relied on the support of the countryside whereas the latter tended to restrict access to the country people in areas where they frequently had age-old rights of way.

Falconry, coursing and deer-stalking all remained outside these petty divisive snobberies, largely because they were much more restricted in numbers of supporters. To take an interest in any of these entailed necessary keenness unrelated to social ambitions, although stalking was perhaps not without its social aspirants. The National Coursing Club was not formed until 1858 and in 1857 the Waterloo Cup, presented originally by the proprietor of the Waterloo Hotel in Liverpool, in 1836, for a stake of eight dogs, was opened up to a sixty-four dog stake, becoming the principal event of the year. The introduction of the Ground Game Act in 1880 resulted in ground with hares becoming much harder to obtain and the sport waned in the last decades of the century, although a keen nucleus of supporters kept it alive.

Stalking, like salmon fishing, developed with the opening up of the Highlands in the latter half of the century, following the royal example at Balmoral. *The Art of Deer Stalking* by William Scrope in 1838, filled with anecdotes of poaching and Highland superstitions, stimulated a good deal of interest in the sport, although a mixture of the old Highland deer hunts and more modern stalking methods seem to have been common still at that time. Naturally enough there was a general desire amongst visitors to the Highlands to sample Highland sports and in the second half of the century stalking, fishing and shooting were often provided by Highland sporting inns, which had developed for no other purpose.

Another Scottish sport which developed enormously during the second half of the 19th century was golf. An increasing number of visitors to Scotland tried their hand at the game and found to their surprise that they enjoyed it. The steadily increasing numbers of Scots in the south who also played the game resulted in a growing number of courses being laid out, especially close to London. The making of golf clubs remained entirely a Scottish craft centred, like the game itself, on St. Andrews in Scotland, but the popularity of golf was already spreading around the world by the end of the century. The death of Queen Victoria and the close of the Victorian age was to be followed shortly by the appointment of the first golf-playing prime minister, A. J. Balfour; the first of many since.

From golf there developed, inevitably, the popularity of the putting green, or clock golf, on the lawn, but this never really achieved the popularity in the Victorian age attained by archery, croquet and tennis. These three, starting with archery and ending with tennis, were in their turn undoubtedly the most popular Victorian games suitable for both gentlemen and ladies. Since there were so few suitable opportunities for mixing the sexes with propriety this naturally made them extremely popular.

The question of dress was all important in archery from the ladies' viewpoint. This was stressed in an article in *London Society* in 1864:

> The costume of an archeress is all important. Not only does it materially affect the pageant, which from a spectator's point of view is a great matter, but it very nearly concerns the shooter. Hence have arisen the numerous attempts made by societies to adopt a distinctive costume. But this has generally been found

The opening of the golf season at St Andrews in 1876. (*Radio Times Hulton Picture Library*)

impracticable. The Bow-women of Wye, the Royal Sherwood Archers, the Harley Bush Bowmen, and many others, even to the extent of regulating the costume to be worn at the archery balls, have endeavoured to legislate on this matter. But a standard of grace cannot be fixed, and now ladies are left to follow their own taste and the result is far more pleasant than any uniformity could be.

"A good and practised archeress," says a lady, who is one herself, "knows that there must not be a string, a ribbon, or a long curl, or a flying feather in the way of either bow or arrow." The same authority declares large crinolines to be very uncomfortable, and those who remember the whimsical effect produced at an important meeting a year or two ago will readily endorse the assertion. It happened that the day of competition on the occasion referred to, was tempestuous. The ladies — many of them with reluctance, be it said — had adopted the prevailing fashion and appeared in the archery field with an exuberance of skirt. Boreas did not neglect the opportunity, and the wind came sweeping over the ground, causing the skirts to touch the bows . . . and promised to make the meeting very unsatisfactory, till a lady, more careful of her fame as an archeress than of her appearance at the moment, very wisely made use of her cord as captain of a target, to tie on the skirts of her dress. And then scarfs, and sashes and cords were impressed into the same service, and there was a field full of ladies whose skirts are said to have presented the novel appearance of so many sacks of flour tied in at the middle. But the reputations of the shooters were saved, and good scores, for a windy day, were made.

A cricket match between Sussex and Kent at Brighton. (*By courtesy of the Chief Librarian, East Sussex County Libraries*)

Just how seriously the archery was taken may be gauged from the above account. The extent of archery parties and the sort of entertainment involved is clearly outlined in the following extract from *Party Giving on Every Scale*, written in 1882, by which time archery was giving way in popularity to tennis and croquet:

"In some counties Archery Meetings are a great feature in the amusements of the summer months and the expenses of these are sometimes defrayed by the club itself; but archery parties are very often given to the members of the county archery club by the gentry of the county. These parties are given on various scales of hospitality, from a mere afternoon-party to a dinner, dance and supper. In the latter light refreshments are served from 4 to 7; a cold collation is served in a lounge marquee at from 7 to 7.30; dancing takes place at 9 in either dining-room or drawing-room. Tea and coffee, etc., are served until 12, when a supper, on the principle of a ball supper, is given. The cold collation, or dinner, is more substantial than a ball supper, as cold lamb and cold beef are given, and bowls of salad, in addition to ham, tongues, chickens, mayonnaises, and various sweets, jellies, creams, pastry . . ..

"With respect to the style of supper given on these occasions it is usually of the simplest order of ball supper; neither hot nor cold expensive entrees nor expensive sweets being provided, as the guests principally comprise very young people of both sexes, and upon whom a supper of expensive dainties would be more or less thrown away. In providing wine . . . considerably less would be required than for an ordinary ball supper . . . for a party of one hundred people, supposing seventy of the number were ladies, 3 dozen champagne would be sufficient in addition to 1 dozen of sherry."

A croquet ground at Gisburne (1865), a popular sport for men and women to play together. (*Radio Times Hulton Picture Library*)

The introduction of croquet in the early 1850s was the beginning of the end for archery, even if archery clubs continued to flourish in some areas until the end of the century. In 1852 a Miss McNaughton is credited with introducing croquet from France to the Earl of Lonsdale. The game was then played with very large hoops and a tinkling bell in the centre. It rapidly became popular, especially after a Mr John Jaques began selling croquet sets in 1856, founding a firm which still operates under the same name. Played in crinolines, it provided endless opportunities for cheating and the game became the source of numerous jokes in *Punch*.

It was only with the gradual introduction of lawn tennis in the 1870s that croquet had any serious competition. However, it was not until the 1880s that lawn tennis had become really established as a popular game, although still played in clothes which were themselves a remarkable handicap. Of course the game in the early days was merely a social pretext for mixing the sexes rather than being in any sense competitive for no lady could possibly expect to compete with gentlemen while hindered by a full length skirt and the absurd fashions of the period.

Another extract from *Party Giving on Every Scale* in 1882, will indicate the attitude of the time to tennis parties:

"Lawn tennis is now generally played at garden parties, so much so that garden parties are often designated lawn-tennis parties. In town and in the suburbs a military band is generally engaged to play from four to seven; in town a military band means the bands of the 1st or 2nd Life Guards, or that of the Royal Horse Guards Blue, and the bands of the Grenadier, Coldstream or Scots Guards. These fine bands are a

The Lawn-Tennis Championship meeting at Wimbledon in 1881. (*Mary Evans*)

great attraction at a garden party . . . The permission of the colonel of the regiment, or that of the 'president of the band' has to be solicited as a matter of courtesy or form, when the bandmaster is applied to for his band, subject to this permission being granted. The cost of the band is regulated by the strength of its numbers, the charge ranging from 10s to 15s per man . . .

"When matches of lawn-tennis are played at a garden party, a table is placed on the lawn, with iced drinks, sherry and seltzerwater for the benefit of the gentlemen. Sherry and seltzer is rather a favourite drink with men in general and 6 to 8 bottles of sherry would probably be drunk, or even less, according to the number of gentlemen present . . . In some remote counties, the gentlemen at a garden party are represented by three or four young curates and two or three old gentlemen, while the ladies perhaps muster from forty to fifty, in which case very little wine is drunk . . ."

A more arduous game which was introduced in 1871 and became inmensely popular, even though limited entirely to males, was polo. First played in England by the officers of the 10th Royal Hussars, the Prince of Wales's Own, amongst themselves, it soon became popular with the 9th Lancers as well and in a short time they had arranged a match. A newspaper account of the occasion read:

## (HOCKEY ON HORSEBACK)

Nearly all fashionable London journeyed from town to Hounslow on Tuesday to witness a new game called "Hockey on Horseback" between the Officers of the 10th Prince of Wales's Hussars and Officers of the 9th Queen's Royal Lancers, who had come from Aldershot.

The game took place at Hounslow Heath and the various equipages quite surrounded the ground allotted to the players. Posts some twenty yards apart marked the goals. The distance between them a little under 200 yards. The sticks used were like those used in hockey. Both sides wore mob caps with different coloured tassels attached. The ball, a little sphere of white bone, was thrown up by a sergeant major of the 10th, who then galloped off the ground. The eight players on each side, who had taken up position in front of their goals, then galloped for the ball at the best speed of their active, wiry little 12½ hands high ponies. The game lasted for an hour and a half with ten minutes interval. The Hussars gained three goals to the Lancers two. Though general remarks make it evident the new game is one most fitted for cavalry soldiers it was more remarkable for the language used by the players than anything else . . .

During the 1870s there was also a surprising craze for roller-skating, which had been immensely successful in the United States of America. Many rinks were opened in England, but due to poor management the sport languished somewhat until the early 1890s when the National Skating Association was founded and the sport taken seriously in hand with first-, second- and third-class tests for skaters. At the same time a large rink was opened at Olympia in Kensington with improved roller skates. The reasons for the popularity of this sport were the same as for croquet and tennis in that it allowed young people of both sexes to mix together freely. By the end of the century the sport had still maintained its popularity, but during the winter ice-skating was generally more popular when suitable conditions prevailed.

Ice skating was a sport at which the English excelled, especially on the frozen canals and fens of East Anglia, but it was not until the 1890s that there began to be any interest in skiing. This was at that time a sport popular in Norway and virtually unknown in Switzerland. There the British residents, who were forced to reside in sanatoriums for "pulmonary complaints," introduced tobogganing as an organised sport. The famous Cresta run at St. Moritz was formed in the 1890s and an *Encyclopedia of Sport* of 1898 noted:

"Tobogganing is a sport which appeals to all Englishmen, as it calls into play all those qualities for which England as a nation is famous. The decision quickly called for and instantaneously carried out, the opportunity of exercising pluck, nerve, resource and activity, the quick eye for a curve, the necessity for hand and eye to work exactly together."

According to the same *Encyclopedia of Sport*:

"Between 1850 and 1860 several men took to mountaineering as a sport. Mr Justice Wills's ascent of the Matterhorn is usually regarded as the first 'important' sporting climb. The highest point of Mont Rosa was reached in 1855 and Mont Blanc was climbed by a new route and without guides by a party of Englishmen in 1865. The Alpine Club was founded in London in the following year. Foreign countries one after another imitated the English institution and thus mountaineering rapidly developed."

Names such as those of Edward Whymper and E. A. Fitzgerald made mountaineering history in the later years of the Victorian age. During the 1860s Whymper, originally commissioned as an artist to make engravings of the French Alps, made a number of startling first climbs, crowning them in 1865 with the first successful climb of the Matterhorn. His book *Scrambles in the Alps* published in 1871, engraved with his own illustrations, inspired many Englishmen to emulate his feats. In the 1880s he went on to climb in South America and thereafter to tackle peaks in Canada, blazing the trail in many areas. E. A. Fitzgerald was cast in a similar mould making a series of spectacular first climbs in New Zealand and elsewhere. Throughout the later years of the Victorian age mountaineering seems to have been

Winter sports became increasingly popular during the century. This is a Cruikshank cartoon of some of the hazards.

Miniature yacht racing
in the Solent near the
Isle of Wight, where
Victoria frequently
retreated from London.
(*Mary Evans*)

Falmouth, a popular
yachting spot, at the
turn of the century.

regarded as a particularly "manly" sport followed with enthusiasm and
dedication by its devotees.

Perhaps the "manliest" of all Victorian sports, however was big-game
hunting. Although tiger and other big-game hunting had been carried on
in India since the eighteenth century, it was not until the late
nineteenth century that sportsmen started visiting India specifically to
hunt big-game. After the publication of Captain William Harris's classic
book *Wild Sports of South Africa* in 1837 and then *Five Years of a*

*Hunter's Life in South Africa* by R. G. Gordon Cumming in 1850, there was a constant procession of sporting Englishmen voyaging to Africa in search of big game. Some, such as Sir Samuel White Baker, preferred hunting wild boar with a knife and hounds in the forests of Ceylon, others, such as Grantley Berkeley, went after bison on the plains of the mid-West. Yet others, such as F. Courtenay Selous, earned their living by their gun in various parts of Africa. The end result of these years of slaughter was that by 1900 the big game, like the bison on the plains of North America, had almost vanished.

One sport, as yet unmentioned, which developed tremendously in the Victorian age, was yachting. The Victorian gentleman's yacht might vary from a well-found, stable steam vessel equipped with bathrooms and suites of cabins, to a small schooner type yacht, down to a small dinghy; for small boat racing became extremely popular during the late nineteenth century. In order to become a member of the Cowes Yacht Club, founded in 1815 and given the title Royal in 1820, the qualification in 1826 was owning a yacht of 30 tons. In 1833 William IV expressed a wish that it should thenceforth be known as the Royal Yacht Squadron and in 1882 the Prince of Wales was elected Commodore. Like the Jockey Club in racing, the Royal Yacht Squadron at Cowes became the arbiter in yacht racing and matters connected with yachting. The Solent, with its wide expanse of water enclosed by the Isle of Wight was ideal for sailing and this south coast area soon became the centre for almost all the yachting in England during the Victorian period.

By the end of the nineteenth century the Victorian class-consciousness had permeated through to the games they played, as had the mania for regulating and codifying a set of rules. Thus cricket, a game never really suited to the English climate, and rugby, were no longer the old somewhat haphazard games they had been, but they were undeniably games for gentlemen. Association football, although played by amateurs was increasingly less of a gentleman's game, though no longer played with an inflated pig's bladder, as it had been in the early days of the period. It was perhaps small wonder that many English gentlemen felt the urge to get away from the country and indulge their basic instincts by pitting themselves against big-game in the wilds of Africa, or else risking their necks in the hunting field. In yielding to the urge to break through the restrictive social barriers erected on all sides they were merely being human.

# CHAPTER NINE
# India and Abroad

In the India prior to the Mutiny of 1857 the East India Company, more familiarly known as John Company, was the arbiter of the British way of life. The amount of corruption which existed and was winked at by all concerned was considerable. Indeed entrenched corruption in the administration of Indian affairs, in the management of business and control of the armed forces was an accepted part of life. At the same time it must be appreciated that the bulk of business transactions and deals between merchants were strictly honourable and straightforward for the simple reason that unless such transactions were conducted honourably business was unlikely to prosper and in general it prospered exceedingly.

On the whole, however, the standard of the English gentlemen in India was not at this time perhaps of the highest. They came to India because they had to, to make their fortunes because they had insufficient money to stay at home. Penurious gentlemen, younger sons, Irish and Scots in general — they would not have come to India unless they had no other alternative. The practice of filling the vacancies among the officers of a regiment posted to India with what were known as "Indian" officers, not wealthy enough to afford a commission in such a regiment at home, was fully exposed when the Earl of Cardigan quarrelled violently with several such officers returned with the 11th Hussars from India to suffer under his command.

From the Earl of Mar and Kelly's unpublished diaries of the period a decade or so before the Mutiny, one obtains a rather startling picture of the standard of the officers in India at that time. Since his diary was a personal record and never intended for publication he expressed some very revealing sentiments about his fellow officers in charge of a regiment of Sepoys. He recorded that the mess was to his liking, for "they had a good billiard table, a pack of half bred dogs and a Book club." This it seems provided all the more important aspects of relaxation the officers required.

Of his commanding officer he wrote:

"Major Bates, who joined the corps for the first time just before me was for a few months very well liked. He commanded us and we were continually calling upon him, but after a while he began to show his real disposition, which was without an exception the most crabbed one I ever knew. He was a little, stout, fussy looking man, elder brother of the comedian. He had certainly a turn for mimicry and I have heard was a pretty good amateur actor. He was a most amusing companion when he liked. Nobody took off eccentricities or sang a better song than he did. He *could* be hospitable too, but he was only a month or so entertaining to us. He was of a most suspicious nature and misfortune had not improved him in any way. When a subaltern he brought charges of cowardice against his Commanding Officer, which he failed to prove to the satisfaction of the Court Martial by which he was sentenced to be dismissed the service ... He was a very ignorant man and used to give us great amusement in the style of his orders. Some time after his return from England he was appointed to the Commissariat and in this department he remained till his promotion to a majority in 1829 so that he could not be expected to know much of his duty. In a very short time he had had a quarrel with nearly all of us. He was always annoying us in the most petty ways. He was unfortunate in promotion and this added to his having a grown-up family of mature children did not improve his temper, indeed his eldest daughter who lived with him and for whom he had the greatest affection was the cause of most of his quarrels with us. She was a perfect vixen ... and they were always fancying we were slighting her (because she was dark, when nothing of the sort was intended). We really hated him. He would publicly wig us for wearing the chin strap of our caps down; or for not handing his daughter at a party. He issued orders that no noise was to be made in the lines *at the christening of sepoys' children* ! ! The grammar and diction of his letters and orders were absurd in the extreme and caused us no end of amusement. He had spies who told him everything we did and said of him, but who they were we never could find out, though we believed them to be the khitmudjars. Poor man he was afraid to take public notice of what he thus heard and the information only maddened him for we were not sparing of our abuse ...."

Having thus outlined what must inevitably have been a very wearing state of affairs for all concerned and hardly conducive to good order and discipline, the diarist went on to give thumbnail sketches of his

An Indian drawing of an Englishman in his carriage. (*Victoria and Albert Museum*)

fellow officers, as follows:

"Carter . . . was adjutant . . .. He is of a morose disposition at times, at others extremely lively and a delightful companion. There is evidently some mystery about him. We never have been able to find out about his birth, parentage or background. He says he was born and educated in Edinburgh, but some have had reason for believing he was an American or had been in America. Since he joined us (17 years) he has never been known to speak of his relations or to receive an English letter. Latterly his habits have been those of a recluse and his temper appeared to get soured.

"He is a man of excellent education and used, until his imagination grew marked of late, to be possessed of sound judgement. He was always eccentric, but until he quite withdrew himself from the world he was not only much liked but looked up to in the Regiment. Now he joins in nothing and is ill and useless to the corps."

According to the Earl of Mar and Kelly the previous adjutant had been no better, of him he wrote:

"Thancart was the best humoured fellow in existence and when I joined the corps he was adjutant for which situation no man could have been more unfitted. He was an ignorant, illiterate man devoted to good fellowship and hospitality to a degree, but addicted to drinking, which grew upon him to such an extent as quite to unfit him for duty. Every night he went to bed the worse for liquor and many is the night I have had to assist in carrying him from the mess. He was also weak in his judgement, liked but not respected by either officers or men. He knew his parade duties pretty well as for as the movements of a corps went . . . but of the internal economy of or arrangements of the Regiment he was perfectly ignorant. The consequence was that the Regiment got into very bad order both in dress and discipline and in 1836 he resigned his appointment or would have been turned out of it . . .."

As regards the rest of his fellow officers he is not sparing of criticism either:

"Patch is a man of inferior mind, of vulgar manners and ideas, not over fond of his duty but devoted to horses.

"Mr Muir is a regular long headed *canny* Scotchman. No man knows better how to look after his own interests. His manners are exceptionally vulgar, particularly so to his juniors in rank; sometimes very overbearing to those who will allow it, but cringing to those from whom he has anything to gain . . . He is a useful member of the corps but not an *ornament.*

"Hunter, or Little Bob, as he was generally called, is a good, quiet, harmless little fellow. Of no use and of no harm.

"Cristofen was a drunken, half-witted fellow, clever and well informed, but fond of low company. He joined the regiment not long before me.

"Andrews: a strange compound, generally speaking gentlemanly in his manners, but not polished and sometimes rude. A remarkably clever musician, plays violin and flute in first rate style, draws neatly, an excellent billiards and cricket player, neat handed writer and beautiful lady-like hand, exceptionally silly, weak and ignorant, active in body, slothful in mind . . .. Very foppish in his dress and yet exceptionally dirty in his person. A young lady once very properly called him 'the dirty dandy' . . .."

It is noticeable that in hardly one instance has the diarist anything really pleasant to say about any of his fellow officers and from this one can draw one's own conclusions. The most charitable is that he had probably been too long in the restricted atmosphere of such a mess and too long in a tropical climate. After something like twenty years in such conditions it is understandable that the mind fastens on the faults rather than on the good points. Even so, the comments are sufficiently truthful and penetrating to make it clear why the Indian Mutiny was at first successsful.

"Hopper, or as we all call him 'Paddy,' " he continued, "is the best natured, hot headed, passionate Irishman I ever had to do with. Very fond of his lass and his glass and is what is generally understood by a good fellow . . .. Laughing or crying, will join in anything, all the same to Paddy. Poor fellow he has since 9 years old been afflicted with a disease which makes him drink to drown pain and care and . . . makes him quite unfit to be an officer.

"Next come Macdougall, a Scotsman by name but a low Cockney by birth.

An Indian painting of two English gentlemen in a tiger hunt. Big-game sporting
became very popular in late Victorian
England. (*Victoria and Albert Museum*)

194

"Marshall comes next. He is all but a fool. In lady's society he is gentlemanly and also among strangers he behaves himself well, but among his familiars he is most gross in his language and his ideas of propriety are very strange. I believe I never met a man who was less bound by rules of propriety. His education has been neglected. His head is remarkably long and flat, his forehead very long and narrow and he once in his cups told me the surgeon informed his mother he had only just escaped being an 'Idiot.' I believe them. Like most idiots he is very revengeful . . .. He is fond of hard drinking and when tipsy which in the past ten years is very often he becomes quarrelsome, quite careless of everything and exceptionally disagreeable. He is boisterous, vain, silly in the extreme, ignorant to a degree . . .."

After such a catalogue of misfits it is a relief to find that he really likes the last three on his list, even if they too each have their weaknesses. He ended:

"Of Richardson I regret to say he is a man quite devoid of principal [sic] and yet a man everyone likes (myself among others). When he begs anything and makes promises to pay it back I really believe it never enters his head it is necessary to fulfill such promises. When you ask him for payment he regrets extremely his inability . . .. When he has money he throws it away or will give it to anyone who asks him for it, but never thinks of paying a debt . . . I fear he spends most of his pay on women . . .

"Poor Carlyon comes next to me. He was rather mean in some money matters; generous in others. Exceptionally careful in his dealings, but always honourable. He was not a man of any education . . .. On the whole he was a good little fellow.

"Bow, our surgeon, from 1825 to 1837, was a married man. A good natured attentive little fellow. Retired in habits, well informed but not clever in his profession. He was much liked by us all and left in 1837."

It is obvious from the Earl of Mar and Kelly's comments that the standard of officers in the sepoy regiments was not of the highest to put it mildly. It is equally plain from his comments that he did not have a high opinion of the natives. Stephen Gilham in his unpublished diaries, however, gives another side to this picture. Writing in 1853 he noted:

"The richest man in Bombay, is, or was, a Parsee; he was knighted by Her Majesty a few years back, which was the first occasion of such an honour being conferred on a native of India. He richly deserved the distinction for amongst that intelligent class the Parsees he was the head. His fortune was something like a million of money; the good he did with it was highly honourable to him; water, which is so great a blessing everywhere, but more particularly so in the burning and parched climate of Hindoostan, he secured to his poorer countrymen by sinking wells and constructing tanks. He built a magnificent hospital and gave some valuable scholarships to the 'Elphinstone College' at Bombay to the advancement of English education generally amongst the natives of all castes at Bombay. And yet this man commenced life only as a 'Patywalla' which I may translate pedlar. He took to buying up empty bottles of which having accumulated a vast quantity he sold them to such advantage at a season of dearth of the article that he made the speculation his starting point to fortune. He afterwards became a large ship owner and speculated largely and successfully in opium to China. He finished by amassing a colossal fortune. He built himself a palace of a residence and . . . everything in it from kitchen utensils to the stables was ordered from and made by the first tradesmen in London. Hunt and Roskel fashioned his plate; Gillow made his furniture; Holland was his upholsterer; Lawrie provided his carriages and Apsley Pellat found him in glassware and china . . . so much for empty bottles and enterprise."

It is not without significance that when Gilham visited Calcutta for the first time in 1853 he recorded:

"Fort William is apparently one of the most strongly fortified places in India. I have heard it said, however, that the number of troops that would be required to garrison it in a time of siege, would be more than could be victualled . . . during a protracted investment of the place, that famine in short, would lead to results that the most potent enemy could not accomplish. It is to be hoped that the question will not be put to the test; it would be a bad state of things, far I trust from any probability or realisation, to see an enemy close to our doors in the East."

In the same year 1853, however, General Jacob wrote in exasperation to *The Times*:

"There is more danger to our Indian Empire from the state of the Bengal Army from the feeling which there exists between the native and the European and thence spreads throughout the length and breadth of the land, than from all other causes combined. Let government look to this; it is a serious and most important truth."

General Jacob knew what he was talking about. By 1856 there were 233,000 native troops and only 36,000 British troops in India, a proportion of five to one, which gave the native sepoy troops, ill-officered as so many of them were, a dangerous sense of their own relative power. It was this as much as anything else, which led to the Mutiny, combined with serious mismanagement of many native matters by men like those described in the diaries quoted. Inefficient white administrators and officers, both venal and stupid, made mistakes that could not always be remedied by the much smaller number of faithful and dedicated competent men, who both loved and understood India and the Indians. Because the majority at this time were inefficient and incompetent, it must not be forgotten that there was a minority of extremely able and effective administrators also present.

The annexation of the Principality of Oudh, from which the bulk of the sepoys were recruited, the prohibition of suttee (the custom of the widow casting herself on her husband's funeral pyre) and of female infanticide (almost a necessity to prevent famine in a land with massive population problems) the spread of Western education and hamfisted forms of revenue control affecting many different classes of Indians, all went to cause widespread discontent with British rule. The introduction of cartridges greased with pig and cow fat, anathema to the religious susceptibilities of the Mohammedans and Hindus, was enough to trigger off a wave of mutiny amongst the native troops. Once started it spread far beyond, until the revolt against British rule was widespread.

The Mutiny started at Meerut in April 1857, when the sepoy troops there broke into open revolt and massacred their officers. Had the British troops then been firmly handled and used to chase the mutineers, the whole affair might have been dealt with effectively on the spot, but the officers in command were old and incompetent. Throughout the whole sorry tale it was too often the same story. Bungling ineptitude, lack of firm command and inefficiency were combined all too frequently with lack of understanding of the native mind and arrogant attitudes on the British side.

When news of the atrocities reached England, there were enormous consternation and demands for retribution. With immediate re-inforcements from England and firm action at last, by 1858 the fighting was nearly over. By 1859 the last notable mutineer had been captured and executed. The most important result was the transfer of power from the East India Company in August 1858 to the British Crown. By November, Lord Canning the first Viceroy had ordered clemency for all except the ringleaders. British rule was to begin on a new note with keen young administrators in control of the Indian Civil Service.

William Russell, the *Times* correspondent, already famed for his despatches from the Crimea, was in India during 1858–9 and in the book he subsequently wrote, entitled *My Diary in India,* he noted:

"To punish 'districts' because evil deeds were committed therein, or because bodies of the enemy selected them to encamp and live in, is as unjust as it is unwise. Many years must elapse ere the evil passions excited by these disturbances expire: *perhaps confidence will never be restored.*"

He was sarcastic about desk bound administrators shouting for blood and vengeance and also mentioned the danger of a "sense of new sprung power, operating on vulgar, half-educated men, aided by the servility of those around them." He was convinced this produced results prejudicial to our influence amongst the natives and cited the case of a chief engineer on the railways of the "head navvy type," whom he found beating the coolies with a stick until Russell intervened.

Fortunately Russell was over-pessimistic about the effects of the Mutiny. In that it forced the British to take drastic action and review their entire policy of government, changing from the old mercantile rule of the East India Company to the direct rule of the Indian Civil Service, it ultimately produced a vast improvement. The diary of a young Victorian, H. M. Kisch, who went out in 1874 to take a post in the Indian Civil Service, is of immense interest when compared with the attitudes of earlier administrators. Pitchforked into controlling a famine almost as soon as he had reached India and before he had had time to get any training, he wrote:

"March 24, 1874: I have under my management as far as famine relief goes, an area of 198 square miles, and for this I shall be responsible. I have full liberty to adopt whatever measures I think necessary, subject only to the very general instructions of the Lieutenant Governor and the Commissioner . . . Every day I have been from seven to eight hours in the saddle riding about from village to village and searching out (1) those who are able to work but cannot find employment (2) those who from weakness or disease can now do no work at all. Of the latter I have as yet fortunately not come upon a very great number, though in some villages it was large enough to be a sad foreboding of what may come and to make me even more anxious than I was before to visit every village quickly. In one of the villages that I visited the condition of some of the people was such that I thought it necessary to have them fed on the spot with cooked food, rather than to trust to their reaching alive the nearest store from which they could obtain rice . . .. Unless I had seen it for myself I could not have believed that anyone could live with so thin a covering to the bones. The very colour of the bone was visible through the thin black film that surrounded it . . .."

He went on to detail the measures he was taking and some of the difficulties he was encountering:

"I have at present three very large grain stores and am establishing smaller grain stores all over my Circle. I am in hopes that the supply of rice, which will be continually replenished, will not eventually run short, but it is now quite impossible to say . . .. There is a great temptation to get in a rage . . . but so powerfully does the doctrine of caste operate on the mind of the Brahmin that he would without a murmur die sooner than work on a tank or road with a common coolie . . ."

"You must not think that the seven or eight hours riding a day which I now have to do — at the imminent risk of knocking up my horses — constitutes all my work. I have to organise relief works, arrange for the erection of store-houses, and give directions as to the distribution of gratuitous relief; besides I have to superintend and control the various registers and accounts that are kept and give endless minute instructions. I have only one clerk who is supposed to know English and he does not know enough to make his knowledge of any use . . .."

As he began to get a fuller grasp of the situation he saw that, despite the effective action he was taking, there was a considerable threat to his area from outside. A fortnight later he was writing:

"April 8th: I have now been to, I believe, every village in my circle; one day this last week I had over forty miles riding . . . Another day I was on my horse from 8 a.m. to 9 p.m. The result is that the horses are getting rather weak . . .. Since I came here I have erected 15 government grain store-houses and opened about 22 relief works. I give employment to about 15,000 men and women per day and am feeding gratuitously about 3,000 more . . . If I could fix an iron fence round my circle I think I might save everyone . . . alive, but I am right in the north of British India and men are journeying down from Nepal to join my relief works. The worst thing I fear is that when hunger becomes very sharp, the men may come over the border in thousands and burn some of the large stores in order to get at the rice . . .."

"An immense amount of rascality goes on in the relief works; coolies get paid only a portion of their wages often, and the man in charge takes the rest for himself. The day before yesterday I arrested three men, who I believe had been engaged in this practice in one of my tanks. It is absolutely necessary that one or two men be convicted as it is very difficult to find out these offences and when found out the only way is to come down hot and sharp . . ."

The tone is that of a public school prefect maintaining discipline amongst the juniors, but the task was a highly responsible one. The extreme youth of the writer and his complete inexperience of the country is plain from the next two entries:

"April 15th, 1874: There is not the least danger in going anywhere alone in India. The great nuisance is that people are so frightened of one that the boys and women as a rule run away . . ..

"August 8th 1874: . . . In the last Government Gazette it was notified that junior civilians, of whom I am of course one, employed on active duty in the famine districts will be considered to have passed the higher standard on condition of their qualifying fully in the higher standard in Bengali and Hindustani within one year of their quitting famine work. I believe I am the only man of my year who has charge of a famine circle in one of the very distressed districts. On the whole it is very lucky to have been sent to famine work as it ought to improve one's prospects materially. It has also enabled me to get over the first examination without the least trouble . . ."

Although by no means everyone would have relished the thought of being put in charge of a famine relief area, clearly young Kisch thoroughly approved of his work and enjoyed it. As if famine was not enough he was soon also threatened with drought and this also he merely regarded as a challenge to his ingenuity:

"Friday August 14th: Since the 12th we have had in my circle only 2.4 inches of rain and the prospects are becoming alarming in the extreme; the scarcity of rain is also very general in this neighbourhood and a telegram arrived yesterday instructing us, if rain does not come within a week, to turn out the whole population and make them dam the rivers and irrigate their lands. There are six rivers in my circle that I shall dam and the work will be rather heavy at the time. I have had sent me a Bengali accountant who knows English thoroughly and ought to be very useful . . .. If I have to dam all the rivers in my circle there will be plenty of work for all the men under me and the work will be very interesting. Altogether I cannot conceive so rapid a system of education as an Indian famine for a new arrival in the country. When I came up to Tirhut I knew no more of how to dig a good tank, or build a grain store, or to store grain so as to avoid injury from the damp or heat, or to do a hundred other things that I have to do, than I have of how to build an English house, or play the piano. Now I can do very well the things I have mentioned above. It is also surprising what a number of small pieces of information one acquires by going about the country a great deal. I am getting quite familiar now with every tree and plant to be found in my circle . . ."

It is pleasant to record that Kisch went to well deserved promotion in his chosen service, but such was by no means always the case. India claimed many British lives from disease or accident, or in trivial frontier skirmishes. Kipling summed it up well in *Arithmetic on the Frontier*:

> A scrimmage in a Border Station —
> A canter down some dark defile —
> Two thousand pounds of education
> Drops to a ten rupee *jezail* —
> The Crammer's boast, the Squadron's pride,
> Shot like a rabbit in a ride!

Unfortunately the sort of dedication shown by Kisch was not always the British way towards the native populations. Although the record of the Indian Civil Service was very high in this respect this was not always the case elsewhere. Isabella Bird in Hong Kong from 1877 to 1882 noted, "Foreigners have misused and do misuse the Chinese. You cannot be two minutes in a Hong Kong street without seeing Europeans striking coolies with their canes or umbrellas. . . ." Lt. Ronald Gower at much the same time, noted young officers of the 74th Regiment treating orientals as if they were a very inferior kind of animal to themselves: "No wonder that we English are so cordially disliked wherever we go."

There was more than an element of truth in this last statement, for without question the Victorian English abroad were frequently very arrogant and tactless. For instance when the Marquis of Hartington visited the United States of America during the Civil War he made so

An Indian painting of the English-built Railway in India. (*Victoria and Albert Museum*)

little secret of his southern sympathies while staying in the north that Lincoln nicknamed him "Lord Partington." A point that is perhaps, however, not fully appreciated is the great extent of Victorian investment abroad. In large part this followed on the visits of the Victorian gentlemen who had seen for themselves where they were investing their money.

In Lady Monkswell's diaries, during a visit to the United States of America, not long after the Civil War, she recorded, "Saturday 8th October: 1881: ... They told us that poor Lord Airlie, whom we left at Denver in rude health, walking about in a flannel shirt — much to the scandalisation of Denver — had suddenly died. Poor man, I am sure it is the very last thing he intended to do. He had been investing largely in the Denver building society and the canal and had set·up a son in a distant ranch. He was a handsome, thin, straight looking man — I can hardly believe he should have died so suddenly."

Paradoxically it was large Victorian landed gentry of this stamp, who invested considerable sums in the trans-continental railway system of North America thus ruining the farmers in Britain by ensuring a supply of cheap grain from the mid-West. On the other hand investment in such ventures as the British South Africa Company, formed by Rhodes, though apparently full of hope and promise of gold and diamonds was never to produce the yields expected. Instead there were a series of tribal conflicts, the Matabele War, and finally the Boer War, when the British were to find themselves ignominiously defeated at first and were only to win eventually after a long drawn-out and bitter struggle.

Nearer at home, on the continent, the British had long acquired a reputation as boors. Thackeray in his *Book of Snobs* in 1847 dilated on the Englishman abroad:

"That brutal, ignorant, peevish bully of an Englishman is showing himself, in every city in Europe. One of the dullest creatures under heaven, he goes trampling Europe under foot, shouldering his way into galleries and cathedrals, and bustling into places with his buckram uniform. At church or theatre, gala or picture-gallery, his face never varies. A thousand delightful sights pass before his bloodshot eyes and don't affect him. Countless brilliant scenes of life and manners are shown him, but never move him. He goes to church and calls the practices there degrading and superstitious, as if *his* altar was the only one that was acceptable. He goes to picture-galleries, and is more ignorant about Art than a French shoeblack. Art, Nature, pass and there is no dot of admiration in his stupid eyes. . . ."

With the outbreak of revolution in Europe in 1848 the British kept away from the continent for a while. The scare did not last long, however, and such favourite German spas as Baden-Baden once more began to draw their regular annual clientele of British visitors to take the waters. There were, of course, always those who preferred Italy or France, or even Scandinavia.

In 1882 an article in *The Queen* noted the development of the Riviera and gave some advice on travel:

> It is only during the last twenty years that Mentone has been so much patronised, but it now bids fair to rival Cannes and Nice. In 1856 it was visited by only fourteen families; while now the strangers' list gives a total of about two thousand families yearly. . . . The hire of a carriage and horses will amount to more than twice the railway fares, even for a party of four; but the views from the old *Corniche* road are much finer, on account of the low level of the railroad and the many tunnels which interfere with seeing much of the fine scenery. Mentone, San Remo, Bordighera, Alassio, Finale Marina and Savona are the best resting places between Nice and Genoa. There is no advantage to be gained in resting the nights at less frequented places and being exceedingly uncomfortable. Discomforts are better met when not tired and in the full light of the sun. The carriages will be vetturino and the horses engaged by the day's journey. You will have to bargain for these beforehand, as the Italian always cheats if he has the chance.

The insular tone of the last remark and the general attitude that only the best is good enough for the English was just the sort of attitude which infuriated foreigners. The Rev. E. J. Hardy clearly was one of

Various resors on the French coast gradually supplanted the English seaside towns in the later Victorian period.

Lucerne. Switzerland became a popular holiday spot.

those who felt embarrassed by the behaviour of his fellow English on the continent. In his essay *Manners Makyth Man*, published in 1887, he wrote:

"A bull in a china shop is nothing compared to a drove of Protestant tourists in an Italian church. You may see, when visiting palaces, a huge cockney lolling down upon thrones and chairs of state, and full of self-complacency, imagining himself Victor Emmanuel, or some greater man. One cannot help feeling for the embarrassment of palatial attendants, whose politeness prevents them forbidding irreverent sightseers from 'touching' fragile ornaments, and sitting down upon almost everything, while at the same time their duty urges them to remonstrate with commoners against making themselves 'at home' in palaces too grand for even kings to feel quite at their ease in."

One of the reasons the Victorians liked going abroad undoubtedly was that they were then able to cast aside many of the irksome conventions which ruled them at home. Like children allowed out of school their conduct then was often riotous in the extreme. Certainly they were often guilty of behaviour abroad which they would never have contemplated at home. Taine noted this different standard of behaviour between the English gentleman abroad and the English gentleman at home and put it down to sheer hypocrisy, but this was not entirely the case. It did not follow that because they enjoyed the greater freedom of life abroad they necessarily behaved badly. In Lady Monkswell's diaries there are some charming examples of life on holiday in Switzerland. They were visiting Sir Alfred Wills, generally known as Judge Wills, the famous mountaineering pioneer, who had been one of the first to build his own Swiss chalet known as "The Eagle's Nest." She recorded in 1891:

"Sunday 30 August: . . . We had a very pleasant breakfast soon after 6.30 . . . and we bid each other farewell to meet again in the evening at the Eagle's Nest: and so we parted, they going over the cricket ground and towards the ridge . . .. It was I suppose about six when we came in sight of the light brown chalet perched on the very end of the valley, nestled in the woods and surrounded by a circle of great rocks rising several thousand feet above it. In front of it was a flag staff bearing the Union Jack, which they lowered to salute us . . .. The first sure sign of an English habitation was the park paling which Sir Alfred had put round his eight acres, which is the extent of his property . . .. I admire the spirit of these people to have actually built their nest here and lived in it for thirty years, but unless you are a first rate mountaineer and crazy about it I do not think it has nearly such a nice situation as, for instance, our dear little chalet . . ..

"This house is about twice as big as our chalet and of course from having been lived in so much, far more comfortable. There is a *grand salon* and a *petit salon*, in which this large party of seventeen has their meals indiscriminately; we walk casually through the kitchen where somebody is always cooking and somebody else feeding. Our bedroom is really perfection . . . beautiful wood walls and ceiling . . . two big windows . . . a balcony outside, a dear little fireplace with a basket standing by filled with shavings and lots of wood so that you can make yourself a fire in a moment if you want to. They have nice large baths here and plenty of hot water, the only thing I miss at our chalet . . .."

Lady Monkswell very amusingly goes on to describe a hair raising expedition with Judge Wills, when she was led up and down cliff faces where she fully expected to fall at any moment. Finally she was expected to climb a steep ladder and here the claims of modesty and safety conflicted somewhat. She recorded:

"The difficulty was to get your legs round and get on the first rung – this done with the smallest exhibition of ancles that the situation would permit, I descended like a lamplighter . . ."

Subsequently she noted wrily:

"The Judge is a dangerous leader, he offers to take you round the garden and soon after you find yourself on the point of ascending the Pointe de Salles . . .."

In a further passage she makes clear why the English appreciated the informality of such a holiday:

"The short but cosy evenings were nice at the Eagle's Nest. After the whole family had helped the one parlour maid to put away the dinner things they pushed the table back, the men smoked, Lady Wills and the girls mended clothes and stockings, everbody talked on Alpine subjects till we very soon retired to our romantic room and comfortable beds."

As the foremost industrial nation, hence also one of the richest, with the British Empire marked in red all over the map of the world, it is understandable that the British were both envied and disliked abroad. It is equally understandable that they often seemed complacently arrogant and overbearing. In fact this was generally far from the truth. Faced with different customs and habits the English usually felt extremely ill at ease. Brought up in a society full of artificial restrictions and restraints, they were unable to adapt themselves easily. Coming from a small island their attitudes were, not surprisingly, insular and narrow.

The behaviour of the British abroad showed the markedly schizophrenic effect of the background and training of the average English gentleman. So deeply were their social habits ingrained that the expatriate British generally continued to behave as if they were still in England, often to the amazement and amusement of the local populace and sometimes with bizarre results. It followed, naturally, that the greatest sin an Englishman could commit abroad in the eyes of his fellows was "to go native," since this implied abandoning the British way of life and standards.

In part at least the attraction of going abroad during the Victorian age was the opportunity to ignore for once some of the restricting social customs endured at home. It was characteristic of the Victorian English gentleman that even if he went abroad for this reason he continued to behave as if he was in England and was unable to avoid making unfavourable comparisons with his own way of life. Having been taught that British was best he had to convince himself it was true.

# Bibliography

Acton, Dr William. *Prostitution.* London, 1858. (2nd Edition, 1870.) *Functions and Disorders.* 1857. (2nd Edition, 1858.)

Aldington, Richard. *Four English Portraits.* Evans, 1848.

Allingham, William. *Life of Rossetti.*

Altick, Richard D. *Victorian People and Ideas.* J. M. Dent, 1974.

Anstey, F. *Vice Versa.* John Murray, 1882.

Arnold, Matthew. *Culture and Anarchy.* London, 1869.

Arnold, Thomas. *Miscellaneous Works.* 1845. (Ed. D. Erskine, Kimber, 1853.)

Ashton, A. J. *As I Went On My Way.* 1924.

Avery, Gillian. *The Echoing Green.* Collins.

Bamford, T. W. *Thomas Arnold.* 1960.

Banks, J. A. *Prosperity and Parenthood.* Kegan and Paul, 1954.

Barrington, Mrs Russell. *Life, Letters and Work of Frederick, Baron Leighton.*

Bax, B. A., *English Parsonage.* John Murray, 1964.

Beeton, Mrs. *Book of Household Management.* 1859–61. (Cape, 1968.)

Beeton, S. O. *The Complete Letter Writer.* 1860.

Benson, E. F. *As we were.* Longman, 1930.

Bent, James. *Reminiscences of a Police Officer.* 1891.

Bentley, Nicholas. *The Victorian Scene.* 1968.

Beresford, E. C. *The Lives of the Rakes.* Couper and Fox.

Berkeley Grantley, F. *A Month in the Forests of France.* 1851.
*Anecdotes of the Upper Ten Thousand.*
*English Sportsmen in the Western Prairies.*

*Recollections.*
*Reminiscences of a Huntsman.*

Besant, Sir F. W. *Fifty Years Ago.* Chatto and Windus, 1888.
Bird, A. *The Motor Car,* 1765–1914. Batsford, 1960.
Birkenhead, 2nd Earl of. *The Life of F. E. Smith, 1st Earl of Birkenhead.* Eyre and Spottiswoode, 1960.
Bist, Geoffrey. *Mid-Victorian Britain,* 1851–75.
Balir's First, *or Mother's Catechism.* 1856.
Blechely, Col. William. *Diary* (ed. F. G. Stokes). 1931.
Blythe, Ronald. *The Age of Illusion,* 1919–1940. Hamish Hamilton, 1963.
Bobbitt, M. R. ·*With Dearest Love to All: Life and Letters of Lady Jebb.* 1960.
Booth, J. B. *Pink Parade.* Butterworth, 1933.
Booth, William. *Darkest England.*
Brander, Michael: *The Life and Sport of the Inn.* Gentry Books, 1973.
*The Georgian Gentleman.* Saxon House, 1973.
*Hunting and Shooting.* Weidenfeld and Nicolson, 1972.
*The Hunting Instinct.* Oliver and Boyd, 1964.
*The Original Scotch. A History of Scotch Whisky.* Hutchinson, 1974.
Brinton, W. *On Food.* 1861.
Broughton, Lord. *Recollections of a Long Life.*
Browne, Matilda. *The Corset and The Crinoline.*
Burnand, Sir Francis. *Records and Reminiscences,* 2 vols. Methuen, 1904.
Burns, W. *Age of Illusion.* Allen and Unwin. 1964.
Burton, Elizabeth. *The Early Victorians at Home,* 1837–61. Longman, 1972.
Burton, Lady. *Life of Sir R. F. Burton.*
Campbell, Col. W. *My Indian Journal.* Edmonston and Douglas, 1864.
Carlyle, Thomas. *Latter Day Pamphlets,* No. 2.
Chadwick, Owen. *Victorian Miniatures.*
Checkland, S. G. *Rise of Industrial Society in England.* 1888. (Longman, 1964.)
Chesney, Kellow. *The Victorian Underworld.* Temple Smith, 1970.
Chesterton, G. K. *G. F. Watts.*
Churchill, Winston Spencer. *Life of Randolph Churchill.*
Clark, G. Kitson. *Making of Victorian England.* Methuen, 1864.
Clive, Mrs. A. *Diary and Family Papers* (ed. Caroline Clive).
Coleridge, E. Hartley. *Lord Coleridge.*
Conrad, Peter. *The Victorian Treasure House.* Collins, 1973.
Cooper, B. B. *Life of Sir Astley Cooper, Bt.* Parke, 1843.
Cox, G. V. *Recollections of Oxford.* 1856.

Croker, J. W. *Correspondence and Diaries,* 3 vols, (ed. L. J. Jennings).

Crow, Duncan. *The Victorian Women.* Allen and Unwin, 1971.

Cummings, George Gordon, *The Lion Hunter.* John Murray, 1911.

Curzon, Lord. *Recollections.*

Dale, W. *Present State of Medical Profession.* London, 1860.

Darwin, Charles. *Autobiography* (ed. N. Barlow). 1958.

Davenant, F. *What Should My Son Be?* London, 1870.

Davidson, A. *Edward Lear.* 1938.

Dilke, Charles. *Greater Britain.* 1869.

Dodds, J. W. *The Age of Paradox*, 1841–51. Gollancz, 1953.

Douglas, James. *Journals and Reminiscences.* New York, 1907.

Drummond, J. A. *The Englishman's Food.*

Eastlake, C. L. *Hints on Household Tasks.* 1878.

Elliott, Major General J. G. *Field Sports in India*, 1800–1947. Gentry Books, 1973.

Ellis, Mrs. *Daughters of England.*

Ellis, S. M. *Wilkie Collins, Le Fanu and Others.* Constable, 1931.

Ellmann, E. B. *Recollections of a Country Parson.* 1912.

*English Landed Society.* Kegan and Paul, 1963.

Erskine, D. *Augustus Hervey's Journal.* Kimber, 1853.

Escott, T. H. S. *Social Transformation of the Victorian Ages.* Seeley, 1897. *Society in London by a Foreign Resident.* Chatto and Windus.

Evans, Joan. *The Victorians.* O.U.P., 1966.

Faber, G. *Jowett.* 1957.

Farrar, F. W. *Julian Home, a Tale of College Life.* A and C Black.

Fearon, W. A. *The Passing of Old Winchester.* 1852.

Ferguson, Lt. Col. A. *Chronicles of the Cumming Club.* Edinburgh, 1887.

Fischer and Boschen. *Modes and Manner of the 19th Century.*

Fischer, Sir J. *Memoirs.* 1919.

Fontane, Theodore. *Across the Tweed.* 1858. (Phoenix House, 1965.)

Freeling, Arthur. *Gentleman's Pocket Book of Etiquette.* 1840.

Fulford, Roger. *Dearest Child,* 1858–61. Evans, 1964.

Garnett, David. *The Golden Echo.* Chatto and Windus, 1953.

George, William. *My Brother and I.* Eyre and Spottiswoode, 1958.

Gilham. *Diaries* (unpublished).

Gloag, John. *Victorian Taste,* 1820–1900. David and Charles, 1972.

Godlee, Sir Robert. *Lord Lister.* O.U.P., 1924.

Grain, Richard C. *Autobiography.*

Griffiths, Arthur. *Chronicles of Newgate.*

Grossmith, George and Weedon. *A Society Clown.* *Diary of a Nobody:*

Hamilton, Lord Ernest. *The Halcyon Era.* Murray.

Hammond, J. L. and B. *The Black Age.* 1934.

Hare, Augustus. *The Story of My Life.* 1896–1900.
　　*In My Solitary Life* (ed. Barnes). Allen and Unwin, 1952.
Harrison, Brian. *Drink and The Victorians,* 1852–1872. Faber, 1971.
Harrison, J. F. C. *The Early Victorians.* Weidenfeld and Nicolson, 1971.
Hawker, Lt. Col. Peter. *Diaries* (ed. Payne Gallwey), 2 vols. London, 1893.
　　*Diaries* (ed. Eric Parker). Allen, 1936.
　　*Instructions to young Sportsmen.* Longman, 1830.
Hawthorne, Nathaniel. *English Notebooks.* New York, 1855.
Hayward, A. *The Art of Dining.*
Heywood, John. *The Trial of Boulton and Park.* 1871.
Hogg, Jabez. *Domestic and Surgical Guide.* 1853.
Hogg, James. *Habits of Good Society.* 1860.
Hughes, Vivian M. *A London Family,* 1870–1900. O.U.P.
Johnston, W. *England in the Mid-19th Century,* 2 vols. Murray, 1851.
Kerr, R. *The Gentleman's House.* London. 1864.
Kilvert, The Rev. Francis. *Diary,* 1870–9 (ed. Plomer), 3 vols. 1964.
Kincaid, Dennis. *British Social Life in India,* 1608–1937. Kegan Paul, 1938.
Knutsford, Lord. *Black and White.* London.
Laborde, E. D. *Harrow School.* Winchester Publications.
Lambert, S. *The Railway King.* London, 1934.
Langtry, Lily. *The Days I Knew.* 1925.
Laver, J. *Children's Fashions of the 19th Century.* Batsford, 1951.
　　*Victorian Vista.* Hulton. 1955.
Leech, John. *Pictures from Punch.* Bradbury, Agnew.
Leslie, Anita. *Edwardians in Love.* Hutchinson, 1972.
Levine, G. *Emergence of Victorian Consciousness.* 1967.
Lloyd, L. *Field Sports of Northern Europe.* London, 1830.
Lochhead, Marion. *Young Victorians.* Murray, 1959.
Longford, Elizabeth. *Wellington.* Weidenfeld and Nicolson, 1972.
Mack, E. C. *Public Schools Since 1860.* New York, 1941.
Mar and Kelly, Earl of. *Diary* (unpublished).
Marcus, Steven. *The Other Victorians.* Weidenfeld and Nicolson, 1966.
Marshall, D. *The English Domestic Servant in History.*
　　*Life and Times of Victoria* (ed. Antonia Fraser). Weidenfeld, 1972.
Maurois, André. *Disraeli.* John Lane, 1927.
Mayhew, Henry. *London Labour and London Poor,* 3 vols. 1851. Vol. 4, 1862.
Millais, J. G. *Life of Frederick Courtney Selous.* Longman, 1918.
Milnes, Richard Monkton. *Biography* (ed. Pope Hennessy).
Monkswell, Lady Mary. *A Victorian Diarist* (ed. C. F. Collier). Murray, 1944.
Moore, Katherine. *Victorian Wives.* Allison and Busby, 1974.

Marley, Lord. *Recollections.*

Munby, A. J. *Man of Two Worlds.* Hudson, 1972.

Munk, W. M. *Life of Sir Harvey Halford.* Longman, 1895.

Nettel, R. *Seven Centuries of Song.* Phoenix, 1956.

Nevill, Lady Dorothy. *Life and Letters.*

Newman, G. *Medical Education in the 19th Century.* O.U.P., 1957.

Nightingale, Florence. *Notes on Nursing.*

Ogilvie, G. *English Public School.* Batsford, 1957.

Palmer, Lord Cecil. *A Mid Victorian Pepys.*
    *Letters and Memoirs of Sir W. Hardman.* 1923.

Parker, Willis Nathaniel. *Famous Persons and Famous Places.*

Pattison, Mark. *Suggestions on Academic Organisation.* 1868.

Pearl, Cora. *Memoirs.* London.

Pearl, Cyril. *Girl with the Swansdown Seat.* Muller, 1955.

Pereira, J. *On Food and Diet.* 1843.

Pinchbeck, Ivy and Margaret Howitt. *Children in English Society.*
    Routledge, 1974.

Raymond, E. T. *Portraits of the Nineties.* Unwin, 1921.

Reader, W. J. *Life in Victorian England.* Batsford, 1964.

Rennie, Sir. J. *Autobiography.* 1875.

Richmond, Sir. A. *Twenty-Six Years,* 1879–1905.

Ritchie, J. Ewing. *Night Life of London.* London, 1857.

Robinson, Sir J. *Fifty-Two Years in Fleet St.* London.

Rogers, Col. H. C. B. *Turnpike to Iron Road.* Seeley Service, 1961.

Rommilly, Joseph. *Cambridge Diary,* 1832–42. 1967.

Roughead, W. *The Bad Companions.* 1930.

Russell, W. H. *My Diary of North and South* (ed. F. Pratt). 1861.
    *A Diary of the Crimea.* 1954.
    *My Diary in India.* 1858–9.

Sassoon, Siegfried. *Memoirs of a Fox-Hunting Man.* Faber, 1928.

Seymour, L. *Florence Nightingale's Nurses,* 1860–1960.

Sherrard, R. H. *Oscar Wilde.*

Sherwood, Mrs. *Life and Times of Mrs Sherwood* (ed. F. J. Harvey).
    Gardner, 1910.

Sitwell, Edith. *The English Eccentrics.* Faber, 1956.

Smiles, Samuel. *Lives of the Engineers.* 1847.

Smith, Woodham Cecil. *Queen Victoria: Vol. 1, 1819–1861.* Hamilton.

Smythe, Palmer. *Mirror of a Gentleman.*
    *Ideal of a Gentleman.*

Soyer, Alexis. *The Modern Housewife.* 1849.

Spencer, Herbert. *Education.* 1861.
    *Railway Morals and Railway Policy.* 1855.

Stanley, A. P. *Life of Arnold.*

Stanley, H. M. *Autobiography.*

Stoker, Bram. *Personal Reminiscences of Henry Irving.*

Strahan, J. A. *Bench and Bar.*

Strafford, E. W. *The Makings of a Gentleman.* W. Norgate, 1938.
   *The Squire and His Relations.* Cassell, 1956.
   *Victorian Tragedy.* Routledge, 1930.

Strickland, Irina. *The Voices of Children,* 1700–1914. Blackwell, 1973.

Taine, H. *Notes on England* (ed. E. Hyams). Thames and Hudson, 1957.

Tayler, W. *Diary of W. Tayler,* Footman (ed. D. Wise).

Taylor, S. T. *Diary of a Medical Student,* 1860–4. Norwich, 1927.

Thompson, Dr. *Health Resorts of Great Britain.* 1860.

Thormanby. *Kings of the Rod, Rifle and Gun*, 2 vols. Hutchinson, 1901.
   *The Spice of Life.* Everett, 1911.
   *Sporting Stories.* Mills and Boon, 1910.

Timbs, J. *Hints for the Table,* 1859.

Vicenius, Martha J. *Suffer and Be Still: Victorian Women.*

Victoria, Queen. *Our Life in the Highlands.* Kimber, 1968.

Wakeman, Geoffrey. *Victorian Book Illustrations.* David and Charles, 1973.

Wallace, A. R. *The Wonderful Century.* 1898.

Warren Arthur. *A London Day.*

Waterton. *Wanderings in South Africa* (ed. J. G. Wood). Macmillan, 1880.

Watt, Margaret. *Diary* (unpublished).

West, George Cornwallis. *Edwardian Heydays.* Quelch.

William, Montagu, Q.C., *Leaves of a Life*, 2 vols. 1890.

Wilson, H. *Memoirs* (ed. Laver and Davis).

Wildon, John. *Life of Sir Henry Campbell Bannerman.* Constable, 1973.

Woodgate, W. B. *Reminiscences of an Old Sportsman.* London, 1909.

Yates, E. *All the Year Round.* 1864.

Young, G. M. *Early Victorian England.*
   *Victorian England: Portrait of An Age.* O.U.P., 1936.

# Index